# AESTHETIC EVALUATION AND FILM

Manchester University Press

# Aesthetic evaluation
and film

Andrew Klevan

Manchester University Press

Copyright © Andrew Klevan 2018

The right of Andrew Klevan to be identified as the author of this work has been asserted by him in accordance with the Copyright, Designs and Patents Act 1988.

Published by Manchester University Press
Altrincham Street, Manchester M1 7JA

www.manchesteruniversitypress.co.uk

British Library Cataloguing-in-Publication Data
A catalogue record for this book is available from the British Library

ISBN  978 1 7849 9125 8  paperback
ISBN  978 1 7849 9124 1  hardback

First published 2018

The publisher has no responsibility for the persistence or accuracy of URLs for any external or third-party internet websites referred to in this book, and does not guarantee that any content on such websites is, or will remain, accurate or appropriate.

Typeset
by Toppan Best-set Premedia Limited

*Dedicated to V.F. Perkins,*

*for whom the aesthetic evaluation of film was a way of life.*


Evaluation ... an entire domain that is properly the object of theoretical, historical, and empirical exploration has been lost to serious inquiry.
Barbara Herrnstein Smith, 'Contingencies of Value' (1983: 6)

# Contents

| | | |
|---|---|---|
| List of figures | page | ix |
| Acknowledgements | | xi |
| Introduction | | 1 |
| PART I: What is evaluative aesthetics? | | 15 |
| 1.1 The origin and definition of aesthetics | | 17 |
| 1.2 The aesthetic attitude | | 21 |
| 1.3 Aesthetic taste | | 24 |
| 1.4 Sensory immediacy | | 28 |
| 1.5 Aesthetic pleasure | | 29 |
| 1.6 Seeking agreement | | 32 |
| 1.7 Imagination | | 37 |
| 1.8 Aesthetic appreciation | | 39 |
| 1.9 Form and style | | 41 |
| 1.10 Aesthetic qualities | | 48 |
| 1.11 Specificity | | 53 |
| PART II: What is aesthetic criticism? | | 57 |
| 2.1 Evaluation | | 59 |
| 2.2 Understanding and interpretation | | 61 |

| | | |
|---|---|---|
| 2.3 | Perception | 68 |
| 2.4 | Experience | 71 |
| 2.5 | Particularity and responsiveness | 76 |
| 2.6 | Description and analysis | 78 |
| 2.7 | Close reading | 82 |
| 2.8 | Comparison, category, and context | 90 |
| 2.9 | Intention, achievement, and skill | 99 |
| 2.10 | Evaluative criteria | 104 |
| 2.11 | Reasons, argument, and objectivity | 107 |
| 2.12 | Subjectivity, contingency, and the relational | 112 |

## PART III: The aesthetic evaluation of film — 117

| | | |
|---|---|---|
| 3.1 | Medium | 119 |
| 3.2 | Constraint | 130 |
| 3.3 | Convention | 143 |
| 3.4 | Choice and expectation | 154 |
| 3.5 | Encouraging perceptual activity | 160 |
| 3.6 | Prominence | 172 |
| 3.7 | Pattern | 187 |
| 3.8 | Relation | 199 |

| | |
|---|---|
| A note on pedagogy | 219 |
| Bibliography | 221 |
| Filmography | 235 |
| Index | 237 |

# Figures

| | | |
|---|---|---|
| 1.1 | 'Fountain' by Marcel Duchamp (replica), Scottish National Gallery of Modern Art, Edinburgh. Photograph by Kim Traynor, via Wikimedia Commons. | page 19 |
| 2.1–2.6 | *Camille* (MGM, 1936). | 66–67 |
| 2.7 | *Kaninchen und Ente* (*Rabbit and Duck*), the earliest known version of the duck–rabbit illusion, from the 23 October 1892 issue of *Fliegende Blätter*, via Wikimedia Commons. | 69 |
| 2.8 | *Man with a Knife (St Bartholomew)*, 1657, oil on canvas, 122.7 x 99.5 cm, Timken Art Gallery, San Diego, CA. | 98 |
| 3.1 | *My Dinner with André* (Pyramide Distribution, 1981). | 125 |
| 3.2–3.3 | *The Rules of the Game* (Janus Films, 1939). | 127 |
| 3.4 | *The Immigrant* (Lone Star Corporation, 1917). | 131 |
| 3.5–3.6 | *The Idle Class* (Charles Chaplin Productions, 1921). | 135 |
| 3.7 | *The Pawnshop* (Lone Star Corporation, 1916). | 138 |
| 3.8 | *The Gold Rush* (Charles Chaplin Productions, 1925). | 139 |
| 3.9 | *Rope* (Warner Bros, Transatlantic Pictures, 1948). | 141 |
| 3.10–3.14 | *All That Heaven Allows* (Universal International Pictures, 1955). | 148–149 |
| 3.15 | *The Shop Around the Corner* (MGM, 1940). | 159 |

| | | |
|---|---|---|
| 3.16 | *The Best Years of Our Lives* (Samuel Goldwyn Company, 1946). | 161 |
| 3.17 | *Boudu Saved from Drowning* (Les Établissements Jacques Haïk, Les Productions Michel Simon, Crédit Cinématographique Français (CCF), 1932). | 165 |
| 3.18–3.21 | *In a Lonely Place* (Columbia Pictures Corporation, Santana Pictures Corporation, 1950). | 170–171 |
| 3.22–3.24 | *River of No Return* (Twentieth Century Fox Film Corporation, 1954). | 178 |
| 3.25 | *The Shop Around the Corner* (MGM, 1940). | 182 |
| 3.26–3.28 | *Written on the Wind* (Universal International Pictures, 1956). | 185 |
| 3.29 | *Marnie* (Universal Pictures, Alfred J. Hitchcock Productions, Geoffrey Stanley, 1964). | 190 |
| 3.30–3.33 | *You Only Live Once* (Walter Wanger Productions, 1937). | 196–197 |
| 3.34–3.35 | *Citizen Kane* (RKO Radio Productions, Mercury Productions, 1941). | 205 |
| 3.36 | *Letter from an Unknown Woman* (Rampart Productions, 1948). | 208 |
| 3.37–3.41 | *Vivre sa vie* (Les Films de la Pléiade, Pathé Consortium Cinéma, 1962). | 212–214 |

# Acknowledgements

This book has grown out of, and immensely benefited from, many people – family, friends, colleagues, students, even strangers – who over the course of my life have conversed with me about why something was good or not. There are so many indeed that I will not attempt to name them for fear of overlooking someone. I do, however, want specifically to express my gratitude to a few people who directly helped with the book. They are: the team at Manchester University Press who enthusiastically commissioned the project; Alex Clayton and Douglas Pye who read the complete manuscript with such care and offered astute advice and amendments; and most of all Vivienne Penglase who made essential contributions, intellectual and otherwise, at every stage of the process. I also wish to thank the Faculty of English and St Anne's College at the University of Oxford for allowing me the time and space to teach and research material which I consider to be of value to my field.

# Introduction

The topic of this book is aesthetic evaluation, and its application to film. What is meant by 'aesthetic evaluation' will become clear as the book proceeds because explicating the topic is the purpose of the project. However, here is a basic definition for preliminary orientation: the assessment, based on close examination, of the merits (or demerits) *of the form* that something takes. An example of an evaluative claim concerned with the form of a work would be this by V.F. Perkins about the structure of *Letter from an Unknown Woman* (Max Ophüls 1948 US): it 'arrive[s] at order and comprehensibility without falling into an impoverishing neatness' (Perkins 2000: 41). Another example, from my own work, claims that the resolution of *The Philadelphia Story* (George Cukor 1940 US) 'is ... satisfyingly worked out, without looking as if it is being ponderously worked through. The film avoids presenting negotiations in series, and appearing too careful' (Klevan 2005a: 42–3). A final preliminary example, by Andrew Sarris, highlights a shortcoming: '[T]here seems to be something more tentative than intuitive in [John] Ford's ideas about ... [*She Wore a Yellow Ribbon* (1949 US) and *Rio Grande* (1950 US)], as if he were drifting in an obscure reverie for which he had not found an articulated form' (Sarris 1976: 156). These overarching claims would have to be substantiated with evidence, and they might lead to revision or rejection, but they are examples of statements that make evaluations about the formal merits or demerits of the films[1].

---

[1] The terms merit and demerit are used throughout the book as they tend to be the formal vocabulary used in the philosophical literature. Although they have other associations, they are probably more neutral and dispassionate than good/bad or

The book is divided into three parts. Part I explores the philosophy of evaluative aesthetics; Part II explores aesthetic criticism, the practical wing of that philosophy, which evaluates the form of individual works. One background purpose of these first two parts is to show that although aesthetic criticism preceded modern forms of critical theory it is not from a naive, pre-theoretical world, nor is it without grounding, secure conceptual underpinning, or self-scrutiny. Part III, the longest part, is devoted to the aesthetic evaluation of film. All three parts are made up of numbered segments, most of which are organised around relevant terms or concepts, for example, 'aesthetic pleasure', 'perception', 'medium' or 'convention'[2]. Some of these segments consist of just a few paragraphs, while others, especially those in Part III, are relatively lengthy. Although the segments are arranged to be read in a particular order, and there is continuity from one section to the next, they are not stages in a single, sequential argument. Each segment is contributing to the whole, filling out a multifaceted picture.

The book becomes more specific as it proceeds, moving from first principles to firm particulars. The reader should not expect substantive exemplification from individual film sequences until Part III. This is because, although the first two parts are disposed towards film, they are foundational and comprehensive. The aim is for the material to be sufficiently general to be widely applicable to all types of films, and not let an extended example suggest special applicability or distract with singular circumstance. The hope is that these two parts will also be of use to those interested in the aesthetic evaluation of things other than films, from novels to furniture (and to those interested in evaluation more generally). At the same time, the material is not simply preliminary or supportive, preparing the ground for Part III; it is presented as worthwhile in itself. Some important ideas are left, and then elaborated upon in later segments: for example, the topic of 'category' is brought up in Part I under 'Aesthetic qualities' and 'Specificity', picked up again in Part II under 'Comparison, category, and context', and then again in Part III under 'Convention'. At

---

positive/negative which have stronger moral and emotional connotations. Merit and demerit may sound blunt, but they are used as shorthand to cover a range of possibilities. For example, demerit may refer to a feature in the work which is not quite working, not fitting, not realised, or not achieving very much; it need not refer to something that is simply bad.

[2] The segments are not encyclopaedic accounts of the use of the concepts in aesthetics and criticism: the focus is on how the concepts relate specifically to, and are illuminated by, evaluation.

the same time, to avoid repetition, Part III, while exemplifying the first two parts, putting their ideas into practice in relation to a specific art, does not necessarily explicitly refer to every idea introduced earlier. They are absorbed into another layer of concepts (that are themselves also applicable beyond film).

The book is a contribution to the philosophy of criticism. This philosophy mainly aims to understand and clarify the vocabulary and methods at stake in evaluation. Most books and essays about the philosophy of criticism are devoted to fine art, literature, and music. Historically the field has tended not to use film as its exemplary art, and the book acts as a rectification. Furthermore, this field is not as prominent as it was in the first half of the twentieth century. There is a thriving field that is entitled the 'Philosophy of Art', but most of its concerns are not those of evaluation. The Philosophy of Art is interested in philosophising about, for example, matters of artistic medium, language, authorship, narration, emotion, and spectatorship and is not necessarily interested in how these matters bear on the principles and processes of evaluation in general, or in how they relate to the evaluation of individual works. An aim is to rejuvenate the philosophy of criticism, partly by exploring it in relation to film, and partly by weaving the various strands of it together (something that was never done, to my knowledge, even when the field was more active). The book rescues its concerns and insights from an interest that is merely historical and, because they are now rarely present in classrooms or in humanities culture more widely, makes them available for use. Even core terms like 'judgement' and 'aesthetic', which are seemingly familiar and often deployed as if they are satisfactorily understood, are in need of enriching clarification and renewed application. One sympathetic colleague poetically likened the project to the removal of limescale from an encrusted filament.

The more important interdisciplinary intention, however, is to introduce the philosophy of criticism to Film Studies. Despite the long tradition within Film Studies of theorising, and the contemporary burgeoning of the field of 'film and philosophy', my experience is that film academia is unfamiliar with what was once an important branch of philosophical aesthetics. Even in previous generations, there was little explicit crossover although some of the concerns and insights of evaluative aesthetics did make their way into film criticism (or they were discovered independently). The book intends to help film evaluation discover an unknown ancestry, or at least foreground a lineage. In 1993, Carl Plantinga wrote an article in the *Journal of Aesthetics and Art Criticism* entitled 'Film Theory and Aesthetics: Notes on a Schism', the opening line of which is: 'The relationship between film theory and traditional aesthetics has been marked to a great extent either by mutual inattention or by open suspicion' (1993: 445). He notes that in the classic film theory readers such as that edited by G. Mast, L. Braudy, and M. Cohen (originally published in 1974) there are few references to major figures in aesthetics such as Immanuel Kant, Ludwig Wittgenstein, or Monroe Beardsley (447). Also missing are references to David Hume, Frank Sibley, and Arnold Isenberg. Their work will be explored in these pages, as will the work of F.R. Leavis from Literary Studies, and Rudolf Arnheim, André Bazin, and V.F. Perkins from Film Studies. They are crucial to the history of aesthetic evaluation, and this book, although primarily conceptual, includes a relaying of that history. Plantinga notes that film theory tended to be influenced by French theorists or non-French theorists influenced by French theory[3]. The reasons for the predilections and occlusions of Film Studies are involved and complex, but Plantinga suggests that aesthetics lacked the political, cultural, and philosophical radicalism of the French theory (449). He also suggests that notable exemptions aside – Rudolf Arnheim, André Bazin, V.F. Perkins – film theory was interested in film 'as a signifying practice', rather than in aesthetic evaluation, artistry, and achievement. He writes, 'In its investigation of conventions and codes of meaning, semiotics has encouraged a shift away from thinking of film as an art toward a conception of film as a signifying practice with important cultural connections' (450).

Even twenty-five years after Plantinga's article, with Film Studies made up of a variety of approaches, aesthetic evaluation is not a distinct component. Although there have been important interventions in this area especially in the formative years of Film Studies, and more recently as interest in the area has revived, they have been disparate. They have also been relatively recessive because of the hegemony of other disciplines and pedagogies. Furthermore, some work in film evaluation was not acknowledged as making an intervention. Perhaps this was because it took the form of criticism of individual films, seemingly promising only specific relevance; perhaps because it did not sufficiently conceptualise, or formulate general principles or conclusions; perhaps because it did not explicitly proclaim its import, or polemicise; or perhaps because it did

---

[3] For example, André Bazin (who is also an important figure in evaluative aesthetics), Raymond Bellour, Thierry Kuntzel, Roland Barthes, Jacques Lacan, Louis Althusser, Michel Foucault, Christian Metz. If he was updating his essay, Plantinga could now add Emmanuel Levinas, Jacques Rancière, and Gilles Deleuze.

not speak to prevailing academic pursuits. At the risk of appearing grand, I would like Part III to construct a field out of individual interventions that have never been brought together. More modestly, I would like to shine a light on an existence that has hitherto been somewhat clandestine and then exhibit it in a coherent form. This will, I hope, help the aesthetic evaluation of film to situate itself in relation to concepts and debates, and move forward more transparently and confidently as a field of research. Although there have been a few books on film advocating individual theories of aesthetic evaluation – such as Rudolf Arnheim's *Film as Art*, or V.F. Perkins' *Film as Film* – this is the first book (in the English language), once again to my knowledge, to explore the terrain holistically.

The book, therefore, intends to connect threads and present a perspicacious picture. It is a work of archaeology. I made my way through a host of essays and books on aesthetics and criticism excavating what was valuable and piecing together fragments. It brings together a wide variety of sources, which are distilled, synthesised, and conceptualised. Sometimes I simply endeavour to elucidate this material and explain through exegesis what is at stake in it. Although the three parts are constructed to explicate each of the main areas – evaluative aesthetics, aesthetic criticism, and the aesthetic evaluation of film – they will also reveal, explicitly and implicitly, what is advantageous in them. Sometimes I elaborate on matters arising, or give the old ideas renewed relevance, often in relation to film. Sometimes I enter into critical conversation, even dispute, with the scholarship. In Part III of the book, much of the film analysis is my own[4]. One important intention of this part is to demonstrate the practice of aesthetic evaluation by engaging closely with film sequences.

I have tried to be as explanatory as possible. The book aims to guide the reader through the subject and its associated skills from its fundamental aspects to those that are more advanced. The purpose is to provide a supportive framework for academics working or teaching in the area and to be accessible to students. The approach and form of address also make the book efficiently informative to anyone unfamiliar with the area, and to those outside institutionalised education. It would be disingenuous to deny that the persistent and detailed scrutiny of form and style that the

---

[4] In a work that includes a large amount of citation a note on referencing procedure might be helpful. Where I employ the exact words of another scholar, I quote directly with the use of quotation marks. When I précis their work I provide a citation at the end of the sentence. If a sentence does not conclude with a citation then it consists of my own observations.

book encourages is made possible by the time and space enjoyed by academia, and the approach to film evaluation it expounds is academically aligned. It does not follow, however, that the approach is not of interest, or cannot be enjoyed and practised, outside the academy.

It is always worth managing expectations in an introduction, so what does the book *not* intend to do? It does not valorise one category or genre of film as superior to another, say the 'art' film over the 'mainstream' or popular film, or serious political drama over slapstick comedy. However, the examples in Part III are taken from the narrative fiction film partly because that is my sphere of expertise and experience, and partly because a lot of evaluative film criticism has developed in relation to it. The concepts and the approach are applicable, or adaptable, to a wide variety of film forms such as documentary, non-figurative film or animation (and to other art forms)[5]. It does not decisively announce the best films ever made, nor the one blueprint which will reveal them, although it does discuss films that have been singled out as having high aesthetic merit[6]. Finally, it does not, unlike many interventions on the subject, proclaim a set of essential criteria that confer merit, although it does highlight criteria that have been central to the tradition of criticism, and remain pressing concerns to aesthetic evaluation. It will show that many individual criteria and theories of excellence are crucially instructive, but not definitive; and if the book has a position or a thesis it is that the aesthetic evaluation of film should be flexibly informed by a cluster of concerns about medium, constraint, convention, choice, perception, prominence, pattern, and relation (all explored in Part III). Correspondingly, the book also advocates and models a type of approach, attention, process, and discourse (rather than espousing a criterion, a theory, or a particular film style).

---

[5] A close study of these forms, however, might throw up different evaluative possibilities, or different priorities. The analysis intends to be exemplary rather than exhaustive. An alternative title for the book could have been 'Aesthetic evaluation and the fiction film', but that would have disguised the presence of valuable transferable aspects.

[6] The films analysed in detail are 'classic' examples that have received an explicitly evaluative treatment in pre-existing criticism (within the Anglo-French tradition). They are used to illustrate the concepts and procedures. Equally good films, from different countries and periods, would benefit from this treatment. Furthermore, the study recognises that *any* type of form and content, beyond that of the films under consideration here, can be subject to aesthetic evaluation and appreciation, and that the concepts and procedures will be applicable. Aesthetic evaluation does not stop with authorised or canonised films.

The book is about the evaluation of film form and is not a neutral study, analysis, or history of form and style. Plenty of distinguished work of this nature already exists. Nor is it about close analysis of form in and of itself because this method is used in many fields of study – from structuralism to formalism to historicism – that are not ostensibly or primarily evaluative. It is also not about all the types of value that inhere in, or are produced by, artworks of which there are many (and too many for one book to encompass): for example, ideological, ethical, cultural, pedagogical, entertainment, or personal value[7]. Aesthetic value is the focus while recognising that it does not exist in a vacuum and that it intersects with these other types. Some work in, for example, ideological, ethical, and cultural studies, does engage with form and value although aesthetic value is clearly not the central concern. Therefore, I will simply be reversing the emphasis. Indeed, where evaluation is practised it tends to be in these fields partly because they can make a more urgent case for relevance. Nevertheless, the *dedicated* attention to the formal detail of artworks in order to ascertain value is hardly an irrelevance. Although the reasons for this dedicated attention will explicitly and implicitly emerge, it is useful to highlight some fundamental ones at this stage. One reason is that such a concentration is stimulating, demanding, and rewarding in many respects: perceptually, cognitively, imaginatively, emotionally, and sensuously. Another reason is that it is responsive to the *kind* of object the work is: one that is made, constructed, *formed* out of many elements (for example, images, shots, sounds, performers, objects, and environments). It therefore brings us closer to the actual work rather than to a resemblance because the form of the work *is* the work. Consequently, it will help with any type of evaluation, indeed any type of assessment. Furthermore, although artworks in general, and films in particular, are made for a variety of reasons, many creative personnel intend to 'achieve substantive aesthetic effects … and in doing that … try to make something of aesthetic value' (Zangwill 2012: 39). Artworks, including films, serve all sorts of 'nonaesthetic functions', and undergo 'nonaesthetic pressures' and intentions, for example, religious, institutional, political, or commercial, but the aesthetic component can still be highly significant, and these other

---

[7] I am using 'artwork' as a catch-all, collective term for any work produced by the various branches of creative activity, for example, literature, painting, sculpture, or music. It is used when making claims that do not only apply to film, and it carries no special honorific meaning. Similarly, 'artist' simply refers to someone engaged in creative activity.

'functions' may well rely on it (47). Aesthetic value can be *distinguished* without being autonomous.

~

Why does the evaluation of artworks deserve to be a sphere of serious intellectual activity (both within and beyond the academy)? What follows is a range of reasons[8]. They are introduced briefly as basic underlying justifications for the book's concerns. Although these reasons can also be taken as encouragements, they are presented in a spirit of inclusivity rather than exclusivity, and to engender parity: they are not intended to usurp – and nor is anything else in this book – the reasons for adopting other approaches and fields.

1. Evaluation is a natural and vital part of human experience. Barbara Herrnstein Smith, the writer who has written the most in-depth study about the evaluation of the arts, and who laments its marginalisation in the academy, states that it is not a discrete act that punctures experience, but rather it is 'indistinguishable from the very processes of acting and experiencing themselves … for a responsive creature, to exist is to evaluate' (1983: 19). Evaluations are 'among the most fundamental forms of social communication' as we assess and reassess in order to satisfy needs (20). In stark terms, survival depends on judging whether something is good or bad for us and assessments are made, sometimes explicitly, sometimes intuitively, about gradations of value all day long. Frank Sibley notes that from early in childhood, '[c]ertain phenomena which are outstanding or remarkable or unusual catch the eye or ear, seize our attention and interest, and move us to surprise, admiration, delight, fear, or distaste' (2006 [1962]: 22). It is reasonable to suggest that these evaluative impulses are not artificially halted when dealing with artworks. It is also reasonable to suggest that some of our analysis of artworks should be satisfyingly continuous with instinctive proclivities and common behaviours while it cultivates and evolves them.

2. An initial response to an artwork is often evaluative, even if the evaluation is undecided, and subsequent enquiries into it may wish to honour this. Mary Rawlinson, in reference to fine art, talks about being 'accosted by the work' and 'being set in motion by it': the experience of, for

---

[8] Not all of them refer specifically to the aesthetic aspect of evaluation.

example, a 'WOW' in front of an artwork 'inaugurates a debate about why a work seems compelling and valuable' (2006: 142). Honouring the initial response would not mean that it is sacrosanct: it could in time be modified or even rejected. Indeed, the aim would be to become more agile at including and testing the initial response.

3   Artworks unavoidably solicit an evaluation by addressing us in a certain way, and we may want to learn how to deal with this. The expressions of artworks are like many communicative utterances which according to Stanley Cavell make claims on us (1999 [1979]). They aim, like utterances, 'to effect particular goals, such as persuading another person to believe something', or come to see something, or react in a certain way (Guyer 2014c: 439). In addition, many artworks are evaluating things in the world including the behaviour of people and situations. How do we feel about the way in which the work wants us to see, react, believe, and value; what do we think about what it 'says' to us, and *how* it says it? In reference to Cavell's work, Stephen Mulhall writes, 'Artworks mean something to us ... in the way people do – we speak of them in terms of love and affection, or scorn and outrage; and they are felt as made by someone – we use such categories as personal style, feeling, dishonesty, authority, inventiveness, profundity and meretriciousness in speaking of them' (2007: 110). As is the case with ordinary human communication, it will take effort and skill to ensure that our response to artworks is apposite and conscionable.

4   Evaluative qualities are experienced as properties of an artwork – 'it is subtle', 'it is crass' – and avoiding them in an account can feel like a distortion of the work's identity and the experience of it. This holds true even if the experience of the work changes, or if one person's experience differs from another. An evaluative approach helps us to be faithful to these ostensible properties of the work and to the experience.

5   Evaluation of artworks can be an enjoyable human practice. It is enjoyable because evaluation can be 'moved by enthusiasm'; because it can be satisfying to be able to weigh up achievements carefully, and consequently feel insightful and just; and because it can be stimulating to work through problems of judgement which are occupying and puzzling (Sparshott 1967: 152–3). Enabling the best features of this enjoyment is worthwhile.

6   Evaluation of artworks can also be a necessary practice. 'Wherever there is a recognizable *kind* of object' or entity – televisions, footballers, restaurants, politicians, *and* the laws they make – there will often be

the need to evaluate and discriminate within a 'field of alternatives' (Beardsley 1981b: 153). This is unavoidable for many reasons, not least for the basic ones of time and money. Personal preferences aside, it will often become clear that one object of a kind is better than another, or differently good, and some people will want to understand and articulate how and why this is so.

7  Artworks, and especially films, are constantly evaluated in everyday life, so it is worthwhile having formal practices that correlate to the informal reckonings. Noël Carroll recognises that 'evaluating films is something that we all do all the time' and he invites the academy in particular to 'talk to the film-goer where she or he lives' (2000: 265–6). According to Carroll, 'it is this aspect of film-going to which recent scholarship pays little attention', and yet it is reasonable for film scholarship to be connected to an activity that is 'part of the typical life of film-going ... [where evaluation] is something that ordinary film-goers care about deeply ... something that they want to do' (266). Everyday evaluations often occur in restricted modes, for example, journalistic reviews, social media, promotional material, award ceremonies, and curtailed exchanges. It is beneficial, therefore, so that they are not the sole evaluating practices, for them to be balanced by more thorough formats. A field of aesthetic evaluation could usefully contribute to mainstream critical culture. This may seem a high-minded fantasy, but it would be an accepted ambition of many educational practices and fields of expertise.

8  Value is often already bestowed on artworks by the critical culture. It is incorporated into the identity of a work by the time it is experienced (Shusterman 1984). Notable examples from the world of film are *Vertigo* (Alfred Hitchcock 1958 US) and *Citizen Kane* (Orson Welles 1941 US) which come to us as 'masterpieces' or 'classics' (or even 'the best films ever made'). Viewing is inescapably affected by this knowledge, and evaluative skills would help negotiate it. The value of these works also then affects the identity and culture of future works. Herrnstein Smith writes that 'stylistic and generic exemplar[s] ... energize the production of subsequent works ... canonical work[s] ... shape and create the culture in which its value is produced and transmitted' (1983: 28–9). In turn, our own identity is over time affected because 'we develop within and are formed by a culture that is itself constituted in part *by* canonical texts' (29). An evaluative practice would scrutinise these formations and transmissions, and fruitfully contribute to them.

9   Some creative personnel are striving to make good artworks. In addition, artworks are often made with the intention to be appreciated because 'making things to be appreciated by others is a fundamental human impulse' (Iseminger 2004: 25–6, 137)[9]. These works are therefore 'constructed to be objects of value; so value judgments [in relation to them] cannot be peripheral and accidental things' (Hough 1966: 8). More specifically, artworks – even quite limited works – are built out of evaluative processes and so it is natural to respond in kind. Herrnstein Smith describes them as crafted, made up of countless 'individual acts of approval and rejection, preference and assessment, trial and revision that constitute the entire process of … composition' (1983: 24). She calls this 'a complex evaluative feedback loop' and because she expands on this tellingly it is worth quoting at length:

> [I]n selecting this word, adjusting that turn of phrase, preferring this rhyme to that, the author is all the while testing the local and global effectiveness of each decision by impersonating in advance his or her various presumptive audiences, who thereby themselves participate in shaping the work they will later read. Every literary work – and, more generally, artwork – is thus the product of a complex evaluative feedback loop that embraces not only the ever shifting economy of the artist's own interest and resources as they evolve during and in reaction to the process of composition, but also all the shifting economies of his or her assumed and imagined audiences, including those who do not yet exist but whose emergent interests, variable conditions of encounter, and rival sources of gratification the artist will attempt to predict – or will intuitively surmise – and to which, among other things, his or her own sense of the fittingness of each decision will be responsive. (24)

In turn, many 'audiences' are struck, moment-by-moment, with whether something fits or not, whether it feels right. Using a simple example, if it is sensed that at a particular moment in a scene a filmmaker *could* have chosen a close-up 'for cheap emotional effect, we may praise her or his intelligence and discrimination in resisting that obvious temptation' (Lyas 2002b: 399). A meticulous evaluative practice can mirror the responsiveness of artist and audience.

---

[9] This is not to deny that many other intentions, for example, commercial or doctrinal, may also be involved.

10  An effective evaluation of an artwork may enrich another person's engagement (especially when it takes the form of a meritorious appreciation), or help them make a more informed assessment. Some works do not necessarily reveal all they have to offer in one sitting: their merits (or demerits) are not immediately apparent. Unlike many objects such as a breadknife that can be evaluated relatively easily by how well it cuts the bread, the functions of an artwork may not be so straightforwardly ascertained. A helpful evaluative discourse is needed, given that time is finite, to illuminate purpose, relevance, and import (Reichert 1977: 182). If we only latently sense something, or there is indecision, assistance may be required to sort out our thoughts, to 'stabilize and clarify' them, and arrive at a satisfactory conclusion (Sparshott 1967: 157). Equally, we may be decided, and it is reassuring to have experiences confirmed especially as initial appraisals are often made in private. Commonality is thereby affirmed – you thought it too. On the other hand, the evaluations of others can challenge apparent certainties. They encourage a dialogue with our assumptions.

11  The careful evaluation of artworks might be required for ethical reasons.

Firstly, one might feel a responsibility to acknowledge the work, and its creative personnel, especially if it is felt that something done well has not been sufficiently understood or appreciated. Vigilance is often required to keep alive works of the past, or works that are difficult, not easily sold to a consumer, or ones that are unassuming, not noisily advertising their significance. Roger Scruton writes that 'we strive ... to extend and enhance the web of sympathy' (1999: 370). Alternatively, a response may not always be sympathetic and the ethical desire will simply be to evaluate fairly and honestly. This can result in a less than enthusiastic appraisal of the work or in reservations about certain features of it. For most of us, it will take training and experience to acknowledge works judiciously.

Secondly, one might feel a responsibility to the self. Improving powers of discrimination may contribute to well-being, and intellectual, emotional, and cognitive development.

Thirdly, one might feel a social responsibility to help foster a culture where knowledge 'of what kinds of success and failure are possible' is shared (Sparshott 1967: 149). Artists too would operate within this more informed evaluative culture, and it might benefit the production and reception of their work.

12 Within academia, the explicit evaluation of artworks would put it in line with its other unmistakeably evaluative practices. Rónán McDonald points out that academia is 'saturated' with value judgements all the way from the grading of student work to appraisals of fellow academics (and their work) (2007: 30). At academic conferences, phrases such as 'she gave a good paper' or the opposite, and a variety of more finessed variations, are omnipresent. McDonald argues that there is then a contradiction, or at least a disjunction, when academia refrains from explicitly evaluating its own objects of study. In addition, implicit evaluations unwittingly abound in ostensibly non-evaluative work. Wayne Booth argues that all writing on artworks is implicitly valuing because even a basic description has made choices about the best way to describe and about what is worth remarking upon (1988: 96). Some analyses which purport not to be in the business of evaluation nevertheless make assumptions about the value of films and other related matters, for example, the values of 'the spectator'. All of this would be less anomalous if there was a visible field of evaluative practice to sit alongside non-evaluative academic approaches. Herrnstein Smith writes that although evaluation is rarely granted its own dedicated disciplinary space, it does occur in academic work and in classrooms. It is permitted 'as long as it comes under cover of other presumably more objective types of ... study, such as historical description, textual analysis, or explication' (1983: 6). This sort of evaluative activity is often transitory, casual, superficial, and without rigour (understandably as it is a relegated concern).

Having introduced a range of reasons that support a developed practice of evaluation, I will now begin my elucidation of the specifically aesthetic variant of this practice.

# PART I
# What is evaluative aesthetics?

## 1.1 The origin and definition of aesthetics

The concept of the 'aesthetic' is best considered as a cluster of interrelated meanings, and Part I will attempt to elaborate its multifaceted nature. Its Greek origin is *aisthesis*, meaning perception by sense, or feeling; more precisely it derives 'from the Greek nominal *aisthetikos*, sensitive or sentient, derived in turn from the verb *aisthanesthai*, meaning to perceive, feel, or sense' (Costelloe 2013: 1). *Aesthetki* is 'the science of how things are known to the senses' and *aisthema* is 'the sensation of any object' (Day 2010: 155). To perceive is to become aware of something through the senses and not only through sight. Thinking in terms of sense perception also links aesthetics to experience: the importance of the experience of the object before us.

The original etymology of aesthetics does not explicitly contain an evaluative component. This is partly why aesthetics is the umbrella title for a range of interests related to appearance and perception (not only of artistic products, but also of other artefacts, of people, and of the natural world). However, the interest in aesthetics that emerges in the eighteenth century is explicitly concerned with matters of value, and in particular the judgement of beauty. This period also marks the beginning of formalising aesthetics as a field of philosophical enquiry. For Alexander Baumgarten (1714–62) the field of aesthetics would provide a foundation for explaining, and justifying, human judgement about what is and what is not beautiful[1]. Paul Guyer defines Baumgarten's work as the 'study of the perfection of and pleasure in the exercise of sensibility for its own sake, as manifested in the production of works of artistic beauty' (1998: 227). There are a number of important elements in Guyer's definition of Baumgarten's work. There is the foundational interest in works of 'beauty', and also the 'pleasure' taken in these works; and not simply pleasure, but a particular type of pleasure, the pleasure taken in the 'exercise of sensibility'; and, furthermore, a pleasure with no ulterior motive than enjoying the production of beauty. Aesthetics would be concerned, therefore, with the beauty of the work and with the pleasure caused by the beauty of the work as it stimulates, and refines, the capacities of perception, responsiveness, and discernment. It might be assumed that artworks exist for these interests, and would naturally attract them, but it is important to recognise that this need not be the case. Aesthetic engagement has not been the only, or even primary,

---

[1] I provide biographical dates for figures of historic importance in the development of aesthetic evaluation to orientate the reader.

mode of engagement with artworks: medieval criticism, for example, was interested in scholarly explication, clarification, authentication, contextualisation, correction, and commentary (see Day 2010: 65–9). These are still favoured modes of engagement, especially in academic study.

*The New Oxford Dictionary of English* defines 'beauty' as 'an excellent specimen or example of something', and the 'best feature or advantage of something' (Pearsall 1998). It means more than simply very attractive. In the contemporary study of aesthetics, beauty is often employed as a synonym for excellence, or as an umbrella term that encompasses the wide array of merit qualities that exist (for example, graceful, subtle, eloquent, or intricate)[2]. As its main definition, the *Dictionary* also describes beauty as 'the combination of qualities, such as shape, colour, form that pleases the ... senses', and there is, once again here, reference to the appeal to the senses, and to pleasure (with the pleasing of the intellect and moral sense also referenced). Another core feature of the aesthetic that appears in this definition is 'combination' (and it is one to which this study will repeatedly return).

The aesthetic should not be equated to the artistic. Firstly, this is because aesthetic interest extends beyond art and artworks. An aesthetic point of view can be adopted with regard to everyday objects, furniture, houses, clothes, nature, food, and people. The form of all these things may also be evaluated. Secondly, it is widely recognised that there are forms of artistic value that are not aesthetic. For example, we might value the knowledge gained from an artwork, the educational, moral or political instruction provided, the personal well-being generated, the emotional experience undergone, the theories or theorisations engendered, or the contextual and historical (or art historical) links created. All these may be of value, but they are not necessarily generated by the aesthetic value of the work. From an aesthetic point of view, a film may not be good, but it may have other good values, and may be valued for good reasons[3]. Equally, artworks, including films, are created with values in mind other than aesthetic ones, and they may be appreciated accordingly. The famous, paradigmatic example from the world of art (and the philosophy of art)

---

[2] Matthew Collings has recently asked the question 'What is beauty?' particularly in relation to fine art, and bravely and fruitfully answered with the following features: simplicity, unity, transformation, animation, pattern, surprise, selection, spontaneity, and a relationship, perhaps internalised, to nature (2009).

[3] Some evaluative disagreement arises because an artwork is being judged within different categories of value (and these categories are often not made explicit)

What is evaluative aesthetics?  19

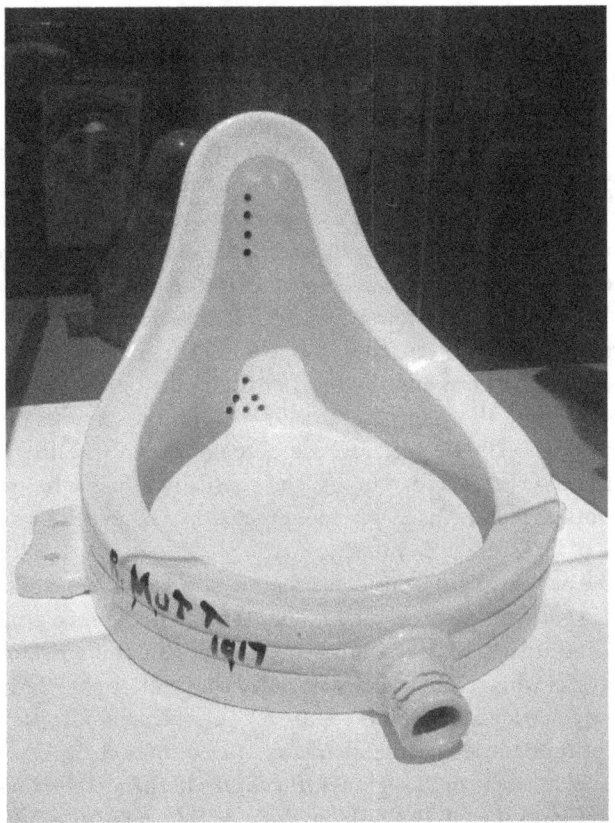

**1.1** 'Fountain' by Marcel Duchamp (replica), Scottish National Gallery of Modern Art, Edinburgh.

is that of Marcel Duchamp's 'ready-made' urinal – entitled 'The Fountain' (1917) – which may have artistic value but not much aesthetic value because the value is exclusively, or nearly exclusively, cognitive, conceptual, and contextual (Fig. 1.1). Indeed, Duchamp's urinal was thought to be deliberately 'anti-aesthetic' because it was not aiming to 'please' the senses through the arrangement of its form[4].

---

[4] There is the possibility of aesthetic value because some formal relationships are created: by the inscription on the urinal; by the urinal's pristine cleanliness in relation to an imagined and customary dirtiness (the absent presence of a urine pool); and

It is important not to fall prey to a popular misconception – that the previous paragraph might also seem to be promoting – that aesthetics is equivalent to Formalism: an adherence to form at the expense of content (for example, subject matter). Nor is it equivalent to Aestheticism if this is taken to mean an exaggerated devotion to beautiful forms, once again at the expense of content. Aesthetics does not discount or demean moral, political, emotional, cognitive, or conceptual content. This content is important, and often essential to an aesthetic evaluation, but *the engagement will be with the value of its expression through the form of the work*. This contrasts with those occasions where, for example, ideological, contextual or conceptual content, even if it relates to formal or presentational matters, is the *primary* concern and the *basis* of the evaluation. Equally, not all values relating to the visual, aural, and sensory, the features ostensibly underpinning aesthetic interest, are automatically of aesthetic value. Something may be visually, aurally, and sensually valuable to some of us at some time for some reason – pornography would be an extreme example – and be of little aesthetic value.

Some people might be interested in the form and media of art while not being specifically interested in value. This is reflected in a disciplinary division. 'Aesthetics' is sometimes used as an umbrella title to cover everything in what might broadly be called the 'Philosophy of Art' which would cover a wide spectrum of topics: for example, ontology, definitions of art, spectatorship, and the characteristics of fiction. If Aesthetics is understood in terms of its eighteenth-century heritage, then these areas may be important to it, but only in so far as they help with judgement. The philosophy of art might be interested, for example, in characterising the particularities of an art or medium. The constitution of an artistic medium could be explored without an interest in the aesthetic consequences; equally, however, this exploration may be put to an aesthetic end of ascertaining what might work well in that medium. A particular story may work well in the short form of a novella, and then perhaps as a film, but not as a longer novel or television series[5]. When undergraduates study courses entitled 'Aesthetics' they are often studying a more expansive syllabus concerned with the philosophy of art; and when they study courses

---

by its placement in the gallery which would establish more varied reciprocation. Furthermore, if Duchamp's urinal is 'anti-aesthetic' as labelled it should not be because it is ugly, coarse, obscene, or improper, as these qualities, for me, are compatible with the aesthetic.

[5] See 3.1: 'Medium'.

entitled 'Philosophy of Art', aesthetics in its evaluative sense may only be one component. The philosopher Robert Stecker divides his introductory book, *Aesthetics and The Philosophy of Art*, into two sections, each reflecting one half of the title. He writes that 'Aesthetics is the study of a certain kind of value. This value derives from certain kinds of experience, and is identified in judgments that an object possesses this value in virtue of its capacity to deliver the experience [...] Aesthetics ... is primarily a topic within value theory' (2010: ix, 7). This is the conception of aesthetics that motivates this study. Nevertheless, someone might be said to have a genuine interest in aesthetics, in *aesthetki* and *aisthema*, in the presentational, tactile, textural, or sensuous features of objects, people, or artworks, without having evaluative intent. Strictly speaking, therefore, it is helpful if the area of aesthetics interested in value is specifically labelled 'evaluative aesthetics'[6].

## 1.2 The aesthetic attitude

The 'aesthetic attitude' or the 'aesthetic point of view' consists of 'adopting a ... voluntary state of mind toward a certain object or event ... when we take an aesthetic interest in it, and appreciate it aesthetically' (Guter 2010: 20–1). There has been some debate in disciplinary aesthetics about whether this state of mind is special or unique, and whether it can be precisely distinguished. There is no need to award it an exceptional or unusual status, to isolate it as a special faculty, obscure and recondite, or to imagine that it 'comprises a single, pure phenomenon' (21). I think of it as a disposition which wishes to engage with the form and style of an artwork, and where there are many aspects to the engagement: for example, sensory, imaginative, intellectual, emotional, pleasurable, and evaluative. The attitude might be adopted automatically because of a predisposition;

---

[6] For the sake of brevity, when I use the word aesthetic from now on I am, unless I specify otherwise, referring to the evaluative sense of the term. In addition, it should be noted that some people are not interested in the aesthetic *at all* when they attend to an artwork: they may be interested in it as a historical document or record, a revealing product of the prevailing culture, or as an exemplar of a theoretical model. They may not, therefore, even regard it as an artwork as such and prefer instead to categorise it as, say, a cultural object. Films are commonly treated in this way in contemporary academic work (and it is the aim of this book to illuminate, and show the value of, an alternative approach). See the following section, 1.2: 'The aesthetic attitude'.

alternatively, it might be encouraged through education or through books like this one. It can be recognised by way of contrast. In my experience, living in the United Kingdom, many academics, journalists, and broadcasters do not *view* films with an aesthetic attitude. Their *prime* interest is not in the form and style of a work, but in its subject matter, or in its milieu, or in the biography of its director or performers, or in the reception of its audiences, or in its cultural or political import, or in its place in a particular history. To perceive primarily from the point of view of these interests is not to perceive from an aesthetic point of view[7].

The aesthetic attitude has been described as disinterested, but this description can be misleading. Disinterest need not imply indifference, or emotional detachment, or lack of care about content or subject matter (although some philosophers of criticism and aestheticians do advocate these implications, for example, Clive Bell with regard to subject matter (1913))[8]. It need only imply attention to the work with no prior or ulterior motive, or broader practical, theoretical, or sociological interest or purpose. There is a famous, simple example, originally provided by Edward Bullough, about a ship surrounded by fog. If the fog presents a danger to the ship then our interest in it is (justifiably) practical; if it does not present a danger then we are free to appreciate the fog's beautiful shapes and textures, and the mood it creates (1912). Some philosophers prefer the phrase *for its own sake* to disinterest: I attend to the film for its own sake, and not for other instrumental reasons. Engaging from an aesthetic point of view, I would not think it is good *because* it is good for me or will improve me as a person, or *because* it is practically useful, or *because* the subject matter is interesting in itself. I may aesthetically value a film about the destruction of the rainforest, but it will be because of its formal presentation of an important topic, not simply *because* the topic is important (or important to me). I may even consider the film's educational or political value – which can exist even if it lacks aesthetic value – is enhanced by the merits of its formal presentation.

The aesthetic attitude aims to be receptive and responsive, to judge something on its merits, and not let prejudices influence. 'Interest' in this context means, 'he knows the student too well, therefore *he has an*

---

[7] These interests, however, may be of value to an aesthetic point of view.

[8] See 1.9: 'Form and style'. An aesthetician is someone who is knowledgeable about aesthetics or about the nature and appreciation of beauty. I use it here to refer to those people who are not strictly philosophers, but who work in aesthetics (for example, some academics in Film Studies).

*interest*; he can't be trusted to judge the student's work fairly or dispassionately'. So, for example, if I love Philippe Starck chairs and they appear in a film, I should not think better of its aesthetic value because I am elated at their inclusion. Perception can be skewed by the disproportionate liking or disliking of features. The aspiration is to adopt a sympathetic disposition: to be guided by the film, rather than by preconceptions and predilections. For Alexander Nehamas, an artwork would not necessarily be approached with a settled sense of self, and there might be an expectation of change (2007: 57). On the other hand, an evaluation of an artwork may be clouded if a viewer is too pliant. It is a balance that is difficult to maintain.

Disinterest is sometimes conceived in terms of maintaining a distance, and without some distance, aesthetic evaluation is not possible. Bullough says that the aim is to be properly distanced. If there is 'under-distancing' the film will be treated inappropriately, like a real event, and its existence as a constructed artefact will be underappreciated (Collinson 2002: 160). If there is an 'excess of distance' judgement will be impaired because there will not be sufficient involvement. Perhaps the word 'attitude' and the phrase 'point of view' imply too much distance: standing outside the work and looking upon it. These labels might give credence to the notion that the aesthetic attitude is a form of aloof contemplation. Distance need not, however, be emphasised at the expense of involvement. The excellence of an occurrence – a glance by an actor, an adjustment by the camera, a piece of instrumentation on the soundtrack at a particular moment – may only reveal itself after getting closer. For Nehamas, the beauty of many things is, at first sight, difficult to discern, disclosed gradually and only through dedication; beauty is not only something that strikes immediately and is obvious (98).

Indeed, the aesthetic point of view will also be characterised by a deepening attentiveness to the form of the work (especially when the work appears to be rewarding the attentiveness). Denis Donaghue, drawing upon the writings of Louise M. Rosenblatt, defines 'aesthetic reading', in the realm of literature, as a slow reading which is responsive to the moment-by-moment experience of sentences (1998: 13). This also implies returning on future occasions to read the same parts again. Rosenblatt contrasts 'aesthetic reading' to an 'efferent reading' that is motivated by what information or meanings it will take away. Therefore, it is usual for the front page of a newspaper to be read in an efferent way (13). An aesthetic reading is interested in the *sense* of the words and the diverse experience they offer given their particular context and their relations (and Donaghue likens this to literary critic William Empson's (1906–84) description of 'complex words' and the variety of possibilities these words hold (Empson 1995[1951]))[9]. Literature is not considered as a static block of meaning waiting to be translated. Words develop a sense within the configuration of the sentence, line, paragraph, verse, or chapter, and are not simply regarded as referential, referring straightforwardly to something they designate. The reader creates a framework into which they 'incorporate … ensuing words and phrases' (Donaghue 1998: 13). They tentatively organise meanings that are undergoing continual adjustment during the initial encounter, the subsequent encounters, and the contemplation in between. This understanding of literary engagement can be appropriated for film, substituting shots and elements within the shot for words. In any particular case, the representational aspect of images may not constitute their richest aesthetic meaning. For example, in my hypothetical film which includes a chair designed by Philippe Starck, some of the film's sense may derive from meanings associated with the chair's existence in the real world. At the same time, under Rosenblatt's suggestion, the chair will also take on particular meanings depending on its place within the configuration of the film's world: its relationship to the performers, to the composition of shots, to the narrative structure, and to the overall visual design. These meanings become accessible when the film is 'read' from an aesthetic point of view[10].

## 1.3 Aesthetic taste

In the eighteenth century, philosophers were interested in the type of judgement that is based on the taste of the one who judges. James Beattie, an eighteenth-century moral philosopher, describes taste as 'the capacity to be easily, strongly and agreeably affected with beauty', and beauty becomes a primary concern for philosophers of taste (Day 2010: 183). Gary Day writes, 'In protestant theology beauty lost its equal status with the good and the true to which it became subordinated. But, in the discourse

---

[9] For more elucidation of a 'complex word', see 3.5: 'Encouraging perceptual activity'. See also 2.7: 'Close reading'.
[10] An aesthetic weakness would be for a film to rely overly on its representational content, or to rely on simplistic, stereotypical, or even offensive representations of people, things, and events that are not redeemed by their configuration and presentation.

of taste, [beauty] seems to have acquired a value in its own right and to have broken free from the domination of ethics and epistemology' (183). Joseph Addison (1672–1719), for example, an influential philosopher on taste, explains that taste 'discerns the beauties of an author and the imperfections with dislike' (183). The philosophy of taste marked, according to Day, 'a huge cultural shift' that is nothing less than 'the birth of the modern' (180). In Britain, there was a change in the approach to artworks: the individual's experience of the work now took precedence over matters of truth, morals, representation, rhetorical effects, or scholarship. Day explains the political dimension of this change: the interest in taste is linked to 'a new freedom of self-determination' where the individual 'exercises ... judgment' and does not 'simply obey' (180).

Immanuel Kant (1724–1804) wants to capture the idea that in aesthetic forms of judgement, when we respond to some item as beautiful or not, we are obliged to judge for ourselves. He contrasts this to a rational judgement. Rationalising is distinguished from reasoning with the former referring to the act of thinking that is in accordance with principles of logic (Kant 1987(1790): §1). The judgement of taste cannot be rationally derived, deducted, or proven from pre-existing rules or premises. Equally, the moral judgement should be differentiated from the judgement of taste because the latter unlike the former is not based on rules of behaviour – 'thou shalt not kill' – which would dictate the judgement. This judgement of taste is based on what has been labelled, post-Kant, as 'the immediacy thesis' (Shelley 2013). 'Immediacy' captures the experiential aspect of the judgement that is based on the senses (akin to the sense of taste). It does not necessarily imply that the judgements are temporally immediate, or instantaneous, and without mental activity, reasoning, or contemplation. Rather, it implies that they are singularly contingent, dependent on events and conditions not yet known. These distinctions are formulated and elaborated in Kant's book *Critique of Judgment* (originally published in Prussia in 1790), also known as the *Third Critique* because it follows two critiques on Pure Reason and Practical Reason. The *Third Critique* is widely recognised as *the* pre-eminent contribution to evaluative aesthetics and is in many respects its fundamental text.

In this philosophical context, therefore, the 'judgement of taste' refers to the individual exercise of judgement and does not refer to a person having correct taste. I mention this distinction because in other contexts being a 'person of taste' might represent someone who knows the rules of taste according to certain cultural and societal norms. Nor is 'taste' carrying the same connotations it does in contemporary discourse where it is often taken to mean a particular preference or liking for something as when people say, 'this is to my taste' (or more commonly say, in expressing dislike, 'this is *not* to my taste'). This conception of taste is closer to Kant's idea of the 'agreeable' which is understood to be a more personal or more private liking (§7). Examples of food and drink are often supplied at this point: liking a particular food should not lead to a judgement that it is beautiful, merely that it is agreeable (to you). In this regard, Roger Scruton (1944– ) writes vividly about the 'spasms of recoil' and 'being contaminated' – he calls it the 'yuk' feeling – on encountering an artwork, or an aspect of it, that is disliked (1999: 386). It might happen, for example, in reaction to the work's attitude to its material, or its tone of address. He considers taste, and more particularly distaste, as important, and necessary, because it shows the 'refusal to be drawn into and compromised by another's desire' (386). Sometimes, we may feel 'presumed upon', and he likens this to 'an unwanted sexual advance', like an unwelcome hand placed on a knee (386–7). I think the usefulness of this response to our aesthetic judgements will be limited, however, if the taste appears to be arbitrary, prejudiced, narrow or too personal. For example, there is a problem if aesthetic taste is anchored in prevailing ideologies of class and education, or is authorised or naturalised by conventional notions of cultural value, and then these influence in advance the considerations of what is, or what is not, of merit. Taste can be a type of snobbery and might take the form of disapproving of entire categories or genres. Many critics were at one time condescending about the aesthetic value of the medium of film. Some may think that only 'art cinema' is worthwhile, or literary adaptations of classic novels, and be appalled by thrillers, Westerns, or female melodramas. Snobbery can work in the reverse direction too, for example dismissing minority films as pretentious while embracing popular blockbusters. These are ingrained attitudes based on a priori assumptions. In contrast, Paul Crowther points out that judgements of taste need not be a product of stubborn isolation, or entail 'a nostalgic lingering amongst established forms and critical idioms' (2010: 114, 112). Taste, for Crowther, is 'an active, developing cultural capacity', and can be affected by 'a comparative ... critical context' (112, 114).

Nonetheless, everyone has preferences. This is the irreducible aspect to what Jerrold Levinson calls our 'aesthetic personality' (2010: 228). Where at all possible it is useful to be aware of this, for example in the case of categories (like genres). One person may acknowledge that a female melodrama is not to his or her taste and hence refrain from engaging in a developed evaluation. Another person who is disposed towards the genre may be more responsive; they may perceive and distinguish aspects that others would fail to, making their evaluation of more use to the reader[11]. Furthermore, particular Westerns by John Ford, Anthony Mann, Clint Eastwood, and Kelly Reichardt may all be of equal aesthetic value, but the Westerns of one may be preferred to the others.

Despite inevitably having preferences, David Hume (1711–76), in his landmark essay *Of the Standard of Taste*, believes that if judges or critics are competent, expert and well trained they will come to intersubjective agreement and produce a standard of taste (2008 [1757]). Many philosophers have challenged the view that 'competent judges' will be more likely to agree than disagree[12]. However, while *a* 'standard' may be neither possible nor desirable, canons do exist. They manifest in lists of classics or best films ever made, or in curriculum choices, and they do influence. Levinson discusses 'the paradox of aesthetic perfectionism': although I might wish to cultivate my taste by following the advice of others, perhaps expert critics or teachers, I also, at the same time, have good reasons not to surrender my aesthetic self (2010: 229). Indeed, one could imagine the logical conclusion of 'aesthetic perfectionism' to be indiscernibility and homogeneity. Levinson suggests, however, that 'perfectionism ... is compatible with a pluralism', as illustrated by the example of the directors of Westerns (232). The important conclusion for Levinson is that the aesthetic personality should be nurtured conscientiously, and refuse to accept any 'ready-made profile adopted from others or from the surrounding culture' (230). Indeed, one purpose of adopting an aesthetic point of view is to be adaptable, and gratefully so, without being chameleonic or compliant.

In a similar way to training a palate to appreciate certain food and drink, there is an acceptance that taste can evolve and become more discerning. My own view is that if we talk of 'improving' or 'cultivating' our taste it would be most profitably understood in the sense of improving or cultivating a multifarious 'faculty'. Therefore, it would be about enhancing skills of, for example, observation, interpretation and comparison, so that I can learn to evaluate effectively for myself, rather than coming to accept works which are culturally lauded, or part of a pre-ordained canon, or those which others consider to be good for me. It may well be worthwhile

---

[11] On the other hand, someone so disposed will also need to be wary of indulgence.

[12] See 1.6: 'Seeking Agreement' below and for further discussion of Hume see 2.10: 'Evaluative Criteria'.

to recognise the merits of such works, but if one does, it should result from a faculty that is well trained, not one that is well behaved.

## 1.4 Sensory immediacy

The sensory element to the aesthetic was built into the original Greek word *aesthesis*, and this element still constitutes one common understanding of the term. Kant thinks that the sensory response is essential to a judgement of the beautiful because it differs to the response derived from a pre-existing rule or concept from which understanding can be rationalised. Judging a face to be beautiful is not the same as knowing that two plus two equals four. The sensory does not communicate in terms of clear rules or concepts, and therefore does not have an obvious standard of correctness on which everyone can straightforwardly agree.

The sensory immediacy of artworks is a fundamental part of the aesthetic experience. The philosopher Mary C. Rawlinson draws on an example from Marcel Proust's *Remembrance of Things Past* (Vol. 5) where the character Bergotte, who is unwell, reads a piece of criticism about Jan Vermeer's painting *View of Delft*. This was a painting that Bergotte thought he knew by heart, but the critic celebrates a patch of yellow wall – 'of a beauty that was sufficient in itself' – which Bergotte had overlooked (Rawlinson 2006: 139). Sacrificing his health, Bergotte is compelled to visit the painting once again. He too is overwhelmed by the wonder of this yellow patch, so much so that he passes away before he leaves the gallery. For Rawlinson, the fictional incident vividly exemplifies a number of matters. The little patch of yellow wall is 'precious in itself' and not valued for an extrinsic reason (140). The artist's perception, in this case, Vermeer's, is palpably embodied. This perception is encountered and recovered by Bergotte, and this encountering is critical – no less a matter of life and death. Rawlinson says that a beautiful thing 'attacks our eyes and makes us desire it, engendering a longing'; it might provoke us to 'sacrifice' things to be in its presence; reproductions are unsatisfactory, and mark its absence; and when lost, like a loved one, 'there is no substitute for the sensuous materiality' (138)[13].

---

[13] Rawlinson also notes that the story illustrates the importance of aesthetic evaluation – and one based in vivid detail – because, as well as Vermeer's artistry, it is the critic who *draws attention* to the yellow patch that 'generously yield[s] the pleasure' to

The medium of film differs from the medium of painting, and what is meant by reproduction, texture, and presence in the context of film is different but, in principle, the same ideas hold. V.F. Perkins (1936–2016) argues against the belief that a film's value is found merely in its subject matter or in its literal statements, and he advises that we should not 'discount … the very things for which one goes to the cinema: the *extraordinary resonances* which a director can provoke by his use of actors, décor, movement, colour, shape, *of all that can be seen and heard*' (1963: 5; quoted and discussed in Gibbs 2013: 130; my emphasis). For example, the evaluation of a line of dialogue would regard not only *what* is said, but the *way* it is said, perhaps the intonation, the pace, pitch, volume, and tone of voice; and *how* it is presented, perhaps the relationship to other features, such as the camera, soundtrack, and other characters; and *when* it is said, perhaps how far into the film or into a particular scene. It is important, however, not simply to equate the acknowledgement 'of all that can be seen and heard' with instances of particularly affective films, or being particularly affected. From an evaluative point of view, the difficulty, with regard to a medium that is disposed towards sensory affectivity, is how the worth of the sensory and the affect is assessed in each case and how it is distinguished from, for example, the asserted, the affected, or simply from instances of visual and aural pleasure. Even though the sensory may be an essential component of aesthetic experience, acknowledgement of it will not secure an aesthetic evaluation.

## 1.5  Aesthetic pleasure

The sensory underpins aesthetic engagement, but for Kant sensory pleasure is merely 'agreeable' and it 'gratifies us in sensation'; it is like being seduced or deluded by a 'charm' (1987 [1790]: §14). Aesthetic pleasure is not equivalent to sensory pleasure, nor is it simply the pleasure taken in the appearance, 'look', or style of things as it is sometimes taken to be in ordinary discourse[14]. So what is the species of pleasure that might be

---

Bergotte (140). In addition, I note that the persuasiveness which returns Bergotte to the work for a renewed engagement, as criticism should, appears to be unwittingly death dealing, and therefore gravely important.

[14] Indeed, the word aesthetic is often used in a limited way to refer to surface appearance, or simply to the general 'look' of something. For example, 'I like the aesthetic of my toaster, especially the pattern of tiny loaves of bread across its front'.

described as aesthetic? According to Levinson, aesthetic pleasure is 1) disinterested, 2) not rule-bound, 3) focused on the formal design of the work, and 4) the by-product of judgement (which is also disinterested and not rule-bound) (2005: 330–4)[15].

Firstly, the pleasure should be disinterested. There is a distinction to be made between a film that may bring me, and perhaps others, some pleasure and one that (I think) is good. Aesthetic pleasure is not derived, for example, from subject matter I find pleasurable (perhaps a film with a story about courage in the face of adversity); nor from features I personally like or desire (perhaps a film containing exotic locations). These may be excellent pleasures, but they are not aesthetic pleasure.

Secondly, the pleasure is derived from the relatively indefinite quality of the engagement. Because the object cannot easily be categorised in terms of a concept or a rule, the arrangement of its formal features stimulates the imagination into what Kant calls 'free play' (1987 [1790]: §9). The imagination is stimulated to make sense of the arrangement of the artwork and this yields aesthetic pleasure. Some works will be particularly stimulating. Malcolm Budd writes:

> one form [may be] better suited to capture attention and reward sustained looking than ... another ... [W]hat matters is that a beautiful form must not offer too little to perceptual contemplation or exploration (as a simple geometrical figure does), or present an array of contours, shapes, volumes, and colours that appear unrelated to one another, so that it is difficult to grasp perceptually as a unified whole. Rather, it must display an appearance of some complexity that invites the eyes to play back and forth across its features in appreciation of the various relations among its aspects ... [A]esthetic pleasure ... involves variety in its ... object, pleasure being taken in the manner in which the various aspects are related to one another (2008: 15–16, 34).

This leads into Levinson's third characteristic which is that aesthetic pleasure is derived from the formal design of the work. Drawing on Kant, Levinson says that pleasure is taken in the design's 'impression of purposiveness' by which he means that pleasure is taken in the purposeful arrangement and development of the form that has not been dictated by a practical

---

[15] For Zangwill, the advantage of an aesthetic approach is that unlike many approaches – for example, institutional, historical, ideological, semantic, and semiotic ones – it intimately and sincerely recognises the pleasurable attraction to artworks (2012: 11).

## What is evaluative aesthetics?

purpose (2005: 330). It is at this point that the *quality* of the formal arrangements also yields pleasure. Thus, aesthetic pleasure may also be derived from 'a property generated by … the relations among [the aspects] (so the experience of a "well-balanced" wine ["well-balanced" being the quality in this case] qualifies, not as purely sensory, but as aesthetic)' (Budd 2008: 34). Monroe Beardsley (1915–85) describes aesthetic pleasure as that yielded by qualities, and more precisely, formal qualities and regional qualities (1981a [1958]: 82–8). Formal qualities are, for example, balance, unity, complexity, or tension, and regional qualities are something like the characteristics – often akin to behavioural characteristics – that are achieved by the formal arrangements, for example, subtlety, eloquence, or vibrancy (Levinson 2005: 331)[16].

Aesthetic pleasure is dependent on the qualities of relation, and it is not normally derived from isolated or detachable effects[17]. Kant believes that aesthetic pleasure should derive from the object's structure or design. At the same time, aesthetic pleasure is not simply produced by a pleasant design. A shot in a film may contain unpleasant, difficult, or sad subject matter, and it may be made more demanding if, for example, it is held still for a long period, denying other viewpoints that might appease. It may be *aesthetically* pleasurable, however, because the difficult material is presented appropriately or revealingly and is productively in keeping with the film's patterns (perhaps a stimulating variation). A relaxation of the form or a softening of the material may cause aesthetic displeasure because the film has betrayed its strategies and its legitimate claims upon a viewer[18].

The fourth characteristic of aesthetic pleasure is the pleasure taken from appreciation. Kendall Walton claims that pleasure is taken *in* the admiration felt towards the aesthetic merits of a work (2008a). Equally, displeasure occurs from the negativity aroused by demerits, and the judgement upon a work becomes more negative as it is blamed for this displeasure. Walton says that 'displeasure and disapproval may thus feed on and reinforce each other, as pleasure and admiration do in positive cases' (13). Pleasure may also be taken in the work getting us to admire

---

[16] See 1.10: 'Aesthetic qualities' below.

[17] This relates to Perkins' claim with regard to the evaluation of film that individual elements should not receive too much praise or blame because what matters for an aesthetic judgement is the network of relationships (1972). This is discussed in 3.8: 'Relation'.

[18] See 3.2: 'Constraint'.

it, although this could backfire if it is going out of its way to please, too easily, at the expense of properly achieved qualities. Scruton uses the example of F.R. Leavis (1895–1978), the seminal British literary critic, who would criticise a piece of literature for trying to elicit a favourable response that was unearned or undeserved. An awareness of this would lead to a reader being unable to enjoy the literature as it is asking to be enjoyed (Scruton 1974: 139–40)[19].

## 1.6 Seeking agreement

Overemphasising pleasure is a worry for Scruton because it risks overlooking the normative urge in aesthetic response: my judgement expresses not only my pleasure, aesthetic or otherwise, but also my conviction that the work is good. The judgement aspires to correctness. The pleasurable response does not explain the wish to persuade others and regard agreement in aesthetic matters as important (243). The aesthetic judgement is not exclusively private or solipsistic. In Kant's terms, I speak with a 'universal voice': you *ought* to think the film is good too (1987 [1790]: §8). For Scruton, this 'ought' reflects the objectivity that is at stake in the aesthetic judgement. Each element of the work is experienced as 'appropriate' or not, suitable or unsuitable (1974: 248). In a film, every shot, camera angle and movement, edit, piece of dialogue, dramatic action or plot development strikes an aesthetically orientated viewer as, to use Scruton's words, 'in place or out of place' (248). He draws on a point that Ludwig Wittgenstein (1889–1951) makes in his *Lectures on Aesthetics*:

> It is remarkable that in real life, when aesthetic judgments are made, aesthetic adjectives such as 'beautiful', 'fine', etc., play hardly any role at all. Are aesthetic adjectives used in musical criticism? You say: 'Look at this transition', or ... 'The passage here is incoherent'. Or you say, in a poetical criticism ... : 'His use of images is precise'. The words you use are more akin to 'right' and 'correct' (as these words are used in ordinary speech) than to 'beautiful' and 'lovely'. (Wittgenstein 1989[1966]: 3, Point 8)

---

[19] This is one reason why an aspect of an artwork cannot be judged to be of merit simply because it is understood to be the fulfilment of a maker's intention. Leavis understood the critic as 'someone able to respond fully to the author's premisses without being gulled by them' (Bell 1988: 114). See 2.9: 'Intention, achievement, and skill'.

It is untrue, in my experience, 'that in real life, when aesthetic judgments are made, aesthetic adjectives such as "beautiful", "fine", etc., play hardly any role at all'. Nevertheless, Wittgenstein downplays the criterion of beauty in order to make the counterbalancing observation that a sense of what appears 'correct' penetrates the aesthetic judgement of artworks[20]. It is the puzzling tension between subjectivity and normativity in aesthetic judgement that so vexes Kant and which he catches in the phrase 'subjective universal validity' (1987 [1790]: §8). The distinguishing feature of aesthetic judgement, as distinct from empirical forms of judgement, is that it is based on individual response and yet it demands 'validity' beyond the self (Zangwill 2014).

It is worth emphasising the distinction between the personal claim that I like something and the more inclusive public claim that something is of aesthetic merit. For example, Andrew exclaims, 'This war film is good because it is graceful' whereupon Edward retorts, 'No. I do not think it is good. It is too graceful. The treatment of war deserves an edgier style and a presentation that reflects the ugliness'. If Andrew then replies, 'Well I like it' or 'I like the gracefulness' that would be 'a feeble rejoinder, a *retreat*' to personal preference because Edward's reasons are 'obviously relevant to the evaluation … and because they are *arguable*' (Cavell 2002[1969]: 91–2, original emphasis). Andrew initially claimed the film was good not merely that he liked it. Andrew will need to counter Edward with reasons for his judgement: that in this case, perhaps, the graceful is in service of the elegiac and the mournful. Andrew and Edward now find themselves in the realm of aesthetic dispute where claims cannot be proven with a fact or a rule[21].

---

[20] For Scruton, judging whether a feature seems right or wrong in its present context makes it not unlike judging the appropriateness of behaviour, and therefore has a moral dimension (1974: 247–8). He adds that, 'We admire works of art, as we admire [people]' for their elegance, vigour, eloquence, perspicacity, or complexity (245, my choice of nouns). It is a matter of importance, perhaps a matter of responsibility too, that others come to recognise these qualities.

[21] This imagined exchange is adapted from an example given by Cavell (2002 [1969]: 91–2). Cavell's example, in accord with many similar examples illustrating the Kantian dilemma of aesthetic judgement, compares preferences in food or drink to claims for aesthetic merit in artworks. For example, if you find chocolate ice cream fails to bring you pleasure, I need not be interested in persuading you to prefer it to your favoured vanilla. However, these examples are misleading because there are also questions of aesthetic merit in food and drink. Whatever the sphere of interest, the important distinction is between claiming to like something and claiming it to have merits deserving wider acknowledgement.

How does Kant think that Andrew and Edward will resolve their disagreement? According to Kant when we respond to the beauty of an object, two of our faculties, imagination and understanding, interact. The imagination is unconstrained, experimenting with various permutations of the elements of the object. The understanding is the better-behaved faculty: it constrains the imagination and supplies concepts and classifications (1987 [1790]: §9). (It might appear as if Kant is contradicting his own claim that the judgement of taste is not subsumed under a concept, rule, or principle. This is not necessarily the case, however, because he thinks that although concepts should not straightforwardly *determine* the judgement, they could be *in play*.) Ideally, the imagination and understanding work together, harmoniously balancing each other. At this point, Kant makes the controversial claim that because all rational beings shared these faculties they would come to a shared position: there is ultimately a *sensus communis*, a 'common sense' (§40). This route to agreement has not proved to be a popular component of the Third Critique. It wraps up the dilemma, which Kant himself astutely recognised, and then philosophically dramatised, too neatly; and it does not sit easily with his idea that each viewer is involved in 'free play' in response to the work. According to Guyer, 'Kant's position that we can reasonably claim subjective universal validity for singular judgments of taste – judgments that are always about particular objects – is not demonstrated' (2014a: 442). It is not clear what the reasoning is that moves us from sharing faculties to sharing a specific judgement with regard to a particular object.

The idea of a universally or commonly agreed position fails to recognise the wide-ranging differences over particular works that clearly do occur between people with well-functioning faculties. Consequently, I suggest that presuming the 'universal' viewer (in the case of film) is something to take care with in aesthetic evaluation. Speculating about how 'a' viewer may react, and how the film may want them to react, might be useful and necessary, but a problem can arise if an individual response is universalised into 'the' viewer, 'the' spectator, or 'the' audience, or into a definite 'we' or 'us'. These terms are harmless when referring to conspicuous information (for example, 'we see the character move towards the right' as a substitute for 'the character moves … ' or 'the film shows the character move … ') or when they carry the implication of speaking on behalf of those who might see the film in a specific way (as distinct from speaking on behalf of everybody). However, they can be presumptuous, and even coercive, when accompanying claims that are not straightforwardly verifiable and where there is opportunity for alternative assessment (for example, regarding an interpretation, an evaluation, or a response to an effect). Conscious consideration of these terms helps to act as a reminder that the responsibility in aesthetic evaluation is to show why and how something might be working, and might work for others, not simply to assume that it does work this way for others (because it does for me). The aim would be to propose an account of what *the film* is doing – rather than what *the viewer* is taken to be doing – for other viewers to take into consideration[22]. Aesthetic evaluation depends on various and mutable viewers because if everyone saw everything in exactly the same way it would lose its influential purpose[23].

Rather than universality, Nehamas prefers to think more modestly in terms of 'communities' of agreement (2007: 81). These communities may be surprisingly capacious because judgements can be transferable across cultures, and be trans-historical, without being all-embracing, permanently transcending, or at the cost of diversity. I think that one way in which a *sensus communis* might be said to be operating is that judgements initially contain, build in, or internalise the views of others. They draw on a stock of sensible and relevant judgement, and this does not imply subservient acquiescence[24]. The judgements of others – viewers and makers – penetrate an individual's judgement, but they do not determine, and this is similar to Kant's idea that rules are not determining in the aesthetic realm. There is an evolving osmosis. The important point for Crowther is not whether universality can actually be achieved, but that it operates as an 'ideal goal' or 'regulative principle' (2010: 98). He writes that 'the claim to universal validity's implicit "ought" ... is a confident willingness to have one's judgement put to comparative test' and not 'a demand for compliance' (110). Indeed, another way of rescuing the *sensus communis* idea might be to apply it to operation rather than outcome: we can agree over what would constitute sound evaluative processes while recognising that these could lead to various judgements. Each of us are in a position to show how our imagination and understanding have been used in responding to a work, and another person could see the strengths or the weaknesses in the mental processes. You might consider my evaluation imbalanced because the imagination has been involved in too much 'free

---

[22] The alternative is to substitute 'we' or similar with 'the film' and not with 'I'. The use of 'I' is useful for indicating a more personal, and possibly idiosyncratic, feeling, but would not be regularly called upon.

[23] See further discussion in Klevan (2014a).

[24] The personnel who made the artwork may also draw on a stock of sensible and relevant judgement (whether explicitly or not).

play', and has been insufficiently regulated by the understanding; or too many constraining rules may have inhibited my imaginative capacity, causing me to overlook enriching connections. Alternatively, you might be satisfied by how I have arrived at my judgement, while accepting it as different to yours, or respecting it as equally viable.

The fundamental point about aesthetic judgement is that an evaluative claim cannot be *proven*. I consider this lack of certainty to be a source of motivation, challenge, and inspiration, and not necessarily the limitation it is sometimes felt to be. People are often stirred to express their view of a film, to share it, and sometimes persuade others to agree with it. One purpose of criticism is to act as a formal vehicle for this impulse. At the same time, people are eager to hear the considered views of others. The possibility of agreement, or simply of enlightening exchange, promises a special type of connection. This is something that would not arise if a decisive regulation existed, or the (re)assurance of a common, universal, or transcendent position.

The urge to persuade is especially powerful if it is felt that a film has been overrated or underrated, or that it is especially deserving of admiration and praise. According to Nehamas, if I fall in love with a person I consider beautiful, I do not (in the normal circumstances of my culture) want *you* to fall in love with them too (2007: 74–5). If I love a film I consider beautiful, however, I want to try to persuade you to love it as well so that in loving the same film we become 'friends rather than rivals' (75). Divergence in judgement may frustrate, divide, and isolate. Friendships have dissolved because of aesthetic disagreement[25]. For Stanley Cavell (1926– ), the lack of conclusiveness in aesthetic judgement ensures that it becomes more fundamentally about the nature of engagement: how do we relate to, or acknowledge, each other?[26] With regard to Andrew and Edward's dispute, Cavell says that if Andrew does not counter with pertinent reasons for thinking the war film is good then he may pay a price in Edward's estimation of him (2002 [1969]: 92). Responsibility and trust come into play: there is a responsibility to find ways to convey my experience to earn your trust[27].

---

[25] This happened to French critics turned filmmakers Jean-Luc Godard and François Truffaut.
[26] Cavell sees the aesthetic realm as analogous to his conception of much human interaction in that it is precariously dependent on the insecurities of interpretation (rather than on confirmatory knowledge) (1999 [1979]; 2002 [1969]).
[27] For a related discussion see 2.11: 'Reasons, argument, and objectivity'.

# What is evaluative aesthetics?

The word 'judgement' can sometimes sound too strict, restrictive, and final. However, *The New Oxford Dictionary of English* defines judgement as 'the ability to … come to … conclusions' which are 'considered'; the judgements of legal judges can be lengthy and involved; and Rawlinson says that judgements can be 'prospective' and provisional, 'an invitation to discussion' and 'critical exchange' (Pearsall 1998; Rawlinson 2006: 150). They can be encouragements to become involved. If Andrew judges his friend Patrick to be intelligent and attractive, a third party would be interested in the possibility of befriending Patrick; they would not merely be interested in confirming Andrew's 'verdict' because the verdict is not important in itself (example based on the insights of Nehamas (2007: 52)). We ask whether we want to make this person, this work, this film, 'part of [our] life' (53). Is it worth our while? If we think it is, then we will want to approach, move forward, and learn about them (75). The hope is that they have more (and more) to offer. Many things we think highly of cannot be fully comprehended: there is always more to learn, perhaps concerning something which has not yet been identified (76). There will also be more to value. Although there can be a desire to deliver a decisive verdict and to come quickly to agreement, this book advocates a form of evaluation which is investigative, receptive, and cumulative.

## 1.7 Imagination

Aesthetic evaluation requires imaginative participation. The use of 'imaginative' may be misleading and even worrying to some because it implies an activity that is too private or personal, or even fantastic or fanciful (as in 'she has a wonderful imagination'). Who knows where the mind will travel while experiencing an artwork? The use of an artwork as a stimulus for creative improvisation can be wonderful, but the risk for those wishing to evaluate is that, even if the imaginative activity is influenced and motivated by the work, it may detach itself from its workings, and sometimes even displace it. The inventive imaginative response, despite being a valuable, even essential, experience, might not be helpful in aesthetic evaluations. John Dewey (1859–1952) writes, characterising an aesthetic experience, that 'the one who experiences the work of art loses himself in irrelevant reverie unless his images and emotions are also tied to the object, and are tied to it in the sense of being fused with the matter of the *object*. It is not enough that they should be occasioned by the object' (quoted in Dewey 2005[1934]: 288, original emphasis). In

Kantian terms, the 'free play' of the imagination can outrun the control of the understanding such that the two faculties are not operating harmoniously. The imagination has lost touch with *the form of the work* and its accomplishments.

Nevertheless, there is no preordained, designated point where it can be said for sure that the imaginative response has gone too far (or too far away from the work). Each response has to be looked at to see whether it 'is fused with the matter of the object' through close attention to its details. The imagination, understood as creative mental capacity, may have to 'play' with the components of a film in a variety of permutations, some of them apparently far-fetched, before the work can be properly appreciated, and evaluated. This shows that the aesthetic point of view is exploratory, rather than single-minded or fixed. The imagination tests out the different ways the film can be perceived: the variety of 'perceptual orientations' that the work's complexity engenders (Crowther 2010: 82). It may be trying to glean, even mirror, the creative imagination that initially produced the configurations. Despite the proliferation of characterisations of the film spectator within Film Studies, few of them give enough credence to this mode of aesthetic engagement. There is a tendency to conceive of film viewing, especially the viewing of narrative fiction films, as a linear, straightforwardly cognitive activity where the story is followed through its twists and turns to its conclusion, or alternatively as *affected*, stimulated by visual and aural excitements, steered by desires, or moved by emotions. Viewing with the imagination, the film is not *received* so straightforwardly and directly. Film spectatorship can be conceived as an imaginative exploration of the film's formal design[28].

Scruton is particularly interested in the way that perception of an object is intimately connected with imaginative activity about it (1974: 155). Encountering a sad film is not the same as encountering a sad person: it is an invitation to use the imagination in association with the understanding to think about the sadness in the film and its ramifications. The difference is caught in the fact that given the opportunity we would not want to cheer the film up. For Scruton, sad becomes a concept and *through this conception* the film is experienced[29]. I do not think that this means that a

---

[28] I am not denying the other conceptions, but pointing out that they may not be the whole story.

[29] This is also discussed in Guyer (2014c: 527). I am not sure I have fully grasped Scruton's discussion of imaginative engagement (even after reading Guyer's commentary upon it), but I think this is one useful element of it.

viewer will cease to feel sad because the sadness may also be felt more directly, and because thought and feeling are interlinked. If a film encourages imaginative thoughtfulness about sadness, then I might be made to feel sad in deep and resonant ways. Indeed, given that many films are affective in an immediate and direct way (some aesthetically worthwhile and some not), it is a merit for a film to be structured so that its best emotional qualities will *only* be released – and felt – pending an imaginative engagement.

## 1.8 Aesthetic appreciation

When aspects of a work are released, we might say that it is *appreciated* anew, or that it is appreciated in a way it was not previously. To appreciate something is not equivalent to liking it. Thinking in terms of people is helpful: saying that Andrew appreciates Vivienne is different to saying that he likes or even loves her. Appreciating her would mean that he takes proper account of her, understands her, and perceives her qualities (and perhaps that he values her highly, and feels thankful for her). Appreciation is not equivalent to pleasure or enjoyment because Andrew could enjoy Vivienne's company and take pleasure in it without properly appreciating her (although, as Walton emphasises, feeling appreciative, like feeling admiration, does in itself tend to bring pleasure (2008a)). This holds similarly for engagement with artworks.

Aesthetic criticism tends to be affirmative, emphasising what is laudable. This is partly because it is often motivated by the desire to explore the reasons why something is of value, and promote this value. Furthermore, favourable appreciation is often a prerequisite for getting the most out of a work because it encourages involvement and deeper understanding. Nevertheless, although appreciation is often regarded as admiring, it need not be: it may also carry the sense, according to *The New Oxford Dictionary of English*, of taking sufficient account of, or 'recogniz[ing] the full implications of', as in appreciating a problem, or appreciating the pressure someone is under (Pearsall 1998). An aesthetic appreciation may sometimes want to draw attention to the less advantageous implications of a film's form, or weigh up the merits and demerits.

In some circles, the word appreciation carries amateur connotations, something undertaken by an enthusiastic connoisseur perhaps, and not appropriate to the professional business of disciplinary study. Stein Haugom Olsen, however, treats appreciation as something more fundamental: as a 'mode of apprehension' (1998). Some philosophers, such as Gary Iseminger, believe that appreciation is at the core of 'aesthetic communication' (2004: 25). This is because he considers that people often make or design artefacts *with the intention* that someone will appreciate them, and 'making things to be appreciated by others is a fundamental human impulse' (137). Therefore, the work has the desire for appreciation built into it, and the aspiration to appreciate motivates engagement. The maker does not simply communicate as they would to express a statement of fact, or simply point something out. The proper reception of a work will depend on appreciating its design, its form, and its character – indeed, its nature or being – a type of understanding that will be different from simply grasping semantic content[30]. For Donaghue, artworks need not only be treated as signs to be deciphered, but also as 'tokens of largesse, acts of grace and flair, to be appreciated as such' (1998: 77). Aesthetic communication is a performance of 'inventive eloquence' where appreciation seeks to esteem the inventiveness (78).

Similarly, understanding a work in the sense of comprehending or interpreting it is not equivalent to appreciating it. The purpose of an interpretation may be to explain the purpose of the work or reveal what it denotes or connotes rather than appreciate its value. Olsen emphasises that someone may give a detailed and precise interpretation of a film and it would not constitute an appreciation; responses from an appreciative point of view, however, interpret 'to recover their value, to experience them as valuable' (1998). Nevertheless, an account, while not necessarily explicitly offering an evaluation, may through the illumination of its interpretation – of a work's meaning perhaps – implicitly attribute value and encourage an appreciation. There might be dissatisfaction though with claims for meaning, even if they are apposite, if the film is considered, for example, pretentious, didactic, ethically suspect, or inappropriately lacking in emotion. In such cases, the interpretive account would be failing to *appreciate* the work as it is experienced or even as it appears. The account may even be expressing the meaning better than the film expresses it,

---

[30] Some philosophers, notably Wittgenstein (2006 [1953]), and more recently Cavell (1999 [1979]), believe that much linguistic communication is similar to aesthetic communication in that it is not straightforwardly meaningful and comprehensible, or syntactically and objectively systematic. For these philosophers, linguistic communication is contextual and relational, and to understand words and sentences we need to *appreciate* the character and context of them and the speaker, and our relation to them. Furthermore, according to Cavell, your words do not merely utter something to me, but make claims on me.

and not satisfactorily showing how it is effectively realised in the form. Indeed, *aesthetic* appreciation does not only interpret the work in order to 'recover ... value', for this is true of all forms of appreciation, but also appreciates the manner in which content is formally embodied (Levinson 2005: 334)[31].

## 1.9 Form and style

Form refers to the shape, structure, configuration, and presentation of the work: the form it takes. David Banner's anger causes him to *take the form* of a bulging, muscular giant. Form sometimes narrowly refers only to shape or structure, and excludes other presentational features such as colour or texture. For this restricted definition, the Hulk's green colour would therefore not strictly be part of his form (because he would have the same shape and structure even if he was pink, though not perhaps the same furious street credibility). Nevertheless, in most cases, form in aesthetics refers to the particular way in which a thing exists or manifests, and this includes *all* the elements that make the thing appear as it does[32]. Therefore, Richard Eldridge usefully defines form as 'involving the arrangement of some stuff – stone or paint or words or sounds or bodily motions or images, as may be – by a maker into a form, so that a certain end or effect may be achieved' (2005: 158). Formal elements combine to produce the form of the work, and for film are, for example, shots, edits, performers, words, pictures, locations, colours, light, and sound. Film form therefore includes not only commonly cited features such as shot composition and arrangement, but also, for example, duration, movement, narrative structure, colour palette, soundtrack, an actor's presence, expressions, gestures, and line delivery, or any constituents of the profilmic.

Kant often uses the word design as a substitute for form; indeed, he writes, '*design* is what is essential' (1987 [1790]: §14). 'Design' emphasises the arrangement or pattern of elements in the work[33]. It also emphasises plan and purpose in the work, what Kant calls 'purposiveness', although to be beautiful it should not merely *fulfil* an extrinsic purpose or a rule (§11). Kant refers to 'adherent beauty' where the object is dependent, or

---

[31] See 2.2: 'Understanding and interpretation'.
[32] Besides, colours are a part of an arrangement, and materials have to be manipulated to achieve colour.
[33] See 3.7: 'Pattern'.

constrained, by some pre-existing forms, rules, concepts, and purposes but not *determined* by them such that they could assure the beauty of its form in advance (§16; Guyer 2014a: 439–40)[34]. Most artworks, arguably all, are 'adherent' in some way. There are general forms within which specific works operate: standard modes of artistic representation and expression, such as sonata form or sonnet form. Genres, like the Western or the maternal melodrama, also offer general forms. Some works also deploy or reproduce local forms, figures, and motifs, from previous artworks, or from other aspects of culture and history. This is sometimes implicit and even unknowing, and sometimes explicit, with the work evoking, referencing, recreating, and regenerating (for example, in order to homage, to pastiche, or to provide period reproduction). The evaluative interest lies in the way the form of the individual work makes distinguished use of the more general or pre-existing forms[35]. A film of merit may be dependent on pre-existing forms, but carves out its individuality; a film of less merit is merely derivative of what has gone before[36].

Dependence (but not determination) leads to a consideration of form in relation to function. Objects and furniture are often considered in this way. Stephen Davies believes that the beauty of form should be at one with the fulfilment of its function: he writes that 'It is a hallmark of great design in furniture, for instance, that the qualities making a chair practically usable are at the same time the source of its elegance, grace, and beauty' (2010: 96). Equally, masochism aside, a favourable judgement about an elegant chair would have to be revised if it was found to be uncomfortable (97). Considering a film in terms of the objectives that it is trying to achieve can be useful in evaluation. If characters need to reconcile in a scene, it may be evaluated according to how well it achieves this function (while recognising that there is no one route to fulfilment

---

[34] This contrasts with 'free beauty', illustrated by flowers and birds, which according to Kant, 'belong to no object determined by concepts as to its purpose', or abstract designs, like wallpaper patterns, which 'mean nothing on their own: they represent nothing, no object under a determinate concept' (§16).
[35] Even if, for example, pastiche is part of the aim. See Richard Dyer (2007). See also Camille Paglia's account (1998) of *The Birds* (Alfred Hitchcock 1963 US) for an aesthetic evaluation that illuminates the merits of the film in terms of the precision and density of its evocations of artworks, artefacts, and cultural styles (despite many of them being in all likelihood not explicitly intended by the filmmakers). For a striking example of the number and range integrated into a short sequence see especially her discussion on pp. 35–7.
[36] See 3.3: 'Convention'.

## What is evaluative aesthetics? 43

because there are many differently good reconciliation scenes). Similarly, a part can be evaluated by how well it functions within the design or themes of the whole. For evaluations that prioritise function, aesthetic discussion would proceed not from formal 'devices to functions, but from functions to devices' (Olson 1976: 143). The advantage of emphasising 'functions to devices' as a direction of travel is that because a viewer is alert to the way a work is functioning she or he is predisposed to evaluating its devices relevantly in a holistic context. Attentiveness to functionality might make her or him alert to whether a device is beneficial or incongruous, unhelpful or superfluous: 'I can (or cannot) see how that camera movement helped the film achieve what I thought it was trying to achieve'. Sometimes homing in on devices and *then* trying to account for their function can lead to undue attention, forced explanation and less pertinent justification. The functionally oriented viewer may also be receptive to a range of devices, some relatively subtle, which serve function, rather than having their attention grabbed by a conspicuous one that proclaims 'Device'. Ultimately, however, good evaluative practice moves in both directions because ascertaining and delineating the functions of a work is often not straightforward, and the interrogation of devices can reveal functions[37].

The occasional philosopher and aesthetician argue that aesthetic evaluation should *only* be interested in form at the expense of content (which in this case means ignoring, or in the main relegating, subject matter or meanings). For these formalists, who advocate formalism, form can be treated in isolation. Clive Bell writes, 'To appreciate a work of art we need bring with us *nothing but* a sense of form and colour and a knowledge of three-dimensional space' (quoted in Zangwill 2001: 66; my emphasis). The extreme formalist position is often derided now as, amongst other problems, logically untenable. To give it its due, as Zangwill explains, the position often begins with a passion for advocating the formal distinctiveness of an artist (for Bell, it was Paul Cezanne). The critic is compelled by the formal originality of a work, and then wishes to impress on others its overwhelming importance. The representational or pictorial content, or subject matter, of the painting, for example a cluster of rooftops, is seen as relatively unimportant (66). Furthermore, and understandably, Bell wanted to demarcate what he understood to be appropriate aesthetic responses as against the frequent overestimation of 'mimetic accuracy',

---

[37] See also 2.2: 'Understanding and interpretation' and 2.9: 'Intention, achievement, and skill'.

and the sentimentality of judgement that results from the attachment to particular representations (Hepburn 2005: 51–2). Unfortunately, formalists, such as Bell, then transpose these concerns into an all-encompassing, theoretical polemic about art appreciation[38]. Although adopting an aesthetic point of view entails the prioritising of form, it does not entail formalism. Indeed, most aesthetic appreciation responds to the way in which content is formalised, even in non-figurative or abstract works, such that it is revealed, explored, illuminated, penetrated, intensified, or transformed.

The aesthetic literature often refers to the 'form and content' of a work. The word 'content' can be misleading in this phrase because the content of the artwork – what is in it – is also its form. However, what is commonly meant by 'content' is either the subject matter of the work or the meanings that are expressed by the work (and different versions of formalism, such as that advocated by Bell, argue that one or both of these features should be relegated). If content is understood as, for example, subject matter, conceiving of form and content separately in order to understand their accord can be useful for evaluative purposes. Sometimes the form/content harmonisation is understood as a work having a suitable form to express subject matter. This will be especially congratulated if, for example, the subject matter is thought to be difficult to express, or recalcitrant. Graham Hough praises the author Henry James for a 'masterful manipulation' of 'obstinate and demanding' material in a literary form (1966: 40–1)[39]. We might also praise films that discover appropriate, perhaps original, forms to represent, for example, marginalised groups of people, relegated points of view, or unfamiliar ways of being; or, alternatively, find productive ways of including them in traditional forms. Sometimes, the form/content harmonisation is understood as a work having subject matter that has been suitably fitted or applied to pre-existing forms as, for example, when a director successfully works new subject matter into her characteristic style. Sometimes, subject matter can be inadequate which creates problems for form, such that it appears to be arbitrary, or

---

[38] Zangwill writes that if the 'nothing but' is removed from the controversial Bell claim quoted in this paragraph then it 'renders it respectable [and] almost always true ... If only Bell had put his point as a *necessary* condition rather than as a *sufficient* condition of appreciation' (2001: 66, original emphasis).

[39] Similarly, Hough says of Empson's poem 'Missing Dates' that 'a heavy lump of painful and almost uncontrollable thought-and-feeling is worked into an intricate argumentative and prosodic form' (1966: 41).

to be working too hard to compensate; alternatively, form may fail to invigorate, investigate, or adequately do justice to promising subject matter. At other times, the harmonisation is understood as simultaneous, one is not conceived as preceding the other: the form and the subject matter appear to come into being and develop together, hand in hand.

Kant conceives of artistic content, in a particularly philosophical fashion, as an 'aesthetic idea'. Similarly, for Georg W.F. Hegel (1770–1831), art makes ideas 'accessible to our senses': it is 'sensuous knowing' (Doorly 2013: 118–19). Diané Collinson, illuminating Kant, explains that the creative artist gives ideas 'the appearance of reality through being represented aesthetically in particular, sensuous, complex images' (2002: 140). She uses the example of a dove which represents peace and by doing so brings out a 'wealth of attributes' and connotations such as 'whiteness, purity, the freedom of flight, soft-voicedness and pastoral quiet', which 'expand and enrich' the original concept (of peace), and stimulate pleasurable mental activity (141). When an idea runs through a work we call it a theme, and one merit of a work is for it to 'expand and enrich' its themes as it develops[40]. Theme and form can tightly intertwine, grow, and mature together, mutually enabling each other to become more robust[41].

Because of the particular way artworks embed content in form, according to Diarmuid Costello, they can be 'intelligible and opaque simultaneously'; they are 'amenable to being understood', while not communicating straightforwardly (2006: 97). It is this 'opacity that differentiates artworks from more transparent forms of utterance' (97). Kant believes that in order for the imagination to work, the form should be organised in such a way as not to present meanings too directly or didactically (1987 [1790]: §49; Guyer 2014a: 450). The dove does not literally *say* 'peace' (although its symbolic meaning is now so conventional that we might imagine it does). Critics such as Leavis and Perkins acclaim work whose meaning and significance is substantially enacted or dramatised in the form[42]. For Leavis, there is an ethical dimension to an aesthetic evaluation, but it is dissimilar to that found in an older form of ethical criticism where certain aspects of the content were singled out for moral approval or disapproval, for example, 'admir[ing] Brutus and Hamlet as "good" characters' or 'condemn[ing] … Cleopatra as immoral' (Baldick 1996:

---

[40] 'Theme' may also refer to unifying images, motifs, or groups of notes (for example, forming a melodic unit).
[41] See 3.7: 'Pattern'.
[42] See 3.6: 'Prominence' and 3.8: 'Relation'.

94). The focus for approval or disapproval is instead on the form in which the content, and the attitude to it, reveals itself. It is the 'manner and movement of the expression' that is judged as being, for example, sincere, serious, complex, or mature, and the 'notion of the moral ... is fundamentally aesthetic' (Casey 2011[1966]: 184, 196).

Sometimes the word 'style' is often used as a synonym for form. However, 'style' carries its own specific connotations and it can be useful not to elide it with form. Most philosophers of criticism deploy the word 'style' when they wish to refer to a particular way or manner of doing something. Therefore, to say that an artwork has a style means that it does not only exhibit a noteworthy form, meritorious or otherwise. It means that the artwork would include elements, qualities, and modes of expression that are consistent, constant, or characteristic, and would have some type of pattern and traits (Meyer 1987: 21; Ross 2005: 229)[43]. As Aaron Meskin explains, style is 'distinguished from form by requiring that the former must involve some sort of regular occurrence not required by the latter' (2005: 496). A style is often exhibited across multiple works, although one film can have a style, as can one scene or sequence. There are individual styles: directors, actors, screenwriters, and cinematographers may have well-defined individual styles. There are also general styles: group, school, period, or regional styles, for example, the style of the rococo or, in film, the style of the French *nouvelle vague* in the 1960s. The Hollywood cinema of the 1920s to 1960s has been understood as a period style, or even a school (and labelled 'The Classical Hollywood Cinema' by David Bordwell et al. (1988)). There are also universal styles such as classicism and realism that may transcend specific places and periods (Meskin 2005: 489). The word 'aesthetic' is commonly used as a substitute for style: the *nouvelle vague* aesthetic, or Michael Haneke or David Lynch or Joseph von Sternberg's aesthetic. A style will also include characteristic content, meaning, concerns, and ideas (496).

Having an individual style is often rightly recognised as a merit because it bestows an identity on the work and marks it out as atypical. Traditionally, film directors with singular styles, productively transferring from film to film, are celebrated. Andrew Sarris acclaims those directors, famously dubbed 'auteurs', who create films where material and

---

[43] 'Style' in this context does not refer to style as elegance or refinement of manners (for example, 'Fred Astaire has style'), or to a fashionable or ostentatious mode of existence (for example, 'They live in style'). Some styles, however, may also 'have style' or be ostentatious.

form are invested and imbued with a world-view, a vision, an attitude, a personality, and feeling (1985 [1968]). For J. Middleton Murry, these impulses will be 'irradiating' the work (1965 [1922]: 42). Filmmakers who achieve distinctiveness within constrained general styles, for example within Hollywood popular genres or within the 'realism' demanded by communist regimes, have been particularly lauded. Having an individual style, however, does not alone confer aesthetic value. As John Gibbs writes, 'That a film is recognisable as the work of a particular director does not, of itself, reveal anything about its merits [...] Being distinctive is not the same as being distinguished' (2013: 28, 240). A distinctive style should itself be evaluated. Because style is often apprehended as expressing a personality, attitude, or world-view, these expressions can be evaluated negatively as well as positively, as with a person (for example, trivial rather than serious, overbearing rather than sensitive). Some aesthetic critics, such as Leavis, are acutely sensitive to the 'existential postures enacted in characteristic uses' of [literary] form (Bell 1988: 128). Aesthetic and moral concerns once again meet because for Leavis the style 'is an enactment of moral identity' (53).

In addition, an indisputable style may exhibit mere stylishness or be a collection of mannerisms; and a style that can be fruitful on some occasions may on others lose its lustre, calcify, become mechanical, or lapse into self-absorption or self-parody. Middleton Murry writes about 'a barren idiosyncrasy of style, when a habit of language or expression is no longer informed by keen perceptions and compelling emotions' (1965 [1922]: 19). Sometimes there is 'atrophy of the central, originating power' and technique 'begins to assume a life of its own', alive perhaps, but like a 'weed' (19–20). The style is no longer animated by substantial content, emotion, insight, or perspicuity[44]. The test of true individuality of style, for Middleton Murry, is that 'we should feel it to be inevitable ... a whole mode of experience that is consistent with itself ... if this ... is perceptible to us, it will be accompanied by a conviction that the peculiarity of style was necessary' (43).

A good style need not be strikingly impressive, and some fine individual styles are modest and relatively impersonal. Some filmmakers choose to operate adeptly within general styles, change style from film to film depending on the material, or devote themselves to best rendering the work of a colleague (for example, a director serving the style of a screenwriter,

---

[44] Middleton Murry particularly pinpoints feeling and emotion as the driving force of good style, but there may be a range of worthwhile motivating features.

or a performer). It should also be acknowledged that a work can still be of formal merit even if it lacks an individual style. Furthermore, the merits of a film by a filmmaker with a recognisable style may be the result of the filmmaker's local execution, timing, or combining of elements, rather than the result of those traits which are most obviously characteristic.

Aesthetic evaluation is also interested in discerning how different styles integrate, or accommodate each other. It might consider the relationship between an individual style and prevailing or universal ones – for example, director Eric Rohmer's personal style within the prevailing style of the *nouvelle vague* and within the universal styles of classicism and realism – in order to assess merit. It might consider the suitability of the style or personality of an actor for the character they are playing or for the dramatic or stylistic context. It might consider the style of the film alongside the style of its source material such as a novel. Because film is a collaborative art, they might also consider how well different individual styles have meshed on one film. For example, doubts have been cast about the Hollywood comedy *Ball of Fire* (Howard Hawks 1941 US) over whether the sarcastic dialogue of Billy Wilder meshes with the undemonstrative, relatively discreet directorial manner of Howard Hawks and whether either of them meshes with the strident deep-focus compositions favoured by cinematographer Gregg Toland (for instance, see Callahan 2012: 139)[45].

## 1.10 Aesthetic qualities

Form and style are tangible features of artworks – patterns, shapes, colours, texture, compositions, movements, figures, devices, and designs can be pointed out – but works also have qualitative features that are less tangible such as discretion and stridency (to use features cited in the *Ball of Fire* example). Noël Carroll believes that engaging in the 'qualitative dimensions of the world at large', including artworks, is a major part of the aesthetic experience, and that 'a great deal of our attention to artworks is devoted to detecting their characteristic' qualities (2002: 189, 199). The most famous aesthetic quality is beauty, but there are hundreds of other possible qualities. For Isenberg, form is often experienced as qualitative so, for example, the Hulk's form is experienced as looming and ferocious (and we might choose

---

[45] See also discussion in Klevan (2013).

## What is evaluative aesthetics?

to describe it in this way rather than in a strictly formal manner, for example, by dimension, density, and curvature) (1973: 36–52; discussed in Guyer 2014c: 383; the Hulk example is mine). Beardsley divides qualities into what he calls 'formal qualities' such as balance, unity, or tension and 'regional qualities', which are akin to characteristics applicable to humans, such as vivacity, serenity, subtlety, and gloominess (1981a [1958]: 82–8). Individual elements, single parts, might have 'local qualities', often homogenous, such as darkness or green, but regional qualities cannot be found in individual parts because they result from combination (Guyer 2014c: 401–2). Qualities may also be divided up into broad 'verdictive' qualities, that is to say umbrella merit and demerit terms, such as good and bad, or even beautiful, and into more precise 'substantive' qualities such as unified, balanced, integrated, lifeless, serene, sombre, dynamic, powerful, vivid, delicate, moving, trite, or sentimental[46]. These are the exact adjectives used by Frank Sibley (1923–96), the most cited and respected writer on aesthetic qualities (2006 [1962]: 1). Sibley's concepts are not only limited to adjectives, but include critical ascriptions such as 'telling contrast', 'sets up a tension', 'conveys a sense of', or 'holds it together' (1–2).[47] Alan Goldman has helpfully broken down aesthetic qualities into more various sub-categories:

Broad evaluative qualities: 'beautiful, ugly, sublime, dreary'.

Formal qualities: 'balanced, graceful, concise, loosely woven'.

---

[46] 'Verdictive' and 'substantive' are terms used by Zangwill (2014). Note that 'a quality' refers to an attribute or a characteristic and it need not be meritorious.

[47] Sibley's papers are a fine example of ordinary language philosophy operating in aesthetics because he is interested in learning about artworks by way of analysing the deployment of vocabulary in relation to them. He does not believe in theorising, a priori, but rather, influenced by the philosophy of Wittgenstein, looks at particular linguistic responses in their contexts. His contexts, in this case, are essays and books on art and literary criticism, although he is also interested in the language used by non-professionals. Like Beardsley, he believes that the discipline of philosophical aesthetics is essentially meta-criticism: Beardsley writes that it is 'concerned with the nature and basis of criticism ... just as criticism itself is concerned with works of art' (1981a [1958]: 6). From this point of view, 'philosophy is a second order, meta-level ... activity', parasitic on 'first order activities, such as chemistry, religion, or history' or, in this case, criticism of artworks (Wreen 2014). One aim of ordinary language philosophy is to *clarify the concepts* we use in our conversations and our writing about things, and indeed Sibley's particular term for aesthetic qualities was 'aesthetic concepts'. Clarifying concepts is not an end in itself, but helps us to better discriminate and articulate, and thereby to better understand and characterise.

Emotion qualities: 'sad, angry, joyful, serene' [the film is sad, the film is angry].

Evocative qualities: 'powerful, stirring, amusing'.

Behavioural qualities: 'sluggish, bouncy, jaunty'.

Representational qualities: 'realistic, distorted, true to life'.

Second order perceptual qualities: 'vivid, dull, muted, steely, mellow (said of colours or tones)'.

Historically related qualities: 'derivative, original, daring, bold, conservative' (1998: 17).

Many qualities are explicitly evaluative. Some of them appear to be non-evaluative, and merely descriptive, such as sad. However, sometimes the implication in using sad to describe a work is that the manifestation of this emotional quality is a merit: 'the film has done well to achieve the quality of sadness'. Some descriptive attributions, stillness for example, may indicate merit or demerit (tranquillity or inertness). On some occasions, a description is assumed to be a merit and it is not clear why it is; this often happens when the quality, for example, 'joyful', 'dark', or 'dissonant', happens to be favoured.

Aesthetic qualities depend on the configuration of what are called 'non-aesthetic properties' (also called 'base properties', or 'objective properties') which are similar to Beardsley's elemental parts. In film, a non-aesthetic or base property might be an edit, a colour, a sound, or a camera movement. Outside aesthetic philosophy, these labels can be disconcerting. This is because in Film Studies, for example, properties such as colour, editing, or camera movement are often referred to as aesthetic elements (and anyone attending to them would be thought to be pursuing aesthetic study). In Sibley's terms, however, and in most aesthetic philosophy, editing as such would be a non-aesthetic, base property. The qualities *that result from* the editing or the use of edits are aesthetic. The recognition of an aesthetic quality can be the route into examining and analysing *how* the film achieves it through its non-aesthetic or base properties. For example, the information on the Criterion DVD case for *Secret Sunshine* (Chang-dong Lee 2007 South Korea) attributes to the film a 'supple' quality, and this, chiming with my own experience, prompts a consideration of how its base properties create this suppleness[48].

---

[48] In Film Studies, the study of the qualitative merit is undeveloped. New work on mood by writers such as Robert Sinnerbrink (2012) is beginning to rectify this, but a mood in a film is rarely an aesthetic quality in Sibley's prime evaluative sense. 'Sad'

# What is evaluative aesthetics? 51

Some important insights result from the relationship between non-aesthetic, base properties and aesthetic qualities. Firstly, Sibley claims there is no logical entailment from base properties to aesthetic properties because even though Olivia and Edward may agree on the base properties in the film, Edward may consider the result of their configuration to be dynamic where Olivia may not. Secondly, there is no logical entailment from aesthetic qualities to more general verdictive qualities like good. Banality would be usually considered a demerit quality. Yet, many great pop songs have banal lyrics that are transformed by musicality and performance so that the banal component appears not merely something to overlook, but embrace. It is arguable that the film *Blue Velvet* (David Lynch 1986 US) conjoins banality with qualities of sincerity, conviction, and earnestness to create unsettling tensions. The riposte might be that the film only uses banality as a means to an end, and as a whole, it is not banal – 'banal' is being used here descriptively, rather than evaluatively, about a feature of the film – but this is not necessarily an easy distinction to draw. Examples using graceful and graceless are more clear-cut: gracefulness may often be a merit inducing quality, but in some films, those that wish to be raw or uncomfortable perhaps, it may detract. What is required is gracelessness[49]. Alternatively, someone might claim a female character to be a merit in a film because she has 'grace' or her behaviour is 'graceful', and although this could be a merit in certain cases, it is not automatically so because gracefulness is also a clichéd or stereotypical mode of female characterisation and presentation[50].

Therefore, aesthetic qualities cannot be deductively derived: deduced from a logical progression such as, 'All films with unbroken camera movements are graceful'. Nor can they be inductively derived: induced from a general rule such as, 'All films, or the women in them, are better for being graceful, or all films are worse for containing banality' (and here there is an echo of Kant's understanding of aesthetic judgement as not conditioned by rules). For Sibley merits are *relational*:

---

and 'sombre' would qualify as moods; 'supple' and 'subtle' would not. See Klevan (2012) for a discussion of the aesthetic quality of fluency (in relation to performance). See also my book on Barbara Stanwyck that is structured around five of the performer's qualities (with a chapter devoted to each): responsiveness, multiplicity, tonal finesse, restraint, and stillness (Klevan 2013).
[49] See discussion of 'crude' in reference to *Written on the Wind* (Douglas Sirk 1956 US) in 3.6: 'Prominence'.
[50] Rather than being based on the requirements of the particular film, the meritorious ascription is perhaps based on an implicit assumption that women should be, and it is good if they are, graceful.

[T]he very same feature, say a colour or shape or line of a particular sort, which helps make one work [of art] may quite spoil another. 'It would be quite delicate if it were not for that pale colour there' may be said about the very colour which is singled out in another picture as being largely responsible for its delicate quality. No doubt one way of putting this is to say that the features which make something delicate or graceful, and so on, are combined in a peculiar and unique way; that the aesthetic quality depends upon exactly this individual or unique combination of just these specific colours and shapes so that even a slight change might make all the difference. (Sibley 2006[1962]: 11–12)

Sibley's claim that 'a slight change might make all the difference' should perhaps be an abiding dictum not only for aesthetic qualities, but also for aesthetic evaluation in general[51].

Qualitative characteristics appear to be properties that are present in the work and, indeed, another name for aesthetic qualities or aesthetic concepts is 'aesthetic properties'. This draws attention to the fact that qualities, such as subtle or crass, are not obvious properties. Aesthetic qualities cannot be straightforwardly pointed out in the way, in normal circumstances, a location can be pointed out, or a physical body, or a colour. Their mysterious existence is the reason they have continued to hold a fascination in philosophy: in the work, but where? Sibley believed that despite aesthetic properties being *in* the work the recognition of them might sometimes require some extra feat of perception: the 'exercise of taste ... or sensitivity, of aesthetic discrimination or appreciation' would lead to a heightened 'perceptiveness' (2006 [1962]: 1). This is why Sibley believes that good descriptions and evaluations – which draw our attention to the manifestation of qualities – will guide and improve our perception of the work[52]. For many philosophers, aesthetic qualities are 'emergent' (Mitias 1988: 28). They are potentialities whose actuality is not predetermined, and they are revealed, manifested, and disclosed in the process of aesthetic perception[53]. Furthermore, according to Walton, qualities also depend on broader categories, genres, conventions, and traditions, outside the work. Some qualities will only be perceived when the work

---

[51] See also 2.10: 'Evaluative criteria'.
[52] This is also why Sibley believes that criticism takes the form of a perceptive guide rather than a systematic or logical proof. See 2.3: 'Perception'.
[53] Both Sibley and Scruton write about this, as do philosophers Mikel Dufrenne and Roman Ingarden. Ingarden understands that aesthetic qualities are 'concretised' in the act of viewing (Chojna 2005: 225; see also Mitias 1988).

# What is evaluative aesthetics? 53

is considered within these broader areas, for example seeing the film through the history of the Western or through other works by the same screenwriter (Walton 2008b[1970])[54]. Therefore, aesthetic qualities are dependent on a series of different relationships: those within the work, those between the work and its perceiver, and those between the work and its wider context.

Despite their indefinite status, Isenberg believes that aesthetic qualities can declare themselves with the same immediacy as, for example, colours or physical configurations (1973: 36–52). A film may be bold or derivative, supple or clunky, lucid or incomprehensible, and any one of these qualities may be experienced as more prominent or powerful than objects, figures, places, and colours on the screen[55]. I consider that Isenberg's understanding of the experience of properties does not contradict the idea that they may be emergent because although properties may not present themselves *immediately*, when they do present themselves they can do so with *immediacy*. Someone might not initially see a film as subtle, but should they come to see it this way the subtlety could be as striking to them (as more concrete features). The idea that qualities are important properties of a work speaks to an understanding of value as embedded in an artwork's existence and an understanding of evaluation as integral to engagement and comprehension. Some people believe that evaluation can be treated as an optional, even idiosyncratic, extra to be added on later, should one so wish, after a range of more secure or definite properties have been accounted for in a work. In contrast, for those that see aesthetic qualities as integral to the work, the lack of a qualitative assessment in an account will be at the cost of an accurate characterisation[56].

## 1.11 Specificity

The recognition of the specific work is one that runs through many aesthetic studies. Michael H. Mitias claims that although qualities are potentialities

---

[54] Such contexts would be needed to ascribe the qualities named in Goldman's 'Historically related qualities' (the final category in his list above). See also 2.8: 'Comparison, category and context'.

[55] Isenberg discusses 'pretentiousness' in this regard (1973: 172–83).

[56] Assessing the character of a work – sentimental, restrained, sincere, or mature – is not unlike assessing a person. This was an important aspect to Leavis's literary evaluations. As Bell states, 'Leavis's best criticism lies in the penetration and accuracy with which he defines moral or emotional quality in the work' (1988: 71).

awaiting engagement, the capacity of the work makes their emergence possible. He writes, 'We can ... say that the [work of art] as a whole exists for the express purpose of creating the right conditions for the emergence of the aesthetic qualities which are potential in the *dynamic inter-dependence of the details which make up the whole*' (1988: 35; my emphasis). In the story about Bergotte seeking out the yellow patch in the Vermeer painting, Rawlinson emphasises the irreducibility of a work's contingent materiality: the way a particular physical and material quality of a work is encountered, here and now, and the way it cannot be experienced adequately in a simpler or reduced form (2006: 138–40). For Crowther, the preoccupation is with how the object 'coheres as a phenomenal *particular*'; it is with the 'form of its *individual* appearance' (2010: 73, original emphasis). For Levinson, aesthetic interest is not in content *per se* because this may be experienced in other works, but in the particular 'complex' of the work's content (2005: 334). For Scruton, aesthetic appreciation is interested in the merits of the individual case: 'the object is *appreciated* for its uniqueness' and no other object will 'do just as well' (1974: 23, original emphasis).

In Kantian terms, aesthetic judgement should not be classificatory: it is not in the business of identifying the object as a particular kind. Kant can be strict about this, but he did concede that an artwork may relate to a concept or category (the idea of 'adherent beauty') as long as it has a singularity that is not consumed by them (Budd 2008: 109). Nehamas writes that aesthetic values are values of 'individuality', hence difference, and sometimes it is knowledge of difference that illuminates the individuality (2007: 91)[57]. The ending of the film *The Woman in the Window* (Fritz Lang 1944 US) provides a simple example. It finishes with the revelation that the story has been 'all a dream' as the lead character wakes up from slumber. The evaluative question, because this is a familiar 'twist' in storytelling, is does the story convention work well *in this case*? I would want to claim that the knowledge that the story is a dream enables the complex presentation of the characters' psychology and desires. It also deepens and enriches formal relationships and dynamics in the film. I

---

[57] In all walks of life, there are those who have the expertise to recognise divergence and distinction where others only see items that are indistinguishable. There are those for whom rap music 'all sounds the same' – the classic despairing cry of the uninitiated parent – and Nehamas writes that they only hear 'a deadly, monotonous beat' while others 'savor the obvious differences between Eminem and P. Diddy' (2007: 94). There will be more differences to 'savor' if Lauryn Hill, Talib Kweli, Immortal Technique, Atmosphere, and Kendrick Lamar are added to the mix (tape).

know from my experience that sometimes this convention might be deployed merely to provide the thrill of the unexpected, to explain a series of mysteries or oddities, or to get the film out of a hole. I also know from experience that the revelation of a denouement may diminish the film as a whole by sealing it up or exhausting it. Later viewings hold less interest than the first innocent viewing (aside from giving the opportunity to register, knowingly, the guile and deception). In the case of *The Woman in the Window*, watching the film repeatedly with the knowledge that the story is a dream improves the experience of the film. The excellence of it depends on its story being a dream, but it does not depend on the revelation that it is a dream[58].

Therefore, similarity might need to be called upon to reveal specificity. Nevertheless, Kant is correct in wanting us, in matters of aesthetic judgement, to draw attention away from what is common about the item's form towards what is particular about it. Kant thinks that the particular form should prompt the imagination into 'free play' – the mind freely considering the possible productive relationships of its components – and this will not happen if the item is *too quickly* subsumed under, or reined in by, a common concept, or a generality (Budd 2008: 112–14). Rawlinson explains that for the purposes of aesthetic evaluation, the work should not be collapsed into a simple universal, to the 'in general' or the 'in common': there must be the sense that this has been done, on this occasion, 'just this way, just this once' (2006: 140–1). Accordingly, the practice of aesthetic criticism endeavours to assess and articulate the formal distinction of individual works. It is in the business of making discriminations. It contrasts to fields of study interested in general forms, structures, or theories that primarily emphasise the similarities across works rather than the differences. It is aesthetic criticism, the practical wing of evaluative aesthetics, to which we now turn.

---

[58] It would be beholden upon me to show, through evidence and analysis, that the film could profitably be regarded in this way. I endeavour to in Klevan (2003).

# PART II
# What is aesthetic criticism?

## 2.1 Evaluation

The etymology of the word 'criticism' points towards an evaluative practice. The word is derived from the Ancient Greek word *krínō*, 'to judge', and *krités*, 'a judge' or 'juryman' (Wellek 1981: 298). The word 'critic' – *kritikos* – is then derived from *krités* (Pearsall 1998). Over time, however, 'criticism' has become capacious referring to all manner of commentary and study of texts, and as a consequence what constitutes criticism is contested[1]. One outcome of the expansion is that the evaluative dimension is no longer central and is in many cases non-existent. 'Criticism' includes, for example, scholarship, philology, contextual/cultural study, historicism, and critical theory[2]. The branch that *prioritises* the evaluation of form and style is aesthetic criticism. Although its differences from the other branches are distinct enough to constitute a particular identity, aesthetic criticism does not operate in a void: it draws on their material and insight, and it overlaps. Aesthetic criticism is the practical wing of evaluative aesthetics.

Barbara Herrnstein Smith writes that evaluation is 'a complex process ... of sampling, discriminating, classifying, comparing, assessing and selecting that constitute the ongoing activities of responsive creatures in their interactions with their environment' (1998). At the outset, it is worth clarifying a common misconception about evaluation in criticism. Although judgements are being made when one evaluates, and judgement is traditionally synonymous with evaluation in aesthetics (for example, Immanuel Kant's *Critique of Judgment*), evaluation is more than making and presenting judgements. Rather than delivering verdicts, it is about a 'complex process'. Aesthetic criticism, unlike much reviewing, is not primarily interested

---

[1] See Smallwood's *Reconstructing Criticism: Pope's Essay on Criticism and the Logic of Definition* (2003) for lengthy and detailed discussion of this contestation.
[2] The word 'criticism' is probably now too encompassing and does not helpfully designate. The evaluative dimension would be less likely to be lost in the broad church if the other approaches referenced by the term went by their more specific and accurate names. As this is often not the case though, it would perhaps be helpful if the wing of criticism concerned with making claims for value was labelled 'evaluative criticism'. Evaluative criticism would properly refer to any criticism that wishes to make, and substantiate, claims for value, and therefore includes some variants of ideological criticism, moral criticism, and cultural criticism. Despite the capaciousness and contestation, I will sometimes refer to aesthetic criticism as simply 'criticism'. This is because the philosophers and critics I cite often use the one word, and also because some of the matters discussed are also relevant to other forms of criticism (especially other branches of evaluative criticism).

in pronouncing discrete judgements nor would it wish merely to praise or find fault. Judgements made, and presented, without careful evaluation may have worth, but as criticism they are unlikely to be useful because they fail to elaborate sufficiently. Despite sharing an evaluative dimension with aesthetic criticism, reviewing involves a limited number of words and viewings (often just one), and this disallows prolonged engagement and involved argumentation supported by close analysis of form. Equally, the reader of a review is often looking for tips about whether to see the film, not looking for interesting ways to regard the film having already seen it[3].

F.E. Sparshott conceives criticism as qualitative not quantitative such that the interest is in the manner of the excellence – as distinct from simply the degree of excellence – that is to say not only in 'how good a thing is', but 'how it is good' (1967: 118). Sparshott is drawn to the word 'appraisal' perhaps because he feels that it encourages the sense of surveying the manner in which something is good rather than giving something a value, or a valuation (121). 'Appraisal' is not necessarily preferable, however, because it still has accountancy associations (tax appraisal), and more contemporaneously managerial ones (employee appraisal). Monroe Beardsley proposes the possibility of using the word 'estimation' – while he nevertheless continues to use the word evaluation – partly because it fits his idea of calculating the amount of unity, intensity, and complexity in the experience of an artwork (1970: 68)[4]. The word estimation suggests a considered opinion, and esteem and respect ('My estimation of her is high') although on balance does not provide an uncomplicated substitution because it evokes the vague or approximate ('I can only estimate'), and does not escape the realm of financial value ('This is my estimate for building your wall').

---

[3] An example of a film review with asserted judgement without sufficient substantiation is Dilys Powell's review of *Jour de Fête* (Jacques Tati 1949 France) for *The Sunday Times* (1950): 'I have now seen *Jour de Fête* three times, and each time I laughed afresh. The fact is that the jokes have been worked out to the last fraction of a second; the gags double back on themselves; at a second look you see some quirk which escaped you the first time. The slapstick has the precision which one recalls in the best work of Chaplin and the other great comics of the silent cinema. And M. Tati, who plays the postman as well as directing, is funny from the word go: funny demonstrating how to erect a flagpole, funny chasing a wasp, funny doing no more than ride a bicycle ... Whether or not people in this country will like the piece, it is not my business to say. But if they don't, I give up.'

[4] See discussion of Beardsley in 2.4: 'Experience' below.

## What is aesthetic criticism?

For many commentators, the value of a work, *abstractly conceived*, is not the important concern of aesthetic criticism. The main aim, perhaps the fundamental aim, is to appreciate the work, and encourage others to appreciate it. Stein Haugom Olsen sees appreciation as not something one might casually adopt, but more fundamentally, as a 'mode of apprehension' that starts with an expectation of value and proceeds as a 'structured perception of value' (1987: 137; 1998). The belief is that paying the work the right sort of attention, something that may require training and experience, will be worthwhile, and lead to a valuable experience (1998). Harold Osborne talks about criticism leading to 'the stimulation and improvement of ... appreciation'; criticism 'stands or falls by its profitableness as an ancillary to direct appreciation' (1955: 21, 23). For Sparshott, criticism enables an 'enlightened and instructed enjoyment' where the enjoyment of a work is caused not simply by the phenomena, but by an 'abstractive and appreciative skill' that is 'brought to bear' upon the phenomena (1967: 113). For Noël Carroll worthwhile criticism should aid appreciation by removing the 'obstacles' that may be restricting our view, and illuminating what is valuable in the work (2009: 45). However, as already pointed out in Part I, although appreciation often presents an admiring view of a work, it need not: appreciation may also carry the sense of taking sufficient account of the work, rather than valuing it highly. Nevertheless, the seventeenth-century critic Joseph Addison believes that criticism should emphasise 'Excellencies' rather than 'Imperfections' (Day 2010: 199). This is true of most evaluative criticism which intends to reveal 'excellencies', and only briefly acknowledges, and often downplays, 'imperfections'. The work or aspects of it are accepted as good and then the criticism explains 'how it is good'. It provides a beneficent, qualitative profile of the work[5].

### 2.2 Understanding and interpretation

In order to evaluate soundly, aesthetic criticism endeavours to understand a work. What is its point and purpose? What does it all mean? What is at

---

[5] Even if the critic does not believe there are any relevant demerits in the work, the notion of demerit may still be in play, because he or she is aware, even if only latently, of *possible* demerits which are being avoided. This cognisance partly aids the recognition, understanding, and articulation of the merit. See 3.4: 'Choice and expectation'. It should also be noted at this point that when using the word 'critic', I am referring to anyone who produces criticism (for example, academic, student, journalist, essayist, blogger, and, given the growth of audio-visual criticism, filmmaker).

stake? How do its different elements come together to make sense? Why is it designed as it is? Sometimes global understanding about the whole is required, for example, disentangling, or grasping, a plot, discerning an overarching theme or a directorial vision, recognising a pattern of imagery or camera perspective, or making sense of a character; and sometimes local understanding about a part is required, for example, about a shot, a piece of continuity, or a character's gesture. Global and local understandings dynamically inform each other.

If criticism wishes to encourage a positive appreciation of a work, it might, for example, explain an obscurity, a perplexity, a complication, a contradiction, or anything it considers mistakable. As well as the difficult or cryptic, it might explain the apparently insignificant or simple, or anything it considers overlooked. It might also expound on something meaningful, a world-view, a tonal demeanour, or anything it considers would benefit from elaboration. These understandings intend to show that a work is significant in ways we may not have sufficiently realised or articulated.

The common presumption is that understanding must precede evaluation because you could not, or would not, evaluate something before you understood it, but it may also work in reverse. A feature of a film may be valued, nebulously perhaps, and *then* a better understanding is sought which thereby enhances its appreciation. Equally, there may be the sense that something is not working and *then* the possible reasons are thought through. Furthermore, some films, such as *Vertigo* (Alfred Hitchcock 1958 US) or *Letter from an Unknown Woman* (Max Ophüls 1948 US), have attracted many different critical accounts because they are considered rich and fecund; sense has already been made of them, but critics want to understand them in different ways (Shusterman 1984). Most commonly in criticism, understanding and evaluation are reciprocal. According to René Wellek, William K. Wimsatt sees 'the critical act largely as an act of explication out of which a judgment of value grows almost spontaneously' (Wellek 1981: 311). Wellek quotes Wimsatt who writes, 'The main critical problem is always how to push both understanding and value as far as possible in union, or how to make our understanding evaluative.' (311).

Understanding a work, important though it is to aesthetic criticism, is not equivalent to evaluation or appreciation (Olsen 1998). I may for practical or professional reasons wish to understand how my computer works, and this need not involve any evaluation or appreciation of my computer (or its workings). It might be argued that artworks in particular

## What is aesthetic criticism?

invite and require an appreciative point of view rather than a functional understanding. Someone, however, may wish to write and read a type of scholarship about artworks that provides knowledge and understanding without evaluation or appreciation. Analysis of artworks often provides explanation without evaluation (for example, 'the work is disrupting narrative expectations' as distinct from 'the disruption of narrative expectations is productive in the early part of the film, but later becomes less productive for the following reasons ... '). Merely to provide an explanation or understanding of, for example, a work's strategies or its design is not necessarily to evaluate (although the provision may be helpful, even essential, in orientating an evaluation).

Interpretation of meaning – for example, semantic, semiotic, symbolic, or thematic meaning – is a pervasive type of understanding[6]. Quite a lot of contemporary writing on the arts, especially within the academy, appears to be more comfortable with interpreting the meaning of a work than with its evaluation. As discussed in Part I, however, accounts of meaning, without explicitly evaluating, may implicitly infer value, as will the 'high interpretive yield' of films of merit (Hinderer 1969: 54; Shusterman 1984). Some canonised works such as *Vertigo* are now rarely challenged – although this was not the case on its release – and are treated like 'inspired sacred text[s]': they are assumed to be special, and are mined for further, or more nuanced, meanings (Hough 1966: 70)[7].

Nevertheless, even beyond canonised works, meaning can easily become the central or only concern and, if the work is receiving an evaluative treatment, '*the* criterion of value' (Seamon 2005: 412; my emphasis). The first problem with this is the possible mistaking of meaning for significance. According to Michael Bell, F.R. Leavis thinks that 'elaborations of "meaning" can sometimes obfuscate "significance" in the apprehension of a work' (Bell 1988: 98). The advantage of thinking in terms of significance, rather than simply meaning, is that relevance and consequence are kept in mind. Furthermore, for Leavis, penetrating further into common readings is as important as the proliferation and 'unravelling' of new meanings; and there should be adequate 'attention to the self-evident', or apparently self-evident (49). Stanley Cavell also urges aesthetic criticism to be alive to those aspects that seem ordinary or straightforward, the significance

---

[6] 'Interpretation' does not need to refer to meanings in this sense. A painting by Mark Rothko, for example, might be interpreted as being about the reverberations between different colours, and not about expressing meanings as such.

[7] The works of Shakespeare would be the most prominent literary example.

of which is so often 'missable' (2005a: 11)[8]. This chimes with an insight by Ludwig Wittgenstein that, 'The aspects of things that are most important for us are hidden because of their simplicity and familiarity. (One is unable to notice something – because it is always before one's eyes.)' (2006 [1953]: 43, point 129).

Secondly, emphasis on meaning may occlude the recognition and analysis of aesthetic qualities, 'the qualitative aspects of works of art', such as 'inventiveness', subtlety, vibrancy, or eloquence (Seamon 2005: 412). Many films of merit, while not meaningless, do not have substantial, complex or profound meaning, nor do they express great truth or wisdom, for example some musicals and comedies, and yet they are full of qualities and achievements (of timing, of pace, of rhythm, of performance, of presence, of energy, of interaction, and of visual and aural arrangement). Similarly, Susan Sontag argues – in an essay entitled 'Against Interpretation' – that the emphasis on meaning eclipses affective merits, those that are sensuous or textural (Sontag 2001 [1961]). She laments the obsessive search for meanings, polemically claiming that to interpret in this way 'is to impoverish, to deplete the world – in order to set up a shadow world of "meanings"' (7)[9].

Thirdly, understanding the meaning of a work *by itself* does not necessarily explain its value. When Leavis criticised the poetry of Percy Bysshe Shelley as 'vaporous', 'monotonously self-regarding', and 'emotionally cheap', he did not take kindly to being told (by René Wellek) that the features that he disliked would somehow evaporate by understanding the philosophical attitude – in this case Idealist – that underpinned it (Leavis 1984 [1952]: 221). In fact, it made him more likely to be concerned about the philosophical attitude, or this manifestation of it.

---

[8] This is also a concern in my own work particularly in relation to the medium of film. See, for example, Klevan (2000).

[9] There is now a strand in contemporary Film Studies, broadly labelled Affect Theory, which pays attention to sensation, the sensuous, and the textural in film (and Sontag's essay is a prototypical example of it). Affect scholars believe that sensory qualities have been overlooked or disregarded. Instead, Film Studies has concentrated on, for example, signification (the meaning of elements), or narrative (the way the story is structured), or classifications (genre, periods, movements), or sociology (the cultural, historical, political contexts). Even when the concentration was on form and style, it was characterised by too much distance, and was too cognitive. Therefore, affective, sensory, and pre-cognitive dimensions, and the value that arises from them, have been insufficiently embraced. According to affect scholars, some films make particularly productive use of film's affective, sensory and pre-cognitive dimensions. See, for example, Shaviro(2006 [1993]) and Beugnet (2007).

## What is aesthetic criticism? 65

Fourthly, straightforward translating or decoding can ride roughshod over the aesthetic experience by simplifying the precise ways meaning operates in the scheme of a work. Cavell discusses the persistent use of *double entendre* in the film *Bringing Up Baby* (Howard Hawks 1938 US) writing:

> While an explicit discussion, anyway an open recognition, of the film's obsessive sexual references is indispensable to saying what I find the film to be about, I am ... reluctant to make it very explicit ... . It is part of the force of this work that we shall not know how far to press its references ... If it is undeniable that we are invited by these events to read them as sexual allegory, it is equally undeniable that what [Katharine] Hepburn says, as she opens the box and looks inside, is true: 'It's just an old bone.' Clearly George [the dog] agrees with her. The play between the literal and the allegorical determines the course of this narrative, and provides us with contradicting directions in our experience of it. (1981: 116–18)

For Cavell, an 'explicit' articulation or transcription would be unfaithful to the suspension and latency, or embedded condition of the meanings, which distinguishes the film, and his experience of it.

Fifthly, the meanings of works can be too severely condensed or abridged in accounts, while nevertheless still being treated as germane, and this can lead to simplification, to the disregard or the misrepresentation of merits, and to inadequate foundations for further assessment. In the film *Camille* (George Cukor 1936 US), there is a moment when Marguerite Gautier, a courtesan, played by Greta Garbo, is slapped by the Baron de Varville (Henry Daniell), and this triggers a series of facial transformations. There are approximately fifteen seconds from the beginning of a close-up, immediately after the slap, to a fade out to black. In this short space of time, she seems to express: a proud, frozen defence; shock kept in check by a steely comportment; astonishment; anger, indignation, perhaps inhibited resentment; some hurt (to her feelings, to her body); relief, a gathering of the self, and resolve; and finally some pleasure in anticipation (of her separation from the Baron) (Figs 2.1–2.6). There is a *movement of meaning* as each expression folds into the next (Klevan 2012: 34–5). One could summarise the fifteen seconds, for example, as being about the economic, physical and emotional abuse of a woman (which it is also *about*), but this summary would not capture the finessed range of meanings achieved by the performer, nor the particular form it takes: the way her response to the abuse is *characterised*, hence the way the abuse, and the

**2.1-2.6** *Camille* (MGM, 1936).

# What is aesthetic criticism?

2.1-2.6  (Continued)

consequences of it, are illuminated[10]. Meaning is a vital component of many works, but aesthetic criticism is concerned with the way it is presented – its embodiment, tone, demeanour, density, prominence, gradation, dissemination, and local transformation – and the consequent merits.

## 2.3 Perception

Aesthetic criticism provides an evaluative perception of the work's presentation. There is often a revelatory component: the work is revealed so that its merit (or demerits) can be recognised. In general, it aims to awaken perception, drawing attention to aspects of the work; it clarifies, articulates or enhances something we were partly or latently aware of, or brings us to see something new. It is interested in the missed, or dismissed (Cavell 2005a: 7–12; and see discussion in Klevan 2011a). Graham McFee writes that 'criticism can be usefully modelled as a kind of *noticing*', and he distinguishes the 'noticing' of 'critically relevant features' from simply 'looking at' (1998, original emphasis). Addison, writing about literature, thinks the 'true critic' ought to discover the 'concealed Beauties of a Writer', and Day explains that '[t]he authority of the critic comes from his ability to see what others overlook' (Day 2010: 194). The philosopher David Hume believes that, 'Many men, when left to themselves, have but a faint and dubious perception of beauty', but are capable of 'relishing' something when it is 'pointed out to them' (2008 [1757]: 110). We are better at appreciation than initial observation.

'Critical communication' according to Arnold Isenberg is a special type of communication where critics want us to incorporate their perception (1973: 156–71). The communication is an expression of an aesthetic experience and the critic encourages us to acquire that experience (Scruton 1999: 376–7). This critical communication depends not on accepting a truth or belief about the work, even if we do, but coming to perceive it *for ourselves*. John Casey likens critical communication to the psychoanalytical procedure where the patient should not automatically accept the psychoanalyst's reading, but must undergo a 'complex change in vision' (2011 [1966]: 22–3, 34). Healing will depend on the patient internalising,

---

[10] See Klevan (2012) on the merits of transformation of meaning, moment-by-moment, in film sequences. See also discussion of 'heresy of paraphrase' in 2.7: 'Close reading' below.

not on acquiescing, or obeying. The patient, like the reader of criticism, needs to *experience* a gradual rearrangement of the data.

The critic hopes, in terms presented by Wittgenstein, that the aspect she or he is pointing out will 'dawn' (2006 [1953]: 166). This sense of coming to perceive the work in a different way links to the notion of 'Seeing As', or 'Seeing Aspects', where the work is seen *as* one thing and then *as* another. Wittgenstein illustrates the notion by way of the much-cited gestalt figure of the duck-rabbit, where the same line drawing simultaneously outlines a duck and a rabbit (Fig. 2.7). Some people perceive the rabbit immediately and not the duck, and vice-versa. Once the duck is pointed out to those people who had hitherto only perceived the rabbit they experience it differently, even though the drawing remains unchanged. Although people perceive different aspects – the duck or the rabbit – both animals are *there* and both have exactly the same base properties (which in this case is the same shape of line and, in the version displayed in Fig. 2.7, the same texture and colouring too). Frank Sibley, a philosopher particularly concerned to explain criticism as an activity which guides perception, enumerates the different things that can be done to get people to perceive the work in a certain way. Firstly, non-aesthetic features such as a cut or a camera movement that may have gone unnoticed are simply mentioned or pointed out. Secondly, an aesthetic quality, like subtlety, is

**2.7** *Kaninchen und Ente (Rabbit and Duck)*, the earliest known version of the duck–rabbit illusion, from the 23 October 1892 issue of *Fliegende Blätter*.

announced, and by using the appropriate term, the suitable perception is triggered. Thirdly, the base property and the aesthetic quality are explicitly linked: 'Have you noticed that the cut coming at this point creates an ellipsis that produces this subtle effect?' Fourthly, similes and metaphors are used. This might be done when trying to describe the behaviour of performers, for example, 'she jerked her head from side to side like an alert bird'. Fifthly, contrasts and comparisons are made: 'Imagine how much less subtle and suggestive the effect of the cut and the ellipsis would have been if the cut had come slightly later or if the new image had started earlier'. Alternatively, attention can be drawn to a similar effect in a different film. Sibley even mentions the use of reminiscences where comparisons are drawn with some (assumed) shared experience in life. Sixthly, repetitions and reiterations are used, so that the same point is repeated with similar words. Seventhly, verbal aspects are used, when delivering the criticism orally, such as tones of voice, nods, looks, or other gestures are used that guide perception, such as the undulation of arm and hand through the air which aids recognition of a melodic line[11]. Written criticism has a sophisticated array of techniques that may similarly gesture, or adjust tone and emphasis[12]. This is why the language and style of criticism – the choice and organisation of words, sentences, and paragraphs – may be crucial in aiding the perception of relevant features. It is not superfluous or idiosyncratic ornamentation (Clayton and Klevan 2011).

Sometimes a value of a work rests in its capacity to be perceived in numerous different ways; it is impermanent and incomplete (in a good sense) (Kuhns 1966: 46). Hence, many works of high merit are thought to be inexhaustible (*Vertigo* again). However, striving for comprehensiveness within a single account – endeavouring to embrace as many features and as many aspects as possible – is forlorn because only a different time, place and critic will reveal new aspects. Most commonly, criticism provides a way of seeing many features from one encompassing perspective (rather than pointing out discrete features). The critic's activity is akin to a detective working out a *solution* from a range of clues and evidence. Realising that a relevant piece of evidence has been omitted or misinterpreted may undermine a particular perspective or render it unpersuasive, and this needs to be distinguished – not always a straightforward matter – from evidence whose salience emerges when a different perspective is adopted.

---

[11] This is my adapted version of Sibley's list (2006 [1962]: 18–19).
[12] This would be also true of contemporary forms of aesthetic criticism such as audio-visual criticism.

According to Richard Storer, Leavis believes that 'reading should be oriented towards … not the indefinite proliferation of different responses without any controlling principle, but collaborative agreement on (or at least movement towards) a shared response' (2009: 89). In addition, the multi-dimensional or multi-perspectival account is not necessarily preferable to one that is distinctive and memorable. The critic is often motivated to present a piece of criticism because he or she believes that they have a point of view that makes sense of the work, makes it cohere, and makes it appear as valuable. They do not require other perspectives or, compelled by their own, and perhaps restricted by it, beneficially or not, are unable to see them. Equally, we may be motivated to read their piece of criticism precisely so that we can come to see, or experience, *the* perspective of *this* critic.

## 2.4 Experience

The individual's experience of the artwork is a fundamental aspect of the aesthetic point of view; unsurprisingly therefore the actual encounter between the critic and the work also underpins aesthetic criticism. Contrasting this to alternative disciplines is useful. Historical or other forms of contextual study illuminate the work by returning it to its origins. The primary relationship is between, for example, the film and its original context, whether that be place, culture, politics, institutions, or people. The individual's aesthetic experience of the work – in the present – is downplayed and sometimes ignored. Theoretical study illuminates the work by placing it within, or reading it through, generalised systems and structures, and this too tends to detach it from the individual's aesthetic experience. Robin Wood contrasts the theorist with the critic: 'The theorist erects systems, the critic explores works. For the theorist, questions of value will be determined by reference to a previously elaborated system; for the critic, a sense of value arises from placing this experience beside that experience in an endless and flexible empiricism' (2006: 17–18). Indeed, aesthetic criticism is experiential all along the line: it recognises that artworks often express or embody experiences, and are often based on an appeal to experience; it is responsive to the experience as the work is encountered; and it intends, ultimately, to contribute to the reader's experience of the work. It is mindful that the experience of the work may be modified by repeat viewings, by new evidence, by other works, by experiences of life, by taking account of the experiences of other people, and by knowledge of a range of contexts (historical, theoretical, cultural, political, social). However, these potentially informing and illuminating contexts will not determine the perspective from which the work is viewed (or evaluated)[13]. Aesthetic criticism foregrounds those aspects of the work, discovered as the work is encountered and apprehended, that remain overlooked or reduced by relatively removed vantage points. Graham Fuller offers the analogy of attraction between human beings where there is an individuated reality that enveloping explanations find hard to capture. He argues that criticism is interested in this 'irreducible' realm (Fuller and Eagleton 1983: 83)[14].

One way of understanding the importance of experience to the aesthetic point of view is to consider how an artwork can remain the same physical entity while the phenomenal apprehension of it will differ. We are once again in the realm of aspect perception. Different periods and eras will experience the same work differently, different people within one era will experience the same work differently, and one person might come to experience the same work differently (over a lifetime or in a matter of minutes). The work itself can introduce something that prompts a reassessment of its earlier parts so, for example, these parts may initially have been experienced as straightforward, well defined, or limited, but are retrospectively experienced as complex, suggestive, or multi-dimensional[15]. Gregg M. Horowitz argues that if a work is to survive in new contexts, to stand the 'test of time', a 'de-contextualized ... perception' is required to disclose fresh aspects (2006: 218)[16]. A work may have merits and demerits that the makers or viewers of the period did not recognise and only emerge in different times and places. Consequently, Horowitz claims aesthetic experience 'enables us to know ... the unconscious of

---

[13] Criticism would not simply *apply* a theory a priori, which is to say in advance of the experience. It understands, however, that some aspects of particular films may be revealed by a theory, for example, Marxist or Freudian theory. This may be because the critic understands a film to be operating in the same or similar territory to the theory, or that a feature of a film is well illuminated by a feature of a theory. Once the link to the theory has been made it remains to be ascertained whether the relation is aesthetically meritorious or not. See discussion of Piso on *Marnie* (2009 [1986]) in 3.7: 'Pattern'.

[14] On the other hand, aesthetic criticism, precisely because it is *involved*, might be blind to insights that emerge from overarching perspectives. Individuation may be seductive and deceptive, and only ostensible.

[15] See Klevan (2005b).

[16] Horowitz contrasts this to an approach that prefers to place a work in its original historical context.

the humanly made' (218). Writers such as Horowitz emphasise how crucial aspects of works may be emergent rather than apparent because they are response-dependent[17].

The relationship between the experience of a work and its value is something that interests Beardsley. For Beardsley, 'aesthetic criticism ... seeks to grasp and expose features of the work that either enhance or diminish the work's power to give ... an experience that is desirable on account of its character' (1981b: 155). Beardsley spent a lot of effort trying to characterise the aesthetic experience. First of all, he claims that it is characterised by 'object directedness' where 'attention is firmly fixed upon heterogeneous but interrelated components of a phenomenally objective field' (Beardsley 1981a [1958]: 527). There is an experience of being guided by the 'objective properties' of the object with a sense 'that things are working or have worked themselves out fittingly' (Beardsley 1982: 288). Then there is 'active discovery' which is 'actively exercising constructive powers of the mind, of being challenged by a variety of potentially conflicting stimuli to try to make them cohere' as well as 'a keyed up state amounting to exhilaration' in seeing connections between the things we perceive and the meanings of them (288–9). Experiencing the way the elements of the work relate – 'fittingly', 'cohere', seeing connections – is particularly important for Beardsley.

In addition to these broadly behavioural or attitudinal dimensions ('object directedness' and 'active discovery'), Beardsley is also interested in locating what he understands to be the qualities of the aesthetic experience. He highlights three which he considers to be overarching. Firstly, there is the experience of 'unity' which includes 'coherence' and 'completeness'. Coherence is the multi-dimensional connections and interrelatedness of different parts: congruence, consonance and consistency, but also something like a logical progression where 'one thing leads to another; [and there is] continuity of development, without gaps or dead spaces, a sense of overall providential pattern of guidance, an orderly culmination of energy toward a climax' (Beardsley 1981a: 528). Completeness is the 'equilibrium or finality ... achieved and enjoyed ... [when] [t]he impulses and expectations aroused by elements within the experience are felt to be counterbalanced or resolved by other elements within the experience' (528). Secondly, there is 'intensity' caused by the 'concentration' of experience that results from the concentration of the artwork. Artworks

---

[17] See 1.10: 'Aesthetic qualities' for a discussion of emergence. See also 2.9: 'Intention, achievement, and skill'.

concentrate by offering, for example, 'a segment of human life', links between occurrences, the framing of elements, and the omission of irrelevancies (527). Thirdly, there is 'complexity' which is experiencing 'the range and diversity of distinct elements [the work] brings together into its unity' (529). Beardsley's conception of the experience is resolutely evaluative: it responds to the merits of coherence, continuity, completeness, counterbalance, concentration, and complexity.

For Beardsley, unity, intensity and complexity are achieved *by the work* but he often discusses them in terms *of the experience*[18]. The value of an artwork for him is the quantity and quality of the aesthetic experience it affords: the '*magnitude*' which is 'a function of at least these three variables [unity, intensity, complexity]' (529). Beardsley's attempt to characterise the aesthetic experience is brave and impressive although it is somewhat restricted by its exclusive concentration on the triumvirate of unity, intensity, and complexity[19]. Another problem, pointed out by his critics, is that although a work may exhibit coherence this does not mean a viewer will equivalently experience coherence or feel coherent, or, as he labels it, 'wholeness'[20]. Nevertheless, even if there is uneasiness about the qualities of a viewer's experience mirroring the qualities of the work, Beardsley's method, by linking it to experiential fulfilment, does attempt to account for why qualities such as unity, intensity and complexity are valued so highly in the aesthetic appreciation of artworks. Furthermore, his

---

[18] It is important to emphasise that when we talk about 'the' experience this should not merely refer to the initial experience, or just one experience; evaluations will often be based on cumulative experience, built up over several encounters with the work (together with intervening reflection upon these experiences). Beardsley does not clarify this, but much of what he writes about experience, and other aesthetic matters, is consistent with it.

[19] Alan Goldman presents a flexible theory of experience that argues that aesthetic criticism will evaluate the form of the work for its capacities to 'engage' the faculties, and to 'challenge' them (2004). (He understands 'challenge' in the broadest sense to mean invite and stimulate, and not only confront or place demands.) According to Goldman, works of aesthetic merit will engage on many levels, for example, perceptually, cognitively, imaginatively, emotionally, and affectively (101). Goldman's account generously includes all these modes of engagement and does not prioritise. Works of high merit will engage and challenge many faculties (106).

[20] Beardsley describes 'wholeness' as a 'sense of integration as a person, or being restored to wholeness from distracting and disruptive influences ... and a corresponding contentment, even through disturbing feelings, that involves self-acceptance and self-expansion' (Beardsley 1982: 289).

experiential descriptions dramatically and vividly get inside the aesthetic state of mind, its aspirations and satisfactions (hence the retention of his own words in the previous paragraph to retain the drama). It is also worth considering, as counterbalance, that this is the same Monroe Beardsley – in association with co-writer W.K. Wimsatt – who warns against overvaluing the direct affectivity of a work. Indeed, he believes in a version of disinterest: another one of his characteristics of aesthetic experience is 'detached affect' which is a 'sense that the objects on which interest is concentrated are set a little at a distance emotionally' (Beardsley 1982: 288)[21]. He writes of poetry:

> The emotions correlative to the objects of poetry become part of the matter dealt with – not communicated to the reader like an infection or disease, not inflicted mechanically like a bullet or a knife wound, not administered like a poison, not simply expressed as by expletives or grimaces or rhythms, but presented in their objects and contemplated as a pattern of knowledge. (Wimsatt and Beardsley 1949: 52, quoted in Guyer 2014c: 394–5)

The aesthetic experience contemplates how the emotions are 'presented' and 'patterned', and this is not the same as feelings *directly* aroused by the work. It is important to recognise that, for Beardsley, aesthetic experience is not equivalent to 'emotional reaction' (Guyer 2014c: 395)[22]. Aesthetic experience is underpinned by the ability to engage the emotional faculties and to apprehend by means of the senses, but this does not mean that the work is simply judged on an emotional response. For Beardsley, therefore, although aesthetic criticism should be concerned about the emotion and feeling achieved *in a work*, it should be wary of measuring its accomplishments in terms of the emotions they arouse *in a viewer*. A film may prompt perhaps joy or sadness for all manner of reasons, some of them personal, and this emotion need not be related to the aesthetic merit or demerit of

---

[21] See 1.2: 'The Aesthetic attitude' for a discussion of disinterest.

[22] Beardsley's worry about affectivity can be linked to his worry about intentionality, once again outlined with his co-writer Wimsatt (1946). Here, he warns against understanding the value of a work by seeking to find out the intentions of its maker. He does not believe that the value of the work is ascertained by what moves the makers, just as he does not believe it can be ascertained by what moves a viewer. Instead of either, the value will be identified by experiencing the presentational and organisational achievements of the work. See 2.9: 'Intention, achievement, and skill'.

the work[23]. Works that emote or are sentimental will unsurprisingly provoke an emotional response while works that express profound emotions will not always provoke the response they deserve.

Although a direct experience of the work will always be required for aesthetic criticism, any reference to the experience will need to be supported by a detailed account of the workings of the work in order to explain and justify the experience and allow it to be shared. The reporting of an experience through affective words – the work is 'powerful', 'memorable', 'arresting' – and merely matching them to an instance in the work will not provide a secure or helpful evaluation. Furthermore, the quality and quantity of the experience are not the only way evaluations are determined. Many evaluations concerning artistry – creative, genetic and functional aspects – such as the execution of a work, the techniques of performance, the relationship to artistic tradition, and originality of generic variation can be made in what Bohdan Dziemidok calls a 'cool' manner (1983: 57). The character of the response will be intellectual and relatively distanced. The two modes are difficult to disentangle, however, because an understanding of artistry, for example the techniques of performance, is partly based on the experiences they have elicited over time. Even if the immediate response is 'cool', the evaluation may still indirectly be drawing on, and appealing to, preceding experiential engagement (64).

## 2.5 Particularity and responsiveness

Aesthetic criticism respects the specificity of the work (even if that leads to an antagonistic evaluation). Helen Vendler claims that the 'aim of a properly aesthetic criticism' is to describe 'the art work in such a way' – its manner, temperament, and texture – 'that it cannot be confused with any other art work' and never to 'conflate' (1988: 2). John M. Ellis thinks that a work of merit will be 'demanding' in the sense of necessitating 'respect for [its] unique emphasis and individuality' (rather than in the sense of it being difficult); and criticism should let the work 'speak for itself, through close attention to *its* emphases' (1981: 24–5, original emphasis). According to David Fuller, William Empson avoids 'any desire to trace a theoretical

---

[23] These emotions might be good indicators of some types of value, for example, personal value, affective value, or entertainment value, but not necessarily the aesthetic value of the work. However, these other types of value may also be, and often are, desirable outcomes of aesthetic value.

argument' for fear that it might 'smooth out the particular and local' detail that only adherence to specific example will respect (Fuller 2006: 156). Leavis insists upon showing sensitivity for the irreducibility of the work, and warns about 'abstracting improperly' (1984 [1952]: 213).

Making the link to the philosophical work of Martin Heidegger (1889–1976), Bell considers Leavis's approach to criticism to be phenomenological, concentrating on the detailed description of an experience that is specific, present, and active (1988: 35–50). Leavis continually emphasises 'direct apprehension': the critic is concerned with the work in front of him (16). Bell elucidates Leavis's approach by comparing it to the sentences in Henry James's novels. James's sentences have a 'responsive plasticity': they seem to follow and record 'the shifts of perception and emphasis *as they arise*' (16; my emphasis). Their shape is influenced by unfolding detail rather than imposed, and although the James example refers to fictional writing, it would be the model for aesthetic criticism. Leavis's approach also joins hands with the philosophy of his contemporary Wittgenstein. Wittgenstein condemns the craving for generality in philosophy: he argues for the particular case and the recognition that all elements – for example words – are occasion sensitive. The meaning or effect of a word or thing shifts depending on the context – the particular sentence, speaker, and situation – in which it appears. The same principle applies to an image, a gesture, a cut, or a camera movement within a film. They are not equivalent to images, gestures, cuts, and camera movements in other films. This is why the critic needs to be phenomenologically responsive to the particular case.

According to Leavis, the critic senses the significance of the work and then 'it must be a matter, first of sensitive response, then of a delicate balancing of one suggestion or intimation against another until the whole, in one's sense of it, has settled into the right inclusive poise' (quoted in Bell: 121). George Steiner, in reference to Leavis's work, describes this as a 'poised vulnerability' where the critic should be 'close' and 'stringent', *and* 'provisional', always 'susceptible to revaluation' (1995 [1962]: 622–3). Leavis thinks that the critic should not simply consider the work, but 'feel into' it and 'become', taking the work as close to oneself as possible in order 'to realize a complex experience' (1984 [1952]: 212–13). 'Realise' was one of Leavis's central terms, and it is multifaceted. The work should be successfully realised by its author so that its purposes and elements are fulfilled, brought to fruition. At the same time, the reader would need to *realise* this. By 'realise', Leavis is referring not only to a realisation of what the work is about or what is at stake in it, but to a responsiveness that consummates. He talks of *realising* as 'sensitively' and 'concretely' as possible that which claims the attention. Evaluating would be implicit in the realising because as the critic's relationship to the work develops she or he asks questions such as, 'How does this stand in relation to … ?' and 'How relatively important does it seem?' (213).

Leavis's principled commitment to responsiveness means that although he believed that this process of realisation is creative, criticism should not become 'a substitute for creative writing' and he disliked 'fine writing' that reflected the critic *more* than the work (Steiner 1995 [1962]: 625, 624)[24]. The critic should not be seduced by anything that might make her lose 'grip on the object' (625). Indeed, Leavis is distrustful of anything that might interfere with responsiveness. The practice of criticism requires vigilance so as not to lose a 'completeness of possession' (1984 [1952]: 213). It is easy for attention to be misdirected, or become muddled by, for example, premature generalising or 'extraneous information' (224). He certainly does not have a problem with learning facts about the text from outside it – Leavis is far from a dogmatically intrinsic critic – and he recognises that his approach has its limitations, but he thinks 'that any approach involves limitations'; indeed, it is by 'recognizing them', and working productively within them, that 'one may hope to get something done' (216). 'Why it is so and not otherwise?' is an oft-quoted question that Leavis said criticism should ask of the work (224). In fact, this quotation is extracted from a sentence that reveals more. Leavis writes that the critic 'is concerned with the work in front of him as something that should contain *within itself* the reason why it is so and not otherwise' (224; my emphasis). Therefore, for Leavis, it is important for the work to be self-justifying, and in order to illuminate this internal achievement, the workings 'within' it will need to be the critic's primary focus.

## 2.6 Description and analysis

Because aesthetic criticism is responsive to the particularities of a work, description is one of its most important tools. For Roger Scruton 'aesthetic description is an immovable part of critical practice' because without it

---

[24] However, writing that is creative *and* germane might well be required *in order to* reflect the work faithfully, and enhance responsiveness. See 2.12: 'Subjectivity, contingency, and the relational'. See also various essays in Clayton and Klevan (2011).

judgements of value are 'presumptuous', emptied of content and ineffectually isolated even if correct (1999: 372–3). The description is required because the reader needs to either undergo the experience for themself, or credibly imagine someone undergoing the experience that has prompted the evaluation (372). Description is rarely a straightforward task, and it is especially challenging for film criticism because film is visual, aural, *and* moving. It is also made up of many artistic forms: it is a narrative art (like novels); a musical art (like music); a dramatic and performative art (like theatre); a recording art (like photography); a framed and compositional art (like painting); a plastic art (like sculpture); and a condensed, contiguous art (like poetry). All of these forms demand specific descriptive requirements and they frequently overlap.

Aesthetic description also has many intentions. It aims to be accurate so as to reflect the work faithfully, evidence any claims, and make clear distinctions and discriminations (for example, 'the camera appears not simply to move, or even start moving, but to *set off*'). It may aim to be telling, persuasively cementing a particular point of view. It may aim to be dramatic, reflecting the drama of the work: its emphases, pace, suspense, or tonal address. It may aim to be evocative and affective to reveal qualities, make their presence felt, and show how familiar figures and forms, perhaps a lateral panning movement, are characterised in a particular context (for example, 'the camera's movement exhibits an ease, and a confident intent; the camera elegantly goes its own way, gliding past the nearby facades of the buildings, carried buoyantly by the music'). In addition, by using an associated set of descriptive terms the critic can show how various features relate and reflect upon each other. At its best, description in criticism can convey the unified variations of the world of the work through deploying closely related vocabulary, and exploiting the malleability of individual words (that is their capacity to shift meaning and effect according to context)[25].

Description, understanding, and evaluation, work together and it is difficult to know which is prior. The assumption might be that something

---

[25] See Klevan (2011b) for an experiment in producing an aesthetic criticism which is copiously descriptive in form, where the intention is for the evaluation and appreciation, rather than always being explicitly explained, to emerge through the description. Wittgenstein believed that insight was attained from endeavouring to provide increasingly more apt and perspicacious descriptions. He writes: 'We must do away with all *explanation,* and description alone must take its place' (2006 [1953]: 40, Point 109). See also Klevan (2011c) for a meta-critical analysis of three passages of descriptive criticism.

is understood in the work and then the effort to describe it follows. However, trying to find the appropriate descriptive words, or deciding between words, is in itself a process of coming to understand the work. One description may lead to another that is more apt and simultaneously more revealing; initially unforeseen descriptions can lead to the realisation of unforeseen aspects. Similarly, a description is sometimes already a basic kind of evaluation. The implication of describing a man as a 'juggler' is that he has certain traits and skills (Booth 1988: 93). To remark on something is to imply something worth remarking upon and, in some minimal sense, 'remarkable' (96). A description of a young boy as 'well-behaved, intelligent, and friendly' is at the same time evaluative (Reichert 1977: 177). Nevertheless, often description of formal features in academic work is seeking minimally to identify and categorise rather than evaluate[26].

Analysis, another important tool of aesthetic criticism, is related to description. A rough distinction might be that description tends to refer to how a work appears: its external, surface features; its qualities, tone, mood; and its general character. Analysis tends to refer to how parts fit, and work, together, how features relate, and to structure and overall design[27].

---

[26] For example, Michael O'Pray describes a film as having 'untrammelled excess, not only in its rich colour and the elaborate theatricality of its mise-en-scène, mixing the exotic, high-art icons and images taken from suspect areas of culture, but also in its blatant sexual imagery culled from performance art, fashion and pay pornography' (2003: 108). O'Pray does not, nor does he go on to, evaluate the merits or demerits of the excess, richness, exoticism or blatancy (in this case), or even minimally analyse the particular ways they are working.

[27] Once again, as with description, analysis of form may not necessarily be in the service of evaluation. For example, in a fine essay scrupulously analysing formal strategies in the films of Roy Andersson, Julian Hanich writes: 'Beginning with *You, the Living* [2007 Sweden] there are ... tendencies to arrange the centres of attention *horizontally* from the left side to the right side of the frame. For the viewer this implies that he or she has to "pan" from one element to the other ... [David] Bordwell calls this type of composition *planimetric* ... The planimetric style – as we can find it, for instance, in Wes Anderson's *Moonrise Kingdom* [2012 US] and Takeshi Kitano's *Sonatine* [1993 Japan] – involves a rectangular geometry with a flat background, which avoids lining up the characters along receding diagonals. Yet, even in Andersson's horizontally arranged compositions, he never reverts to pure instances of the planimetric style. I would prefer to speak of *planimetric layering* in his case, which gives weight to the fact that Andersson even in his horizontally arrayed images stages in depth' (2014: 39, original emphasis).

This type of analysis of form would be an important *part* of aesthetic criticism, but Hanich does not, in this instance, provide an evaluation. Elsewhere in the essay, he implicitly and occasionally explicitly evaluates, making claims for the films'

However, they overlap and inform each other: description already contains analysis, and it is partly used to convey analytical findings accurately and vividly. Analysis is often presumed to be more secure and objective than description which is more impressionistic and personal whereas, as many scientists will testify, analysing is no less prone to subjectivity, preference, and bias than a description (Daiches 1969: 167). Both may be more or less accurate, helpful or penetrating when evaluating a work. I have seen marking criteria in schools and universities that (ostensibly) punish 'description' and reward 'analysis' whereas both are essential to aesthetic criticism, and can be executed well or less well[28]. Nevertheless, what I think is sensibly discouraged is indiscriminate and unstructured description that is neither purposeful nor revealing. Functional or informational description that merely conveys features of the film – for example, points about plot or character behaviour – can substitute for description that improves or adjusts perception. This is encouraged by the fair assumption that the film may be unfamiliar to the reader of the essay or absent at the time of reading, but it can result, especially in work by students new to film study, in extended passages of obvious exposition. Ideally, the aspiration would be to achieve both at once so that perfunctory necessities are contained within revealing description. A related, but less recognised, pitfall of description is that in the understandable need to make things explicit and clear for the reader, the less definite or defined qualities of a work, for example, the indirect or implied, are lost. Aesthetic criticism has to take care that in highlighting and foregrounding in order to reveal it does not distort significant variations in presence.

While it need not disfigure, description will inevitably be selective and partial. A film, like many things, can be described meticulously and faithfully in many different ways depending on purpose and perspective. A plant will be described in diverse yet accurate ways by a botanist, chemist, dietician, horticulturalist, or an artist (Osborne 1955: 28). In aesthetic criticism, description supports an appreciation or an evaluation. Given that a description will necessarily be incomplete – providing an exhaustive

---

complexity and the perceptual activity they stimulate. Often, however, his purpose is to explain and illuminate the form, and the processes of viewer comprehension they elicit, through stylistic analysis. I choose this segment to exemplify a distinction not to draw attention to a limitation.

[28] Contemporary ideological assumptions and prejudices probably influence this pedagogy. In different times and places, description, often referred to as *ekphrasis*, was regarded as a valuable skill requiring formal training.

description of a film would be impossible – it should be judged by an occasion-sensitive 'standard of adequacy' and relevance (Sparshott 1967: 105). It is faithful to a critical purpose, as well as to the work. Scruton pushes this point further by distinguishing between the 'material object' and the 'intentional object' of aesthetic interest. 'Intentional' is being used in the phenomenological sense of the object before us towards which attention is directed. The aim is to describe a material reality *and* to 'express' and 'recommend ... a particular response to it' (1999: 372). Aesthetic criticism therefore describes an aesthetic experience of the work, or perhaps more precisely, describes the work as it appears during a particular experience of it.

## 2.7 Close reading

The combination of describing and analysing the form and style of a work attentively, often moment-by-moment, is known as 'close reading'. The practice of close reading for aesthetic criticism aims to adjust perception and bring to light the previously unseen (or unheard), explain inner workings, refine interpretations, justify and evidence evaluative claims, and deepen the experience. Close reading is sometimes referred to as 'practical criticism' a term derived from the British literary critical tradition, 'new criticism' from the US literary tradition, and 'explication de texte' from the French tradition (and it is occasionally referred to as ontological, formalist, or technical criticism). In Film Studies, close reading is often referred to as 'textual analysis' which should not be confused with the same term in Literary Studies which refers to the scholarly practice of comparing existing manuscripts, printed versions, and folios (sometimes to establish the most 'accurate' version of a written work). All these labels have different histories and emphases. 'Practical criticism', for example, originally referred to an extreme version of intrinsic close reading, developed by I.A. Richards (1893–1979), where students were given poems, or passages from poems. These passages were decontextualised, and the students were asked to analyse without the benefit of extrinsic knowledge (1973 [1929])[29].

Close reading became an important pedagogical tool in schools and universities. Apart from the aesthetic benefits of students attending closely

---

[29] Richards used their responses as part of a quasi-scientific, psychological experiment he was conducting.

to the form and style of a work, the approach would help legitimate arts subjects challenged for being too unscientific and lacking discipline. Students could be trained in an analytical method that was procedural and rigorous, and which demonstrated and evidenced claims. The *practical* in 'practical criticism' brings out valuable dimensions of close reading: non-theoretical, hands on, useful, adaptable for general purposes, and amenable to improvement through practice. As a teacher within the academy, I am committed to the approach for all these reasons, and because most students are not likely to encounter, rehearse and perfect the skills outside an academic context. In my experience, students are receptive to describing and analysing form and interpreting its meaning (and many of them perform this analysis and interpretative work at a remarkably accomplished level especially given the short time periods within which they work). They are less comfortable, however, with the evaluative dimension to close reading which even if integrated by teachers into the exemplification of the approach is more difficult to formalise or to model. As A. Alvarez has written, in a discussion of some of the problems arising from the institutionalisation of close reading, 'Method, of whatever brand' with its 'clear teachable elements', 'is always easier to teach than discrimination' (Davis 2008: xxvi)[30].

The first proponents of literary close reading reacted against what they understood to be an old-fashioned and amateur form of loose, impressionistic appreciation in Literary Studies. This amateurism was characterised by comments on the plot and character, references to 'artistic touches', and expressions of personal enthusiasms and moralistic prejudices (Logan 2008: xi–xii). They instead argue for a forensic attention to the detail of the work. The work must be properly scrutinised, and indeed the name of Leavis's journal, which practised this form of criticism, was *Scrutiny: A Quarterly Review* (1932–53). Critics would concentrate on individual words and their placement, and show how slight changes in a phrase would make all the difference. For example, Leavis examines a not obviously impressive line from a Samuel Johnson poem – 'For such the steady Romans shook the world' – and praises the use of the word 'steady' which 'turns the vague cliché, "shook the world," into the felt percussion of tramping legions' (1972 [1936]: 112). Leavis 'homes' in on a 'familiar word', the significance of which might go unnoticed, one that seems to be there simply to make up the 'required number of stresses' (Storer 2009: 90). Instead, however, the word contributes to 'a vivid image – both auditory

---

[30] See 'A note on pedagogy' at the conclusion of this book.

and visual – of a powerful and disciplined military force on the move, the specific force on which the Roman Empire was based' (90). This analysis is 'a constructive or creative process' of *realisation* guided closely by the evidence, and not simply an interrogation and 'dissection of something' assumed to be 'already and passively there' (Leavis 1943: 70; quoted in Storer 2009: 87). Rather than gliding over the surface of the work, Leavis takes us inside its workings and inside the creativity, and this privileged position allows more to be perceived.

Indeed, brought close to the poem by Leavis's analysis, I am now in a position to discern even more aspects of it by myself: the way in which, for example, the inclusion of 'steady' gives the phrase alliterative force – 'such', 'steady', and 'shook' – which adds to the 'felt' percussive quality. Furthermore, the contrasting 'steady' and 'shook' are conjoined – through the alliteration – providing the paradox, economically and unassumingly expressed, that steadiness can shake. Close reading notices details that might be passed over, and avoids the 'stock responses' (a phrase used by I.A. Richards 1973 [1929]: 235–54). It is a way of thoroughly experiencing, understanding, and articulating the intricacy of the work and therefore is at one with evaluating it. The assumption is that the work is worth looking at closely (although a work thought to be failing in some respect could also be examined meticulously)[31].

New Critics emphasise local effects: paradox, oxymoron, irony, ambiguity, and other tensional occurrences, often in poetry, an art form that is already relatively terse and condensed. One of the American New Critics, John Crowe Ransom, makes a distinction between 'structure' and 'texture': structure, the 'logic' or 'functional argument' of the work, is essential, but it is there to support the texture, the 'heterogeneous detail', that gives it 'full density' or 'body' (Baldick 1996: 83). One of the critiques of New Criticism, made especially by the Chicago School of critics, is that it is too obsessed with local detail and improperly relegates the bigger picture which is essential for orientation. The Chicago critics elevate larger-scale matters of structure and form such as genre or narrative (which became a 'master term' in Literary Studies and Film Studies). Rather than linguistic qualities, they are interested, for example, in the way works adapt features of traditional genres, or overcome challenges presented by the structure (120). For those critics irresistibly drawn to

---

[31] Close reading need not serve evaluation. If the word criticism is taken in its evaluative sense, then it might be said that some writers practise 'close analysis' rather than 'close criticism'.

the moment-by-moment distinctions in a work it is useful to be reminded of the benefits of a flexible movement between the local part, the larger structure, and general forms. However, as Literary Studies and Film Studies progressed there was often what Chris Baldick calls 'a drastic 'standing back' from the local particulars of a given work' (1996: 133). Attention to categories, classification, and structure became dominant – eventually leading to various forms of structuralism – and evaluation, especially of local effects, was unfortunately no longer a concern.

The New Critics were also criticised for downplaying or excluding another aspect of the bigger picture: the socio-historical context of the work. To be fair, the New Critics were themselves correcting a prevailing emphasis, reacting against Literary Studies as a form of historical scholarship and warning against reducing literature to cultural history. Wherever the emphasis is put, on 'text' or the original socio-historical context, each can be intelligently informed by, and benefit from, the other. Because this study's emphasis is on evaluating the form of the 'text' (with the socio-historical context relevant in so far as it serves that purpose), the arguments that Leavis puts forward for 'textual' emphasis are worth mentioning. Firstly, Leavis worries that socio-historical context might dominate perception at *too early* a point in the encounter making one prone to see the work as typical rather than exemplary, and/or failing to see a view more advantageous to its appreciation. Secondly, he thinks that the work, as it is currently experienced, is the thing that is shared in the present moment, for example, in a classroom. Even if this current experience is incomplete, or thought to be misguided, and would benefit from the socio-historical knowledge, the present moment is the time and place where perceptions and judgements can meet and be exactly located, and where perspectives may be finessed in the light of the evidence (before us). This is why close criticism has been also labelled 'ontological criticism' because it calls attention to the work's ontology: the *being* of the work, its material presence, in relation to the current reader (Johnson 1998). Thirdly, Leavis thinks that even if one draws upon socio-historical context, close attention to the text is still necessary to assess how a work is, for example, creatively deploying or challenging a prevailing feature (of the period)[32].

---

[32] The points in this paragraph emerge from Leavis's argument against F.W. Bateson. This argument concerns poet Andrew Marvell's use of the Body and Soul emblem in his poem 'A Dialogue between the Soul and the Body', in the essay 'The Responsible Critic: Or the Function of Criticism at any Time' (Leavis 1986 [1953], 184–206). See also 2.8: 'Comparison, category, and context'.

Indeed, it is only through close reading that the *particular configuration* of all the elements that meet in the work may be carefully evaluated. Cleanth Brooks and R.P. Warren in their New Critical textbook *Understanding Poetry* argue that the meaning and effect of elements is discovered by examining how they relate (1976 [1938]). The word 'steady' in the Johnson line, not particularly noteworthy in itself, gains its value from its relationship to 'shook'; and, furthermore, 'shook the world', a clichéd phrase, according to Leavis, is revitalised by 'steady'. In this way, close reading specifies and articulates the *precision* of placement and conjunction. Sometimes, if the work warrants it, it will be able to draw out its *richness* by noticing the variety of relationships even in a short passage or sequence. Empson was celebrated for extracting the variety of associations between congregating words in a concentrated space. Rónán McDonald writes about his ability to recognise, through close reading, the capaciousness of a work, and its 'prismatic variegations' (2007: 95).

The worry, expressed by some critiques of close reading, and exemplified by some of Empson's analysis (according to the critiques), is that the mining of the work becomes proliferating, and without perspective or pertinence[33]. This has rarely been a problem in the tradition of film criticism, and most films of merit would benefit from more rather than less local examination. Besides, for the close critic, escalation is a risk worth running in order to give the work a chance to open up and display its wares. Accuracy sometimes depends on pushing apparently farfetched hypothetical constellations with a view, if necessary, to reining back. Brooks and Warren had supposedly preferred *Experiencing Poetry* or *Reading Poetry* to be the title of their New Critical textbook rather than *Understanding Poetry* (the one they settled on) hence encouraging 'a continuous and mutable process of discovery' rather than a finalised comprehension (Johnson 1998). Close reading is the formalised method of slow, 'aesthetic reading' (highlighted in 1.2: 'The aesthetic attitude'). It is for those people who want to give a work prolonged attention, dwelling on it, returning to it, allowing the imagination, intellect, and emotions to work on it, so as to permit different

---

[33] Although I am grouping critics together, it is worth noting that there are variations of approach and emphasis amongst the close reading critics (even within the American New Critical version of the movement). Leavis, for example, is suspicious of what he takes to be the 'knowing' exegesis of Empson's close readings that value 'semantic ingenuity' and 'punning virtuosity' in both the works and the criticism (Christopher Norris, 'Editor's Foreword' in Bell (1988: xiii)). The attractions of ingenuity and virtuosity 'affected [Empson's] critical judgement' (xii).

qualities or aspects to emerge. It discourages premature understanding and judgement. It happens on different occasions and not commonly at one single sitting. The definitive moment is held off: the work reveals itself, for better or for worse, over time.

For the New Critics, poetic form and style instantiates content, and does not simply convey it. Consequently, form and content, technique and sense, are inseparable. The work does not only reflect a preconceived experience outside itself. It is a dynamic, autonomous entity that 'dramatizes experience within the theatre of its form' (Baldick 1996: 83). A work's style is regarded as a failure if it is found to be ornamental. Therefore, close reading for these critics is not simply a critical method for analysing texts, but allows the achievements of form/content indivisibility to be divulged. New Critics also insist that the expression of a work is at one with its particular medium, and should be evaluated accordingly: a poem should be judged *as* Poetry by attending to the multitude of technical aspects that constitute this particular art (for example, rhyming, line breaks, and stress)[34]. This means that there is no straightforward translatability between media (for example, between poem and novel). It also means that any translation or shift in the discourse of communication, crucially that between poem and critical essay, should respect the form of the medium within which the original work expresses itself. Both form/content indivisibility and medium applicability explain the dismay shown by New Critics towards paraphrase in critical accounts – they famously railed against the 'heresy of paraphrase' – which would inadequately summarise the content of a poem and not attend sensitively enough to its formal configuration, which is the very thing that makes it a poem[35]. This disembodiment would result not only in a simplification of the work, but probably (perhaps necessarily) a distortion of it, and more worryingly an incorrect or inappropriate evaluation. T.S. Eliot (1888–1965) insists that poetry is 'an intense fusion of associations within the complex concentration of its images', and not merely 'a versified idea' (summarised by Baldick 1996: 78). Decades later a group of English film critics, writing for a journal called *Movie* in the 1960s (first issue 1962), insisted that film is 'an intense fusion of associations within the complex concentration of its images', and not merely recorded ideas, stories, or events. Failing to recognise this was leading

---

[34] See 3.1: 'Medium'.
[35] 'The Heresy of Paraphrase' is the title of the final chapter in *The Well Wrought Urn*, an influential work of New Criticism, by Cleanth Brooks (1975 [1947]).

to the considerable qualities of films, especially Hollywood films of the classic era (1930–60), being undervalued. Film evaluation is especially prone to paraphrase as shown by the ubiquity of the shrunken discourse of promotion, reviewing, and popular dissemination, and the nature of this discourse can seep into more extended considerations.

The other side of the same coin, according to the *Movie* critics, is that certain films are overvalued. In these cases, content is *too* easily extractable, and therefore not sufficiently bound to form and style. This might make a film too obvious, or too conspicuously declare its significance, perhaps by way of 'important' subject matter, and this would lead to undeserved acclaim and prizes dispensed from certain sectors of the establishment. The Hollywood films that the *Movie* critics celebrated had their content deeply embedded in action and image, and this contributed to their underestimation or dismissal: their actions and images, which permitted a subtlety of expression, were mistaken as superficial or *generic* (and they were often genre films). Close reading would unlock the films' merits, and in any dispute with reductive reviewing or establishment taste it would substantiate argumentation.

It is remarkable how this group of film critics resemble the movement of close reading critics in Literary Studies. Although Leavis is acknowledged as an influence – for example, by *Movie* contributors Robin Wood and Andrew Britton – the movement more widely, and its methods, are not explicitly acknowledged in the *Movie* work[36]. It seems that despite the lack of a deliberate appropriation, the *Movie* group replicated the literary movement in reference to a different medium. They expressed the same rebellious intent through a journal, not unlike *Scrutiny*, the *Kenyon Review*, and *Sewanee Review*, that was positioned, and published from,

---

[36] The moral component of Leavis's criticism particularly influenced Wood and Britton who also added an explicitly contemporary ideological dimension. One important evaluative criterion for Leavis was 'moral seriousness'. At its best, moral seriousness refers to a complexity of expression that leads to a complexity of thought about life, and can be distinguished from moralism (although the cruder form is not absent from Leavis's criticism, nor Wood's). Leavis's philosophy of criticism, set out in many position essays, and cited in this part of the book, is actually uncannily close to Perkins' views, even though Perkins never acknowledged an influence. Indeed, he may have kept his intellectual distance because he was wary of being associated with 'the literary': films treated by critics as if they were novels or poems. He also regarded the dismissal of 'the popular' and the medium of film, by people such as Leavis, as wrong. The work of the *Movie* critics shows, however, that despite Leavis's conservatism, his understanding of aesthetic criticism is eminently transferable.

outside the establishment[37]. V.F. Perkins, a key member of the *Movie* group, wrote a book entitled *Film as Film* which is a pivotal contribution to the aesthetic evaluation of film (1972). The book derives its precepts from a specific conceptualisation of the film medium: an intertwining of recording aspects (by the camera) and creative ones (for example, arranging the set, composition, and editing). It nevertheless advocates a range of critical tenets that the literary critics held dear for works of literature. These include: the use of close reading (then a radical idea in relation to film); the distinct treatment of the medium (hence *film as film*); the indissolubility of form and content (one chapter is entitled '"How" is "What"'); the recognition of authorial achievement from the text (rather than from extra textual information); the recurrent emphasis on a work's internal relationships, its *synthesis* of elements, and on the coherence and credibility of these relationships; and the explicit concentration on evaluation and appreciation (Penguin's subtitle for the book was 'A Superb Introduction to the Appreciation and Criticism of the Cinema').

Perkins also warns against the 'heresy of paraphrase' (without using the phrase). He close reads a sequence from the film *Johnny Guitar* (Nicholas Ray 1954 US) which involves a character seeking revenge. His analysis encompasses aspects of action, colour, framing, object, and narrative context, as well as showing how the sequence is informed by the handling of an earlier occasion in the film. Following this analysis, Perkins writes, 'The example under discussion, stripped of all that it gains by its presentation in movie terms, amounts to nothing more interesting than this: "Emma arrives on horseback during a dust-storm"' (1972: 79). For Perkins, 'In order to comprehend whole meanings, rather than those parts of the meaning which are present in verbal synopsis or visual code, attention must be paid to the whole content of the shot, sequence and film' (79). The claim against paraphrase leads into the claim for close reading because only through the close reading is the achievement of synthesis suitably comprehended. Form and meaning are inseparable, as are shot, sequence, and film, but so are achievement and critical method such that the 'extent to which a movie rewards this complete attention', Perkins writes, 'is an index of its achievement' (79)[38].

---

[37] Film discourse also necessarily operated at this time, unlike literary discourse, outside the academy and was not yet institutionalised as Film Studies.
[38] Both the book *Film as Film* and the benefits of close reading for the aesthetic evaluation of film are explored and exemplified in Part III.

## 2.8 Comparison, category, and context

The emphasis so far in this study has been on the importance of attending to the individual work. Looking beyond the individual work is also a part of aesthetic criticism, and one aspect of this is the use of comparison. Leavis believes that as the critic feels her way into a work she is naturally placing it in relation to other things, and weighing up how relatively important it seems. Comparison is implicit within discriminatory activity, drawing upon cumulative experience. Awareness increases as films are viewed over time: the critic becomes more knowledgeable about variations within similar instances and about possibilities in the art form. Booth believes that ascertaining value in artworks is similar to ascertaining value in persons: 'by *experiencing* them in an immeasurably rich context of others that are both like and unlike them' (1988: 70, original emphasis). The evaluative process is unavoidably comparative even when comparisons are not consciously being made, and is set against 'a backdrop of [a] long personal history of untraceably complex experiences' (71).

What are the correct points of comparison? Carroll argues if works are judged within categories, and by categories he seems to mean genres (and sub-genres), then evaluative practice would be more stable (2009)[39]. In a moderate sense, this is fair because it would be odd to evaluate a slapstick comedy by the same criteria as a comedy of manners. They have different points and purposes. Similarly, different values are expected in different genres: a character without psychological complexity would probably be a failure in a psychological thriller, but it would be less damaging, and perhaps necessary, for a more abstract work, one dealing with archetypes and where other qualities, unrelated to psychological complexity, are central. Knowledge of genre is also important for gauging the merits of those aspects of originality, variation, hybridity, and expectation that are based on genre, and particularly important for those works which especially elicit a comparison within their genre. However, Carroll understands the role of genre less moderately because he considers it a

---

[39] Carroll's examples and most of his discussion seem to imply that he primarily means genre. His argument would also appear to depend on this because if it referred to any of the multiple categories a work could be viewed within then there would not be the stable categorisation that, for Carroll, secures evaluative judgement.

fundamental and substantial part of the evaluative process[40]. Carroll sets out the argument as follows:

1a)  Harold Lloyd's *Safety Last* [Fred Newmeyer, Sam Taylor 1923 US] contains (let us agree) many successful pratfalls.
1b)  *Safety Last* is a slapstick comedy.
1c)  Given the purpose or function of slapstick comedy, slapstick comedies that contain many successful pratfalls, all other things being equal, are good ...
2)  Therefore, *Safety Last* is good ... (167)

Unfortunately, one flaw in this argument occurs in proposition 1a) which assumes that the pratfalls in *Safety Last* are 'successful' whereas this is precisely what would need to be ascertained[41]. This assumption makes the conclusion, within the limited terms of this example, tautological (the pratfalls are successful, therefore, the film is good). Slapstick comedies with Harold Lloyd and slapstick comedies with The Three Stooges contain pratfalls, but I consider those in the former to have more merit, for a variety of reasons, than the latter. *Merely* allocating a film to its genre, and knowing that genre's traits and purposes, does not automatically help with the evaluation. It would need to be ascertained what makes for a 'successful' pratfall. Pratfalls may be mistimed, badly orchestrated, repetitive or lacking intricacy, and an experience of a wide variety of slapstick comedy will help an evaluation. Nevertheless, knowledge and judgement about, for example, timing, choreography, variation, and intricacy will be required, and these features are not genre specific, nor medium specific. Indeed, Beardsley's triumvirate of unity, intensity, and complexity crosses generic categories and media. When comparing a film adaptation to its source novel, for example, a judgement can be made about in which medium a quality available to both – fluency of narrative progression or credibility of characterisation perhaps – is best rendered.

The specification of generic or categorical features sometimes masquerades as evaluation. For example, Martine Beugnet acclaims a

---

[40] Carroll has more recently (2016) adjusted his position. He now argues that ascertaining 'purpose' is the most important aspect of evaluative practice. Category identity, however, is still an integral part of ascertaining purpose. See 2.9: 'Intention, achievement, and skill'.

[41] My aim in critiquing Carroll's argument is not to pick at his work, but rather to serve the wider purpose of illuminating the limitations of generic classification for evaluative criticism.

series of French films from 1997 to 2006 which are concerned with sensation and transgressive subject matter. She makes a collection of observations, sometimes via reference to individual films, which accurately, and often vividly, identify this corpus: for example, they have an 'organic ensemble of "blocks" of sensations rather than a chain of logically articulated narrative moments ... a series of ... fragmented sensory experiences'; their 'editing ... of the sequences never explicitly attempts to locate an event ... the montage tends to catch the characters already in action, without recourse to links or establishing shots'; and they exhibit a 'foray into the unconscious ... [a] world of repressed drives' (2007: 168, 128). These characteristics are sometimes also implicitly presented as evaluative claims, reasons for why the films are of merit. They could equally hold though for routine films in the category, and presumably, not every film that adopts these traits is of merit. Beugnet discusses a sequence in the film *Trouble Every Day* (Claire Denis 2001 France) where a young man is a victim of a vampiric murder during lovemaking. She notes that 'conventional shock tactics are denied by the length of the takes shot in close up, by the increasing obscurity of the image, and by the soundtrack, which combines a graphic evocation of pain with the haunting tune of the *Tindersticks*' music. As kisses turn into bites, the sound, like the image, veers towards the formless' (107). However, all these features could result in demerits: 'shot[s] in close up' could be exploitative or gratuitous; the 'obscurity of the image' could be a sign of ineptitude; and 'haunting' could signify cliché. By 'formless' Beugnet is referring to the attribute of the amorphous rather than implying that the film lacks form, but once again it is not clear why a 'veer ... towards the formless' is a merit in this film (even if it is). Formless is not an evaluative criterion. Beugnet does hint at the sequence's merit in merging and shifting: in relation to the soundtrack, she refers to the 'graphic evocation of pain with the haunting tune' and 'The young man's cries turn from begging for mercy into an incoherent howl that mingles with his killer's moans' (107). Yet, little more is offered by her to substantiate the implied merit. What do the close-ups effectively obscure? How do the many different sounds I can hear mutate, conjoin, and transform (hysterical laugh, guttural rasp, joyous yelp, animalistic moan)? What is the role of the cutaways to the victim's friend in complicating the reception of sight and sound? How does the music coordinate with the image, and contribute to strategies of involvement and separation? What are the effects and moods created by the shifting prominence of the various instruments (double bass, violins, trumpet, synths, and maracas)? Illumination would help to individuate and evaluate the significance and merits of the formless, a characteristic of the category, in this case[42].

Carroll claims that many evaluative disagreements would dissolve once the interlocutors agree on the correct genre within which the film should be judged[43]. What the Beugnet example shows, however, is that a lot of evaluative work still has to be done even when the generic category has been agreed upon. A lot of work also has to be done because genres tend to be capacious in their concerns even when narrowed down into sub-genres. A Western might be interested in, for example, character intimacy or cowboys chasing Native Americans or in the shaping force of landscape and each one of these interests will be have to be recognised and evaluated on their own terms. Sometimes works within a genre are dissimilar, or more profitably compared to something outside their genre to crystallise what is of value. The critic Raymond Durgnat has compared Laurel and Hardy's short films to the plays of Samuel Beckett in order to emphasise their abstract quality (1976: 141). Charlie Chaplin's use of physical choreography, especially the way in which his body interacts with objects, may have more in common with Fred Astaire than with his colleagues in slapstick. Some of the films of Jerry Lewis, for example, *The Ladies Man* (Jerry Lewis 1961 US), with its bravura reflexivity including the doll's house presentation of Herbert's home (where he lives with a group of women), might relate to some of the films of Jean-Luc Godard more comfortably than to other Hollywood comedies (contemporary or otherwise). Booth points out that within genres, creative personnel are aiming at quite various forms, effects, and shapes that may be more salient than the genre's trappings (1975: 208–9).

In addition, Carroll's argument tends to presume that recognising the genre at an early stage will act as a guide – in his propositional progression 1b) simply asserts it – but it is sometimes not straightforward within which generic category to place a work[44]. Interpretations and evaluations may have to be made *first* in order to find the genre within which the film

---

[42] I select Beugnet on *Trouble Every Day* as an illustrative example because there is an implicit and explicit evaluative component to the work. A lack of detailed substantiation may not harm many of her other intellectual and scholarly purposes, and, for the record, I share her positive regard for the film (and the particular sequence).

[43] See Carroll (2000).

[44] In the case of genre hybridity, Carroll writes 'the realization of the points and purposes of the different kinds should be calculated in terms of each category's proportionate influence on the overall outcome of the work' (2009: 182).

is most advantageously appreciated. For example, *Black Swan* (Darren Aronofsky 2010 US) might be considered crude and bombastic if treated as a female melodrama, but unusual and imaginative if treated as a piece of body horror. Cavell allocates a series of Hollywood film comedies, previously designated 'Screwball', to a genre he called 'Remarriage Comedy' (1981). He considers that the cognisance of this new category leads to a better appreciation of the films than the familiar label. To justify this new category he must have *already* evaluated the films in a certain way (without benefiting from, and possibly distracted by, a pre-existing category). More radically, he believes that the films have been created with a concern – albeit perhaps without explicit articulation – for the generic traits, themes, and formal qualities of the category he seemingly later constructs.

The argument that different merits of an artwork will emerge when it is perceived within different categories is made in a much cited essay by Kendall Walton entitled 'Categories of Art' (2008b [1970]). One purpose of Walton's essay is to show that aesthetic qualities, of the sort discussed by Frank Sibley, depend on the context and history of the artwork as well as on immediate or proximate perception[45]. Walton believes we often evaluate works by comparing them within categories to see whether they are standard examples or interesting variations (198–9). Knowing the history of an art form allows the distinctive to be distinguished from the conventional. Features that were once original or radical deviations are now, with repetition, considered clichés. The use of black and white cinematography in Hollywood films of the 1930s is seen as standard, but its use in a film of the present day, given that colour stock is the norm, would make it 'contra-standard' (Walton's term). This will have evaluative ramifications unavailable to an immediate perception that lacked that knowledge.

Walton's account of the usefulness of category to evaluation is flexible and productively indeterminate. He argues that there are many categories that a work may fall into from broad ones like 'film' to narrow ones like 'short films with lead characters from Manchester', and he does not equate category to genre (genre is just one categorical possibility). For example, *Diary of a Country Priest* (Robert Bresson 1951 France) has often been understood and explained, understandably and valuably, from within the thematic category of Catholicism (particularly matters concerning the soul and grace). I argued in a piece of aesthetic criticism on the film that it can be appreciated within two other categories – which were not

---

[45] See 1.10: 'Aesthetic qualities'.

necessarily unrelated to the religious viewpoint – the everyday, a thematic one, and the undramatic, a formal one, which foreground merits of the film that, if not overlooked, had not been sufficiently regarded (Klevan 2000). Other categories which may reveal merits are 1950s French films, Robert Bresson films, French countryside and village films, transcendental films, or George Bernanos adaptations (which include *Under Satan's Sun* (Maurice Pialat 1987 France) and *Mouchette* (Robert Bresson 1967 France)). Walton wants to draw attention to the variety of different categories which might disclose a work's value. Some categories may reveal the work to be more aesthetically 'pleasing' and stimulating than others (Walton 2008b [1970]: 212; also see Laetz (2010: 295)).

T.S. Eliot values a creativity that is not only a matter of expressing individuality, but stems from the artist accessing and realising a tradition. He also believes, concomitantly, that criticism is not about the personal judgement of the critic, but about attuning her or his sensibility to the artistic tradition from which she or he will gain authority (and objectivity) for judgement. Criticism amounts to 'a cultivated entente with precedent' (McDonald 2007: 83–4). Leavis, influenced by Eliot, believes that creativity of the artist arises from operating within 'inherited forms', and with intention embedded in tradition he or she 'serves' this as much as 'selfhood' (Bell 1988: 112; Day 2006: 137). The artwork organically relates to other works, and the critic values the work through understanding its place in a developing organism. For E.H. Gombrich (1909–2001) many critical terms, for example, original, experimental, clichéd, or derivative, require historical judgement. They are made against a background of knowing the traditions of the art form, and they involve an understanding that creative personnel operate within those histories, making aesthetic choices, or *moves*, within them. Gombrich thought that any activity, for example, cooking, fashion, pop music, ballet, jazz, acting, or cricket has a circle of devotees 'who argue among themselves about excellence' (1978: 42). These arguments are linked to an intimate knowledge of the history of the activity, and an experience of it, from which comparisons are made. Aesthetic criticism is a formalised version of this knowledgeable devotion.

At the same time as believing that the individual work should be recognised within a tradition, Leavis does not believe it should be justified by some past context. What matters is how the work lives within the present circumstances, and how active it can be within the contemporary mind. One of the purposes of evaluation for Leavis is to keep alive the tradition of an art, not by being indiscriminately respectful to works of the past, but by illuminating their *relevance* – another central Leavisite word – in the present (1986 [1953]: 201). For many teachers an important pedagogical principle is exposing students to works of the past that they might not come across in the ordinary course of their lives, and which they might find valuable. The hope is that these works may be freshly appreciated. (The appreciation of these older works may also affect, for the better, the perception and creation of contemporary works.) This hope is related to the evaluative criterion of the 'test of time' – extensively elaborated by Anthony Savile – which understands that the best artworks are those which open up to different generations (1982). The 'test of time' guards against fashion and trends which in the short term skew perception and perspective, and instead encourage us to see the bigger picture. It also ensures that the criterion of originality does not predominate in judgements because the 'new' might turn out to be of limited value, or ephemeral, and a technique that once appeared to be radical is exposed as merely novel or gimmicky.

Canons should be pliable, with works constantly subject to the 'test of time', and open to the inclusion of works, old and new, previously excluded. Canons are useful because, however incomplete, they open up histories, especially for those new to art forms and set standards for current artists and critics[46]. Nevertheless, canons can also monumentalise works, and even indoctrinate the uninitiated thereby discouraging active critical engagement. Furthermore, sometimes a film is canonical or 'classic' because it is a fine model or exemplar (of something), or good in obvious ways, rather than necessarily the best. (I am not yet convinced that *Citizen Kane* (1941 US), brilliant and exceptional though it is, is better than Orson Welles's following film *The Magnificent Ambersons* (1942 US). The former, however, is canonised in a way that the latter is not.) Aesthetic criticism should be respectful towards canons, but also productively antagonistic, especially once the critic has gathered experience of the art form, so that it can re-evaluate the misunderstood, the overlooked, or the overrated (and it should therefore be, at the same time, in a dialogue with previous criticism). For Harold Bloom, a work deserves to be canonical if it engenders, or has engendered, excellent criticism (1981).

For aesthetic criticism, the present context in which the work is viewed is equally important to the one that is past. Aspects of works that were once central to their effect may be lost. There are references in

---

[46] When I was first learning about jazz and how to listen to it, I was grateful to canonical lists of personnel and 'best albums'. See Doorly (2013) for an extended discussion of how canons have contributed to excellence in fine art.

## What is aesthetic criticism?

works that, although knowledge may bring understanding, will not be experienced with the immediacy and relevance of an original audience (for example, the targets of satire). Equally, the critic can become aware of qualities that only later come to light so that, for example, subsequent films by a director or performer may lead to their earlier ones being reconceived. McFee argues that criticism is alert to what Arthur Danto called the 'retroactive enrichment' of the artwork – McFee labels the process 'forward retroactivism' – where later events alter the perspective of past works (2011: 119). Roland Barthes believes that works of merit contain semantic possibilities capable of sustaining more than one sense over time. Providing that the configurations and patterns of the work are respected, the critic should be responsive to these possibilities, and not beholden to some apparently correct sense recoverable from the historical context (2004 [1966]; also Davidson 1968: 98–9). Concomitantly many creative personnel are sympathetic to their works being appreciated in diverse and unexpected ways and contexts. Wilhelm Emrich judges a work's artistic quality in terms of a flexibility over time that stems from its 'fabric of interrelations':

> What constitutes the specifically artistic quality of a work ... is the fact that the various contents and forms which the [creator] utilises or produces out of his imagination are combined into a fabric of interrelations. This fabric, made from structure and [the] language [of the art], liberates the various contents and forms from their specific historical context and opens up an inexhaustible wealth of meanings which, in turn, can develop representative or symbolic meanings that are equally applicable to other periods, other forms of life, other ideas. What constitutes a ... work [of less merit] is the fact that the reflection it contains does not represent an endless continuum, but breaks off very soon, or reaches its end because its contents and forms do not point beyond themselves, do not contain a multiplicity of meanings, but remain within an unequivocal realm which is quickly exhausted. There is no need for any further contemplation or exploration and, therefore, none takes place. (Quoted in Jacoby 1969: 122–3)

Meyer Schapiro also illuminates how a figure, despite carrying initial connotations, can take on a range of senses once it is embedded within the work. For Schapiro, knowledge of 'the identity' of a figure in a work might not be needed 'in order to admire the *realization of individuality* by [artistic] means', even if that identity was essential in rendering the original realisation (1966: 11–12, my emphasis). Schapiro gives the example

**2.8** *Man with a Knife (St Bartholomew)*, 1657, oil on canvas, 122.7 x 99.5 cm, Timken Art Gallery, San Diego, CA.

of a beholder, looking at Rembrandt's painting entitled *Man with a Knife*, who although he is 'unable to say whether it's a portrait of a butcher or an assassin or of Saint Bartholomew who was martyred by a knife, he can still [recognise] the painting as a beautiful harmony of light and shadow, colour and brushwork, and appreciate the artist's power of making the figure visible as a complex human presence steeped in feeling and revery' (11) (Fig. 2.8). Similarly, either because of ignorance or lack of interest in religious figures, the specific features of a French Catholic priest in *Diary of a Country Priest* may be lost, but a viewer may nonetheless still appreciate the film's rendering of tenderness, altruism, youthfulness, naivety, self-consciousness, and self-harm. This appreciation will be possible even though other features of the work may seem removed or may not be deciphered. For Schapiro, the force of the work's form, and the sense conveyed by that form, overcomes knowledge. Nevertheless, this decontextualised inclination needs to be balanced by a recognition that knowledge of grace or of the martyrdom of Saint Bartholomew may also give access to important merits, perhaps to those that were initially intended[47].

## 2.9 Intention, achievement, and skill

Of all the matters that lie outside the work arguably the most important for aesthetic criticism is the intention of the creative personnel. Aesthetic criticism recognises that the artwork has taken work, and is worked; it has been *made* by people, and is made well or not so well[48]. It also recognises that the work is designed to achieve some end(s) which may or may not be achieved, and therefore it often talks in terms of achievements. Sometimes an achievement will be dependent on skills therefore criticism responds to how skilfully it considers a film has been *executed*, appreciating, for example, that a difficult line of dialogue is delivered convincingly or fluently, a familiar situation is dramatised without collapsing into cliché, a sentiment is conveyed without tipping over into sentimentality, or a group of figures is arranged in the frame so that the composition does not look incongruously stilted. (Part of being skilful will depend on learning a craft, and films involve great craft at every stage of the process.) Some things are harder to achieve than other things and the recognition of this, perhaps implicit, becomes part of the assessment. Patrick Doorly is eager to understand the history of fine art as high quality endeavour where artists seek excellence. When an artist paints a face, she is not simply copying a face, before her or from memory, but creating a face by adapting, for her own present purposes, conventions, forms, and techniques learned from other painters. The artistic tradition is one of accumulated experiences

---

[47] Research can be carried out into earlier contexts to reclaim meanings or understandings in order to reveal former merits. Indeed, this activity would constitute part of a history of evaluation. Such meanings or understandings might even be revivified and incorporated into a current aesthetic experience.

[48] Sparshott claims that there is criticism about paintings and not sunsets, and about music and not birdsong, because 'criticism of anything other than a human act seems doubtfully relevant' (1967: 40). Presumably, however, there are components of aesthetic criticism such as explanation, description, and comparison, which can be used to appreciate birdsong. Furthermore, the singing of the nightingale in my garden *might* be less accomplished than the one seemingly responsive to the lovers in London's Berkeley Square. And according to Bawden (2015) nightingales are performing.

of how best, through an improvement in skills and a process of trial and error, to execute and achieve (2013).

For Sparshott, criticism is fundamentally underpinned by a conception of the artwork as an intended 'performance' (1967: 40–3). Sparshott means to emphasise the way in which criticism tends to treat an artwork, even a painting or a novel, as something 'performed' to a public who then judge the success of the performance. I think this understanding of criticism (and artworks) is too sweeping, but it is a useful notion in relation to the dramatic arts because of its more literal applicability. In the fiction film, the filmmakers are presenting a dramatic performance (although this suitability is easy to overlook because fiction films are often treated as narratives or as signifying entities rather than dramatic performances). Morse Peckham finds expressions such as 'suspension of disbelief' and 'dramatic illusion' misleading because they emphasise the fictional absorption at the expense of recognising the non-fictional performance (which the work also exhibits) (1981: 46). He uses the example of applauding a *performer* in an opera when they finish singing despite being deeply involved with their *character* (46). Similarly, when viewing a fiction film there is a flexible movement between, for example, engaging with the character and evaluating or appreciating the performance of the character (Klevan 2005a). Maybe 'movement' does not quite capture the dual apprehension as both are perceived simultaneously. This is true for many features of fiction films: for example, there is a recognition that the train of events is also a story being told, that the place is also a set or location, that the clothes are also costumes, that the action is also staged and choreographed, that spoken speech is also (often) written lines, and that the character is also the actor (who may also be a star). Consequently, in the matter of judgement, attribution may be difficult: for example, is awkward behaviour a failure of performance or an achievement of characterisation?

Leavis believes that the critic should not only attend and react to 'the completed work', but respond to a sense of the author's creativity and choices, to 'the implied activity of [the work's] composition' (Bell 1988: 47)[49]. He suggests further that the critic might need *to identify* with 'the impulse' to make the work (47)[50]. Leavis is not only referring to the critic

---

[49] This approach is common in the work of English film critics such as Wood and Perkins, and critical responsiveness to filmmakers' choices has been recently addressed by Gibbs (2006). See 3.4: 'Choice and expectation'.
[50] Leavis is specifically referring to the single, literary author, but his argument has wider applicability.

identifying with the personality of the author, implied or otherwise, or with their thematic preoccupations, but with the intentional process being enacted in the form of the work. Creative personnel will 'struggle ... to bring the material to a focus' and this struggle is 're-enacted in every fully responsive' engagement (87). This is suggestive because with regard to film, identification by a viewer is often thought to be predominantly with characters, or with the stars that play them. Yet, the identification can also be with the process of *filmmaking* (primarily the directing, but also with any other creative aspect such as the screenwriting, the cinematography, or the performing). The latter is especially forceful in works that have a distinctive authorial style where the mark of the filmmaking is a prevailing feature for viewer and critic.

Trying to exactly ascertain and assess the intentions of creative personnel has been a perennial challenge for criticism. It is difficult because the actions of creative personnel often cannot be observed directly and therefore must be inferred. It is also difficult because many different intentions are operating simultaneously, for example, those relating to meaning, address, design, and quality. As well as global intentions (for example, an overarching theme), there are a multitude of local intentions or micro-intentions in a work (for example, how to execute a gesture). The web of purposeful activity is complex and intricate. Another complicating factor is that creative personnel may act intentionally and skilfully without conforming to 'previously formed intention[s]': they come up with ideas as they make things, '[t]inkering and experimenting', and responding to circumstance (Zangwill 2012: 45). This is true of filmmaking which has so many working parts and where even the best-laid plans may have to be reformulated, and is especially true of filmmaking on location which, as Alain Bergala vividly reminds us, is 'necessarily in negotiation with rugged reality' (changes in light, weather, geography, and countless practicalities) (2016: 78). Bergala writes, 'The act of decision making in cinema is always a mix of rationality ... intuition, instinct, reflex' (86). He goes on, 'To be a good filmmaker is to have good reflexes, to make the right decision at the right moment, which sometimes passes in a fraction of a second, even if you don't know exactly why you are making that choice' (87)[51]. It is also the ability 'to soak in what this location, this light, can bring anew to the preconceived idea that [the filmmakers] formulated

---

[51] Bergala also adds that it is during the editing process that 'the filmmaker is in a much better position to think through and rationalize his choices, to call them into question, to make them and remake them' (87).

for the scene', and this would also be true in a more controlled environment such as a studio where the director might have to 'soak in' the atmosphere of the set that has been constructed or the demeanour of actors (111). In turn, even the most prepared of actors needs to be contingently responsive to the filmmaking environment. Many films of merit are the result of an alchemy that only results when all the participants finally come together on a shoot. This does not prevent the possibility of design, pattern, and intelligent form – indeed it is a wonder that given the unpredictability of filmmaking so many films are even minimally coherent – but rather means that, like the filmmakers, they are modifying. Modification and accommodation might be seen as compromising aesthetic creation and achievement, and yet they are an integral part of it[52].

Learning about what the filmmakers intended from interviews or commentaries can help the critic understand the work, and appreciate it better. Criticism uses whatever information will usefully contribute to a fair and reasoned evaluation. However, the statements of the creative personnel cannot be the authority. For a start, it might be a problem for the work if, for its appreciation, there is too great a requirement to inquire. The work may be solipsistic, failing to make its features intrinsically expressive to a satisfactory degree. In addition, quite understandably, not all creative personnel will want, need, or be able to give, helpful, accurate or adequately multifaceted accounts, and some may actively mislead. They have, after all, chosen to express themselves through the work and through a particular medium. Makers may or may not be cognisant of the multifarious components of their agency, and the intricate, entangled interrelations that constitute it on any occasion.

Although Leavis believes that criticism should be responsive to the artist's choices, he thinks that there is an aspect to creativity 'which overrides the conscious choosing self' (Storer 2009: 81). Without a 'deep animating intention', which the author may not declare, or even reflect upon, a work could be calculated, contrived, or 'willed' (Leavis 1984 [1952]: 225). Cavell writes, 'To say that works of art are intentional objects is not to say that each bit of them, as it were, is separately intended' (2002 [1969]:

---

[52] Something good in a film may have been the result of an accident or even a mistake, and therefore will not straightforwardly be an achievement by the filmmakers (and this is one reason why not all merits should necessarily be attributed to intention). On the other hand, recognising a happy accident and choosing to keep it in the film will be an achievement, as will creating an environment that fosters the fortuitous.

236). Alex Clayton extends the thought with regard to *Psycho* (Alfred Hitchcock 1960 US), a film he considers to have many merits: '[I]t is unlikely that many ... details ... are the result of defined premeditation in each case ... Rather, it seems more credible to suppose that their intuitive "rightness", their lucidity and density of suggestion, their preservation of dramatic logic and inflection of dramatic mood, issue from a more general commitment and clarity of purpose on the part of the filmmaking team' (2012: 78).

A writer, director, or actor may intend all manner of things, but may not necessarily be conscious of them at the time or conscious of their ramifications in the future. Some durable works seem to have a *built-in* capacity to disclose new merits, and this capacity is regarded as part of the original achievement[53]. We do not always consciously know what we intend; to use a psychoanalytic analogy, a patient's refusal to accept an interpretation about his behaviour does not entail its falsity (Casey 2011 [1966]: 148–9). A film may exhibit purposive 'patterns of intention' that its makers deny (149). In the way that analysts (or friends and family) may better discern our intentions from the way we appear or behave, so too attentive viewers and critics may better discern intentions from the appearance and behaviour of the work. Intentions are disclosed and discovered as the work is experienced.

Not everything that manifests within the work, however, is intended (consciously or unconsciously). A director may intend profundity, and the result may only be portentousness; a performer may wish to be powerful and rousing, and only end up being loud and strident. The road to hell is paved with good intentions. Therefore, Richard Wollheim talks of evaluating works according to their 'fulfilled intentions' (quoted in McFee 2011: 93). However, even if the intentions have been 'fulfilled', they may be anything from limited to abhorrent, and thereby result in a negative evaluation. Equally, it is sometimes a blessing that intentions have *not* been fulfilled: a director may intend a restricted effect, and end up unexpectedly or unwittingly achieving something multifaceted. This is why a work cannot simply be evaluated in terms of it appropriately satisfying or fulfilling intentions[54]. It is also why it is often worth separating what a work does from what an artist does – something that Beardsley emphasised – and

---

[53] This point is made and discussed arrestingly by Cavell (2002 [1969]: 225–37).
[54] Even if a work is suitably fulfilling one intention it may be failing to satisfy another, one which is perhaps more crucial (and this suggests that it is important for criticism not only to discover intentions, but to figure out which should be prioritised).

this is why I mostly refer to '*the film* doing, or meaning, or achieving this or that'[55].

## 2.10 Evaluative criteria

Philosophers who believe in essential evaluative criteria are known as 'generalists'. Beardsley is one of a handful of aesthetic philosophers to believe that there are general criteria for evaluation – unity, intensity, and complexity – that are transferable from work to work. These are unquestionably far-reaching and outstanding criteria, but it is difficult to make the case that they are universal. A work that was sentimental in a variety of ways, each way unifying to create an intensity of sentimentality would not necessarily be of merit (Sibley 2006 [1962]: 113). The majority of commentators, known as 'particularists', to distinguish them from generalists such as Beardsley, believe there are no evaluative rules or laws that hold for all works a priori and prescriptively apply (for example, 'complexity *must* be exhibited in all works', thereby possibly prejudicing ones exhibiting simplicity). Instead, numerous criteria for excellence will be deployed depending on the work. From the point of view of a couple of notable categories, and broadly speaking, a classical work will be valued for exhibiting propriety, balance, and symmetry whereas a romantic work will be valued for exhibiting originality, sincerity, and intensity. Even though the films of Fred Astaire and R.W. Fassbinder both contain vigorous physicality, it would not be useful to evaluate them by the same criteria. Although it is rare now to see the generalist case being explicitly proposed, a generalist attitude is evident in formal and informal evaluations where similar criteria are commonly cited in relation to dissimilar films. For example, in contemporary Film Studies, subversive, transgressive, and radical are frequently applied evaluative criteria (sometimes carrying the implication that they are essential to a work's merit).

Indeed, many good critics, despite believing in, and advocating, 'particularist' principles, do have favoured criteria. Leavis repeatedly values intelligence, sensitivity, maturity, vitality, spontaneity, realisation, and concreteness. The New Critics value tensional complexity in, for example, irony, paradox, and ambiguity. Although these criteria are ideal at revealing

---

[55] See Wimsatt and Beardsley (1946). Another advantage of this locution is that a film is the symbiotic result of many significant personnel, and disentangling attribution is often difficult and unnecessary when making an evaluative claim.

the merits of certain types of novel or poem, other types which might be lit up by different criteria can unfairly suffer. Nevertheless, they do have more than local applicability, and it would be wrong to call them niche or idiosyncratic. This is partly because, without claiming universality or permanence, many of the criteria are relevant and rewarding beyond an isolated work or category, beyond the critic's sensibility and preference, beyond one time and place, and beyond artworks. The criteria have turned out to be of repeated value in criticism and across different mediums: Perkins, for example, lauds precise tensional complexity in a selection of Hollywood films of the 1950s as the literary New Critics once had in the poems of John Donne. The criteria are inclusive while being discriminating, and this is particularly true of the most general ones such as unity, intensity, and complexity[56].

Nevertheless, there is no one criterion, or selection of criteria, that will ensure the perfect work. This is akin to the problem presented by Wittgenstein of defining a game: there are many games, all deserving of that categorical label, but it is impossible to come up with one definition that will include all activities accepted as games (2006 [1953]: 27, point 66)[57]. William Righter historically charts how most efforts to award primacy to one particular criterion have come unstuck. He emphasises how criticism is characterised by its 'open character' and should not sacrifice 'sensibility', developed through experience and education, to a 'general concept' (1963: 116, 98)[58]. It should therefore also take care not to be 'assimilated' into the procedures and languages of other studies 'which make claims upon it' – something film criticism has been susceptible to for various cultural, institutional, pedagogical, and medium related reasons – and which might introduce criteria that unduly dominate, or be prejudicial (116). More profitably, rather than being armed with pre-ordained criteria and ready to pounce, the critic senses that something is or is not working in the work and arrives at the suitable criteria from the proximate experiential stimulus. Suitable criteria will often emerge as the critic engages with the work and its critical context (for example, building on, or challenging, previous accounts of a film). Hence, Bell's understanding, through his

---

[56] This might partly explain the apparent contradiction in Leavis's viewpoint: on the one hand, he argues for responsiveness of judgement while on the other he consistently advocates, much to the frustration of his adversaries, quite particular criteria.
[57] For example: they are played on a board, they must include two or more people, there must be a winner ...
[58] Sensibility is defined in *The New Oxford Dictionary of English* as the ability to appreciate and respond to emotional or aesthetic influences (Pearsall 1998).

explication of Leavis's work, that criticism is phenomenological – reacting to the phenomenon as experienced – rather than essentialist – coming to the work armed with essential criteria which must be fulfilled. Booth believes the critic should ask the question: is *this* device good for *this* task in *this* work? In discussing irony, he gives the vivid example of Jane Austen using an unusually lengthy passage of speech for Mr Collins's proposal to Elizabeth in *Pride and Prejudice* (1975: 198–9). Booth argues the speech is not evaluated by some set requirement of how long passages of dialogue *should* be or for how irony *should* operate in this novel or novels of this kind (*pace* critical methods prioritising category). According to 'proper proportion', the speech is too long, but he considers it just the right length for *this* character 'at *this* spot in *this* novel' to do 'its full comic job' (198–9, original emphasis). Booth elaborates on how its length conveys a variety of the traits and mannerisms of 'a grasping foolish clergyman'; it enables the reader to experience the intolerable tedium that Elizabeth is feeling; and it makes possible the 'anticlimax' where her value is clumsily expressed in terms of money (198–200). In principle, criticism is conditional, practical, and pragmatic. Christopher Ricks writes that it deals in 'living adjustments, allowances, re-adjustments, apprehensions, and concessions' (1996: 315). It also proceeds by way of example, context, and circumstance. For Wittgenstein, this manner of procedure is not inferior to, or less rigorous than, abstract definition and general statement[59].

This is why aesthetic criticism is dependent on *principles or standards of critical practice* rather than set, absolute, or universal criteria. Critical evaluations should be judged by the way the critic goes about his task, not proven by a set of rules. This is an important insight of Hume's seminal work of the eighteenth century, *Of the Standard of Taste*, where he considers that judgement is grounded by the community of competent critics and it is their qualities and procedures that are paramount (2008 [1757]). Hume crisply announces that a '[s]trong sense, united to delicate sentiment, improved by practice, perfected by comparison, cleared of all prejudice, can alone entitle critics to this valuable character' (109). He therefore recommends that the critic should have – in relation to his or her particular art – a refined and developed sensibility, experience, perceptiveness, comparative skills, and be free from prejudice so they will not judge from their own idiosyncrasies (as far as possible). Centuries after its publication aesthetic philosophers and critics are still adding traits to Hume's list.

---

[59] See Byrne (1979: 265–70); and Shusterman (1986: 93–7) for relevant discussions of the Wittgensteinian understanding of the use of criteria in criticism.

James Grant particularly emphasises 'imaginativeness' and 'communication skills' (2013: 66, 50). Skills of communication are needed to produce criticism as distinct from judgements: somebody can be an excellent judge without being an articulate critic or without being a critic at all (50–1). Imaginativeness will be needed both to enhance the communicativeness and to produce assessments which are 'unobvious' and therefore worth communicating in the first place (70; and Chapter 3 more generally). Stephanie Ross adds 'emotional responsiveness' (2014: 591). Hume believes that, except in some special cases, the community of critics, thanks to their qualities and qualifications, would come to agreement and thus reveal the best works, and produce a 'standard of taste'. This belief may not be as unfounded as some commentators have suggested, as there is more convergence or at least more cumulative, cooperative understanding than is often acknowledged. I think, however, that Hume's more valuable insight is that evaluations are secured by the quality of the critic's treatment of the work, and not by fixed evaluative criteria.

## 2.11 Reasons, argument, and objectivity

In the absence of absolute criteria, the critic provides reasons to support their response. Yet, it is repeatedly emphasised by philosophers of criticism that the reasons provided are to recommend the same response in others, and not simply to justify an evaluation (Budd 2008; Isenberg 1973; Radford and Minogue 1981; Reichert 1977; Righter 1963; Scruton 1974; Shusterman 1986). These are my reasons for coming to see – *to regard* – the film in this way; prescriptively, this is how the film *should* be seen, or more moderately, how it *could* productively be seen (and heard, and experienced). It is worth being reminded of the psychoanalytic analogy: the patient should not simply accept the account provided by the analyst, but make it work for him (Casey 2011 [1966]: 150). Criticism is aspiring to be inclusive as well as to be correct.

Colin Radford and Sally Minogue focus on the nature of persuasion in criticism, and give an instructive example from Leavis's writing on a line from a Shelley poem *Ode to the West Wind* (1981: 44–5). The line is, 'Loose clouds like earth's decaying leaves are shed' and comes from the following section of the poem:

> Thou on whose stream, 'mid the steep sky's commotion,
> Loose clouds like earth's decaying leaves are shed,
> Shook from the tangled boughs of Heaven and Ocean,

Leavis questions Shelley's comparison of 'loose clouds' and 'decaying leaves':

> In what respects are the 'loose clouds' like 'decaying leaves'? The correspondence is certainly not in shape, colour, or way of moving. It is only the vague general sense of windy tumult that associates the clouds and the leaves. (44)

Contesting Leavis's evaluation, R.H. Fogle writes:

> To Mr. Leavis' objections to the comparison of 'loose clouds' with 'decaying leaves' *one can only assert* that there are quite adequate resemblances between them. The clouds and the leaves are carried in precisely the same fashion by the power of the wind. Furthermore, the resemblance holds for shape and colour as well as movement. Swift-flying clouds may present the same angularities as leaves, and leaves flying horizontally through a grey sky will take the hue of their surroundings. (45; original emphasis)

Personally speaking, Fogle does not persuade me to adopt his perception. He does not convincingly show that the clouds and the leaves are 'carried in precisely the same fashion'. The poem says that both clouds and leaves are 'shed', but it is not straightforward to imagine a shedding cloud. In addition, it is not self-evident that 'swift-flying clouds', even when wispy, present the same angularities as leaves. Fogle does not bring me to see the resemblances perhaps because he feels that 'one can only assert'. Alternatively, it may be because he is content for the imagistic correspondence to be *only* 'quite adequate'[60]. Sparshott writes that criticism is perhaps 'less aptly described as evaluative discourse than as discourse of a kind that adequately grounds evaluations' (1967: 37).

Some readers may be more convinced, or feel that even if his reasons are not conclusive, Fogle suggests enough to allow a more generous reading than Leavis. Some may be satisfied with the 'vague sense of windy tumult' and do not feel the poem requires a more exact or resonant association between the clouds and the leaves. (This would be difficult to sustain, however, given that the line sets up a direct comparison.) Furthermore, the example would not alone be decisive in damning the poem because this simile may be anomalous rather than characteristic (although Leavis considers it typical). Even if it is characteristic, the poem may exhibit

---

[60] It is also not clear what Fogle's standard of adequacy is.

merits that outweigh its weak similes[61]. An important, and difficult, skill of critical judgement and argumentation is weighing, within the segment being appraised and within the work as a whole, the relative importance of merits and demerits. How significant or inconsequential is a merit or demerit within the work's scheme?

Although criticism need not necessarily proceed by way of an actual argumentative dialogue, the critic often speculates argumentatively. Therefore the critic may take a feature that appears to be a demerit or that they imagine might appear to others to be a demerit (an apparent cliché perhaps). They then provide an account which shifts the perception of it by showing how and why the feature is in fact meritorious. While an evaluation may ultimately not persuade, the endeavour to persuade is advantageous as the critic and the reader are forced to become increasingly specific.

Ultimately, the reader has to come to her or his own conclusion – hence my 'personally speaking' – showing that choice is an integral part of the critical process. Righter calls criticism the 'art of choice': 'We choose not only among works of art themselves, but among arguments, insights and points of view. Because there are no rigorous logical procedures that govern reason giving, we choose among reasons' (1963: 79). I think that the lack of fixed criteria results in an indecisiveness that is productive. It requires that nothing should be taken for granted and this means that each individual can take responsibility to work through the claims and evidence presented in any piece of criticism: they test them for themselves (against the work). Far from being a limitation, criticism's participatory character is democratic and invigorating.

In aesthetic criticism, both the critic and the reader of the criticism are regarded as distinct individuals. The critic offers *his or her* perception of the film based on study and analysis of it for *me* to respond to. It is common in academic Film Studies for writers to explore a film indirectly, for example, by assessing it through its historical or cultural context, or through theories. Some of these theories are about 'the spectator' and their responses. There are gains from detaching in these ways, but also losses, and some inevitable circumlocution and ventriloquism. In aesthetic criticism, the exchange is direct, and relatively unmediated: between actual spectators – the critic and the reader – rather than hypothetical, recreated or amalgamated ones. The critic proposes ways for me to perceive the

---

[61] For a discussion of this see Radford and Minogue (1981: 44–8).

film, but she does not assume presumptuously that I do perceive it in those ways or that I ever will.

Criticism has an ambivalent relationship towards agreement: most critics seek, even crave, consent, for their own evaluations, but recognise that, for the many reasons already discussed, there will be varying, legitimate responses. Hume understood this to arise from 'diversity' that is 'blameless' (2008 [1757]: 110). Some have considered this irreconcilable aspect to be troublesome, even fatal, for criticism and have concluded that its findings are not objectively verifiable. In fact, although criticism is undoubtedly community and culturally dependent, as most discourses are, it has many features and procedures that might reasonably be called objective. Individual viewers may actualise aspects, but the potentiality of these aspects must lie within the work, and therefore are verifiable. Through skill and experience, wine tasters 'discern real differences' in the quality of different wines (Lyas 2002a: 372). Some people are better at recognising things in particular arts than others, and we can train ourselves to be better; indeed, that is one of the aims of an aesthetic education. Even if aspect perception may vary – and many works of merit encourage a variety of aspects – some possibilities are more revealing than others and many can be excluded. The famous line drawing is both a duck and a rabbit, but it is clearly not a tiger, a frog, or an elephant. Those who see the duck and the rabbit are both right and both (objectively) accurate. Barthes believes that even if an evaluation is peculiarly idiosyncratic it would need to be attuned to verifiable patterns of imagery, forms, and themes (Davidson 1968: 99). In this sense, although good critics refrain from adopting pre-ordained systems, they are often systematic because they wish to think in an ordered way about the way the artwork has been ordered. Furthermore, although much fine criticism exhibits individual creativity and imaginativeness, both in engagement and in articulation, recognising that a sequence in a film is subtle, or well-paced, or ill-conceived, or that a correspondence is inexact (as in the Leavis/Shelley example), and explaining why with reasons, is not accurately described as personally creative[62]. Booth tells of an experiment he did with a class where he changed some of the words in W.B. Yeats's poem *After Long Silence*. The actual opening lines are, 'Speech after long silence; it is right,/All other lovers being estranged or dead,' and Booth adjusts them to, 'Speech after long silence; it is appropriate,/All other lovers being estranged or passed to the other side,' (1988: 102). Every student in the class agreed that the

---

[62] For a discussion of reason giving in criticism see Kupperman (1966).

changes made the poem worse (for reasons of rhythm, tone, and suitability of vocabulary). Booth concludes that when we replace relatively abstract questions such as "Is this poem absolutely good ... ?' and 'Is evaluation objective?' with contextually circumscribed questions such as 'Are these lines better than those, *in this poem*' there can be remarkable 'consensus' (1988: 103).

Value judgements in the arts are frequently assumed to be damagingly 'subjective' in that they exist only as perceived, and not of, or in, the object; such judgements are dependent on the mind of the thinking subject or on an individual's perception for their existence (one definition of subjective in *The New Oxford Dictionary of English* (Pearsall 1998)). Nevertheless, we assume (we hope) that it is not self-generating subjectivity that leads a judge or a jury, after examining and arguing over the evidence in a trial, to arrive at a judgement that a person is guilty. Whatever the faults in any particular legal system, there is supposed to be a procedure that leads to an 'impersonal verdict' that does not merely exist in the minds of the judge and jury, nor merely 'express the[ir] feelings' (Macdonald 1965 [1949]: 103). The legal analogy with criticism is instructive. The court is trying to understand the meaning of events that are rarely obvious or certain. Evidence needs to be presented and interpreted. The case is treated as special, but within a finely grained network of precedent. Judgements may be incorrect or unjust, and verdicts can be reversed when new evidence becomes known[63].

Another lament is that criticism is not scientific enough. It may, however, have more in common with science than is commonly supposed. The lack of a single truth does not mean that its procedures are not in some respects scientific. The critic often responds to a perplexity: she or he wonders about what the scene means, about the thematic purpose of the story or drama, or about why the moment seemed to be working well. According to Max Black, certain 'hypotheses' then come to mind which are tested while looking closely at the work (1966: 32). These hypotheses might be supported or refuted by an 'observation' (32). New pieces of criticism build on previously established understandings, and might even overthrow them. Criticism may have different purposes and import to science, but at its best, like scientific research, it is 'tentative, exploratory', and responsive to data (32). Black argues that like science, criticism is a 'protracted process of progressive correction of defective

---

[63] This is an elaboration based on the legal analogy made by Macdonald (1965: 103). I also deploy it for different ends.

preliminary insights'; and Karl Popper argues that they both 'share the same basic method of trial and error' (Black 1966: 33; Popper in Shusterman 1984: n.p.).

## 2.12 Subjectivity, contingency, and the relational

As well as being objective, aesthetic criticism also depends on the individual person and personality apprehending the work[64]. Compared to some other approaches to artworks, it has a well-balanced combination of the personal and impersonal, and this is one of its distinct attractions. From a pedagogical point of view, it encourages skills of impersonal and rigorous analysing and evaluating of evidence through close reading; at the same time, it encourages the development of a personal voice so that the student does not feel like he or she is working on an assembly line (or that they are the product of one). Whether this personal perspective is described as subjective would depend on the extremity of the definition of subjective being offered. Criticism never *only* belongs to, or proceeds from, the person offering it. As previously discussed, a work is often multi-dimensional and indeterminate, and it leaves matters undone; different critics will realise and complete it in different ways. Any piece of criticism will be necessarily partial, but a partial view is not equivalent to an inadequate, inaccurate or unjust one.

Some individual imaginativeness – which is not the same as exercising an idiosyncratic imagination – will be necessary to recognise aspects and merits of the work that may not be obvious to others and to communicate them eloquently (Grant 2013). Beyond this minimal level, criticism has been regarded as actively creative so like legal counsel, the critic does not simply represent the client's case, he or she designs it, or at least constructs a particular version of it, and affects how it will be perceived[65]. A less manipulative way of analogising this creativity is likening the critic to a concert pianist who draws out the 'value of a sonata' by playing it in her or his own particular manner (albeit while following the original score) (Macdonald 1965 [1949]: 111). This is similar to Leavis's understanding

---

[64] This is also true of science where insights of great significance and value have depended on the personalities of individual scientists apprehending and interpreting the world.

[65] The critic is a multifaceted figure: detective, counsel, judge, and jury all rolled into one.

that appreciating a work is akin to an inward performance of it. Criticism is therefore also performative as well as analytic, descriptive, and prescriptive. Like other performances, it may be well done or not, and judged accordingly. When paraphrased, the interpretations and evaluations offered in several critical essays may be broadly similar, but one may be preferred to the others, because, like an artwork, it may exhibit a range of admirable qualities (which enhance the work or the engagement with it): for example, coherence, lucidity, intensity, or dynamism. Part of critical argumentation will require expressive rhetorical literary skills (or, in the case of the currently expanding world of video criticism, audio-visual ones).

This rhetoric, more potent for being, perhaps, ardent and committed, might motivate somebody to examine and appreciate a work in a way that a detached account would not (Shusterman 1984). This is one reason why some commentators believe that the critic *should* be personally invested in the work. Another reason is that an intense connection may well be more fertile than one that is dispassionate. Criticism often begins with an impassioned response to the work, positive or negative, or to somebody else's response to the work (and this is compatible with disinterested judgement). The critic is, for example, inspired or angered and then compelled to write. The account 'draws forth ... from a deep level of the self' (Smallwood 2003: 146, on H.A. Mason). The personalities and preferences of critics will make them more or less suitable to tackle particular works. This does not disqualify criticism from operating in educational frameworks providing teaching, curricula, and assessment are appropriate. There need be no loss of discipline. Some commentators believe that the critic *must* sympathise or empathise with the work because only then will its spirit be entered into, and only then will it be seen correctly, and evaluated fairly (for example, Johann Gottfried Herder cited by Wellek 1981: 300). Some go further and say there needs to be an identification with the work, even an initial surrender. If one begins in a doubtful, sceptical or suspicious frame of mind then the work will be inaccessible, essential data will not be recognised, and there will be no possibility for objectivity (Booth 1988: 32). Even a form of projection by a viewer, in the psychoanalytical sense, which might actively distort, could result in verifiable and shareable revelations (Krieger 1968: 34). Oscar Wilde believed that the critic could only penetrate further into the work by 'intensifying' his or her own personality (Day 2010: 250). This might be regarded as too solipsistic, but Wilde thought that a virtuous circle operates where the work gives 'new insight into ourselves' and that in turn opens up 'new insight into the work' (250). Leavis and, more recently, Cavell think that the critic should be present in the writing to *self-consciously* and dramatically enact, and thereby expose, the processes of response, understanding, and evaluation. The moment-by-moment 'interior drama', which goes hand in hand with attentiveness towards the work, should be presented to the reader (Bell 1988: 74). This 'running presentation' might be regarded as an unnecessary and irritating record of deliberations that could be condensed or erased, and too much of an imposition of personality; for Leavis and Cavell though, in their different ways, it 'constitutes a clear and open-handed source of authority' (74–5).

In this conception, the critic is transparent about his relationship to the work, openly declaring the relation between them and it. Regardless of how much or how little one should explicitly map private meditations, aesthetic criticism is relational at every level: it evaluates how different parts of a work relate, and how the work relates to the creative personnel that made it, to other works, to the previous criticism upon it, and to the critic who engages with it. Everything is interrelated and each aspect unavoidably affects the others. Criticism embraces all the dynamics involved and does not aim for fixity or security. History shows that today's consensus over works, or features within works, is tomorrow's source of disagreement. Later generations modify or challenge the evaluations of previous ones. Even within generations, received opinion will be challenged. Critical positions and sometimes consensus inevitably become part of the way a work is perceived, in the long term as criticism on a work accrues, and in the short term as reviews and promotion are internalised. The latest criticism reacts to previous criticism, established understandings, and reputation. Much of Leavis's criticism is oppositional, motivated by vehement conviction, by what he found himself *urgently* needing to say. Many of his critical essays are mounted against 'The Enemy' (Steiner 1195 [1962]: 629). They are written in opposition to particular critics, mercilessly unpicking their failings of judgement, sensibility, and approach (and are not for the fainthearted). The Enemy was also an establishment that included different elements of the media, the British Council, and parts of academia where he thought that critical opinion formed in cosy, clubby cliques and coteries operating for 'mutual adulation' (629). Within film criticism, the *Movie* critics, as previously discussed, were also motivated to challenge what they took to be establishment taste best represented by *Sight and Sound*, the film journal of the British Film Institute[66]. For all the radical changes

[66] See Perkins (2010) for a vivid, at-the-coal-face account of these rebellious motivations.

to the media landscape, this context has not changed, and through, for example, social media bandwagons and incessant award giving, judgements about what constitutes *aesthetic value* in films – and not simply what is enjoyable or entertaining or socially valuable – are established and take hold. This is why there is still a necessary role for detailed, careful, aesthetic criticism, with space to elaborate and test received claims, especially those that have been cemented too quickly in hurried contexts that are often capsulated, hyperbolic, and promotional. Leavis's oppositional strategies may have operated at an extreme, but there is a non-conformist element even in moderate criticism. The critic feels the work has been overrated or not rated highly enough and this misjudgement needs rectifying in order to gain fair recognition. This is more than an academic intervention; it is felt to be an ethical imperative.

Therefore, revaluation – the title of one of Leavis's books – is a part of the critical process (1972 [1936]). Criticism depends on debate, exchange, and persistent questioning that leads back to an examination of the work. Leavis's pithy encapsulation of the critical exchange was 'This is so isn't it?', 'Yes, but ... ', and a piece of criticism might be thought of as a contribution, albeit a formalised and elaborate one, into a continuing conversation[67]. This is one reason why aesthetic criticism operates within ordinary language – aside from using the terminology and language of its art – and resists being unduly determined by discourses from other disciplines[68]. It is therefore able to maintain its continuity with two associated activities: the creative processes of making artworks and the everyday evaluative exchanges about them. Although the previous paragraph characterised the process as combative, criticism also operates productively within environments of 'collective and cooperative seeing', where understandings and evaluations are compared, refined, built upon, and transformed (Schapiro 1966: 15). The ideal is not a coterie or a clique, but a likeminded community – Ross calls them 'critic clusters' (2014: 611) – which may extend across periods and places where each individual within the community may not know (of) each other. Alternatively, the members of the community may be in direct collaborative contact – through journals, websites or within seminars – where actual conversations and discussions can take place. Creative personnel are also part of these communities so

---

[67] I try to enact this 'Yes, but ... ' in Part III where my own examination of film sequences tests pre-existing evaluative claims.
[68] Such discourses might be necessary to present a *radically* alternative account of artworks, to present, for example, a Marxist critique.

that filmmakers make films that respond to other films and filmmakers, contemporaneous and historical, working within contexts and histories of techniques, styles, and genres, to which critics, in turn, respond. In theory, such groups are accessible, and open to renewal and diversification. Wittgenstein insisted that our statements only make sense against this background of our social practices. Herrnstein Smith thinks evaluative claims can be testable, plausible, useful, and valuable, without them being 'fixed', 'given', 'inherent', universal, or *absolutely* true; and that these immutable ways of conceiving evaluative claims are a distraction and a false impediment to worthwhile evaluative practice (1983: 27, 22–3). The fact that evaluations are context dependent and contingent is disciplining and exacting, and need not be destabilising. Consequently, we now turn to the specific contexts, practices, and processes associated with the aesthetic evaluation of film.

# PART III
The aesthetic evaluation of film

## 3.1 Medium

A medium is a means or agency for communicating something. As Eran Guter describes, 'Literally meaning something that stands between two other things, the notion of medium implies the possibility of transference of something from one side to the other, or mediation between the two sides. Hence the idea of medium patently gives rise to the idea of content, i.e. that which is transferred by the medium' (Guter 2010: 126). The medium of film is all the elements that contribute to the particularity of the transference. This is capacious, extending from traditions and conventions (existing prior to the individual film), to creative personnel, to physical materials, to the conditions of screening and viewing. The medium of the artwork is nothing less than its ontology: the nature of its being (and its coming into being). The aesthetic evaluation of film therefore is concerned with how a film communicates *as a film*, by way of images and sounds, and more particularly by way of, for example, the screenwriter, the director, the camera, the actors, the costumes, the location, the lighting, and the mode of recording and reception. 'This is a good film' does not simply refer to merit; it does not only mean that this film is *good*, but that it is a good *film*. It is a good example of a category, namely film. The claim is about a film as distinct from a claim about a novel or a play or a piece of music.

Early film theory was keen to establish the new medium as a distinct art, and was therefore necessarily evaluative. Each theorist argued for the merits of a film based on what they thought was the most important feature or capacity of the medium. If individual films took advantage of this feature they would help cement the medium's status as an art. For example, put simply, André Bazin (1918–58) thought that photographic realism was the pre-eminent feature of film and therefore he valued films that took advantage of this to explore reality. Alternatively, Rudolf Arnheim (1904–2007) prioritised film's ability to manipulate: it is too easy to rely on film's photographic basis and therefore the good film must find ways to imaginatively shape reality[1]. Arnheim was wary of the introduction of sound because he thought it would further predispose films to lazily replicating reality. Sergei Eisenstein (1898–1948) emphasised the medium's facility for montage and stark juxtaposition, between, and within, frames. This would produce collisions in the composition and shocks to a viewer that

---

[1] Arnheim only advocated manipulation up to a point; the film should still keep in touch with reality.

would stimulate new ideas. Consequently, Bazin prefers films that maintain the continuity of reality, Arnheim those that expose the veracity of reality, and Eisenstein those that change our ideas about reality[2].

Sometimes important features of the medium are taken to be *essential* features, for example the capturing of reality on celluloid. However, many have challenged the idea that film has essential features, or that a single feature would constitute its essence. The physical materials that make a film, and the viewing contexts, have changed. Films were once 'silent' (although not viewed silently), now they have integrated sound; they were once filmed on celluloid, now they are recorded digitally; they were once projected, now they are broadcast via a variety of screen-based devices. The word 'film' continues to be used even though many films do not even use film, that is to say celluloid, as their recording medium. This thing we call 'film' is inclusive, flexible, and historically contingent. Each different feature will have possibilities and limitations, and an evaluation will need to respond accordingly. Traditional medium-based evaluations, however, can be prescriptive and deterministic rather than responsive: a film is good because it conforms to notions of what a film should be (based on what film essentially is).

Materials, while important, do not determine a medium, and they may contribute more or less to the achievements within it. Graphite can be used to draw pictures or write stories, but it is more aesthetically significant to the former than to the latter (Gaut 2012: 288). The achievements in poetry depend on the use of words (the means), not on the handling of a pen (the material). The relevance of a material will depend on use and outcome. Discussions of the film medium tend towards emphasising the recording process above all else, for example celluloid versus digital, although film deploys many 'materials' such as actors, objects, locations, light, and sound. For example, a performer's behaviour may often be more important to the general character of a film's communication, and its aesthetic value, than whether he or she was recorded photographically or digitally[3].

---

[2] Staples of film theory, most film textbooks will lay out the theories of these writers in more faithful detail. They are introduced cursorily to permit some general observations about medium-based evaluation. Specific evaluations by Arnheim and Bazin are explored below (see sections 3.2, 3.5, and 3.8).

[3] The practice in fine art commentary is instructive in the way that it breaks down the different materials for each artwork so that the viewer can evaluate how well each has been deployed. This can be seen in the descriptions which accompany works in galleries, for example, 'The work is made with charcoal and human hair on papyrus'.

In the desire to distinguish film from other art forms, there was also a tendency in early film theory to make claims for *unique* properties. Most arts share properties, however, and a medium is usually made up of many media. Film is particularly hybrid. It combines, for example, storytelling (novel), performance, costume, set (theatre), composition (painting), images of the world (photography), and sounds (music), and it is difficult, if not impossible, to pinpoint what is unique to it. More moderately, even if a feature is highlighted as particularly important (rather than unique), for example, the presentation of moving images, it is not straightforward to derive appropriate evaluative criteria. Will it be a merit for a film to have a lot of movement (because it is encouraged by the medium) or to limit it (because it comes too easily to the medium)? What should be encouraged to move: the image or the contents of the image? What should be the nature and speed of the movement? It will depend on the film. Isolating particular elements may be less important than recognising film's ability to combine many diverse features into a whole where they satisfactorily relate.

Nevertheless, medium-based 'theories' of evaluation are sometimes less a priori, deterministic, and theoretical, than they appear. Bazin was an accomplished critic observing many films that he thought had substantial qualities; he then constructed a quasi-theoretical position based on the evidence. It is arguable that this way of proceeding is also true of later medium-based theories of evaluation: for example, those presented by V.F. Perkins in *Film as Film* (1972) and by Stanley Cavell in *The World Viewed: Reflections on the Ontology of Film* (1979). These books begin by presenting a theory of film and then work outwards to examples, although this may be misleading as the progression of thought is probably the other way around. The writers derive the advantages of the medium from films they consider to be of exemplary merit, and the theory is therefore constructed from evidence and critical analysis. This may not overcome omission and disregard, but the position is less of an imposition, and less determined than it initially appears. The potentialities of the medium are discovered by observing how well they have been realised. Indeed, Cavell's view elsewhere is that 'the most significant films' will 'most significantly *discover*' the 'nature of the medium' which cannot be preconceived (Cavell 1996: 122; Mulhall 2007: 111; my emphasis). Furthermore, because many of 'the most significant films' may not demonstrate or declare their discoveries, aesthetic evaluation helps to reveal them.

Despite being prejudicial, medium-based theories of evaluation also valuably draw attention to significant features of films. Murray Smith says that we can sensibly talk about characteristic features of the medium or ones that play, or have played, a central role, for example, words for literature, or moving images for film (2006: 146, 142). Taking the case of Bazin's writings, the photographic technology of film was dominant for a century and he recognised the possibilities it offered for subtlety of expression, ambiguity of meaning, freedom of perception, detail of texture and materiality (for example, real-world concreteness), complexity of relationship (for example, people to their surrounding world), even the nature of 'being' itself[4]. Based on film's recording of reality, David Thomson proposes, in Bazinian vein, that a particular performance mode has been successful. '[T]he most effective actors and actresses in the cinema,' he writes, 'are those who can achieve such a degree of external and internal relaxation while being filmed that the camera records their nature without defining it' (1967: 123). Thomson is not patient, and he believes the film medium is not patient, with the sort of artifice in performance that is more suitable for the theatre. Although it is arguable that many unrelaxed and unnatural performers have also been effective on film – for example, Bette Davis, Greta Garbo, James Dean, and Christian Bale – Thomson does recognise an important quality that the medium enabled. (Equally, the performers I name as counterexamples tap other potentialities.) In addition, recognition of medium difference can gird analysis. For example, unlike characters in novels, characters in fiction films are usually performed by actors, so evaluations of film characterisation are inextricably bound up with performance, being, and presence. This may seem a straightforward point, but in assessments where it would be relevant it is sometimes overlooked (for example, a character's role, behaviour, and attributes in the narrative will be discussed, but not their dramatic presentation).

The medium is vital to the generation of the artwork. Smith claims artists work through media as 'sources of inspiration' (2006: 144). Aesthetic evaluation is interested in the ways in which artists handle their medium (or media); as well as the ways in which they explore their medium and enable their medium to explore content. A viewer's consciousness of which media are being used helps them appreciate the way the work is made. A viewer's knowledge of materials, for example, may reveal achievement. Berys Gaut uses the example of fresco painting where the

---

[4] Because the recording of reality has continued apace with the advent of digital recording – as shown by the numerous home movies shot on digital cameras or mobile phones – despite the shift from celluloid many of Bazin's understandings about film reality are still relevant to aesthetic creativity.

painting has to be done relatively quickly because the paint is applied directly to wet plaster (2012: 293). This leaves limited opportunity for reflection and refinement in the process, and the knowledge of this might affect an evaluation. Each material and technology presents its challenges that need to be overcome. However, not all achievements are practically difficult: the accomplishment might be in *conceiving* of things that work well in the medium (or work well with particular materials) and are relatively easy to achieve in it. Conversely, something may be practically difficult to achieve, and the feat may impress and the skill dazzle, but the achievement may be little more than technical. Hence debates over the value of virtuosity. In addition, because film is an art built out of various complex technologies many basic, commonplace occurrences on film require plenty of technical craft – for example, as most amateur filmmakers will readily admit, constructing a convincing conversation between two people – and yet this is not something that an evaluation will often need to dwell upon. On the other hand, many things that are difficult to achieve in craft terms are worthy of note, but look effortless because the hard work is effaced. This effacement is one way of measuring the artistry of an endeavour.

It is understood, from an aesthetic point of view, that it is a merit to make use of features of the medium. However, using features demonstratively or using too many features may result in an effortful or cluttered film. It is important to use the features of the medium well, not simply use them (or use them up). This would be a truism were it not that effusive demonstrations of the medium are sometimes automatically accepted, as Perkins claims with disgruntlement, as 'models of filmic creation' (1972: 26). This bears on the matter of the 'cinematic', an oft-used but perilous word, because it is frequently deployed to valorise an unrestrained use of film technique. Hence, Bruce Kawin decries the 'tyranny of the "cinematic"' (1981/2: 63). Gaut considers the film *My Dinner with André* (Louis Malle 1981 US) 'uncinematic' because it 'does not exploit in any *interesting fashion* any distinctively cinematic devices such as montage, elaborate framing techniques, camera movement' (2012: 295; my emphasis)[5]. After a brief prologue, the film consists of one dinnertime conversation in a restaurant over the course of an evening between playwright Wallace Shawn and director André Gregory (who play fictional versions of themselves). Gaut falls into a trap because the film *does* exploit possibilities of

---

[5] Gaut is responding to the essay by Smith (2006) cited previously, which refers to the film.

the film medium, just not ones that would make the film ostentatiously 'interesting'. The fact that it is highly constrained does not necessarily make it less cinematic[6]. He considers that the scenario would have been more suitable for the stage. However, the film routinely observes the characters' faces in close-ups which is not possible in the theatre (without the inclusion of screen-based media). Equally, because neither of the actors needs to project, as they would on stage, they can perform their roles less expansively, for example, by lowering their vocal volume. Indeed, the film is partly an investigation of conversational intimacy under laboratory conditions.

The film actually does use a form of montage, albeit discreet, with the shifts in camera angle and distance bringing different aspects of posture and gesture into view[7]. This is one part of a strategy to analyse, through the analytical editing, the dynamics of speaking and listening, of address and response. Near the beginning of the film (twelve minutes in), André is telling his story about working with theatre practitioner Jerzy Grotowski. At one point, after showing a close-up of Wally sipping his drink, the film returns to a wider shot from behind his shoulder (Fig. 3.1). This angle of view has already been established as the one that directly shows André speaking while Wally looks and listens. On this occasion, the film cuts back to this angle just as Wally removes the glass from his lips to replace it down on the table. The replacement is steady and deliberate and shows his careful respectfulness, and possibly, despite his genuine interest, something effortful in his listening. The move to the more removed shot introduces the relatively expanded field *at just this moment*, and nudges towards an expanded awareness of Wally's behaviour and character. Therefore, Wally's action might catch a viewer's attention even though it

---

[6] Many structuralist films are minimal and one of the aims of the filmmakers is precisely to *experiment* with aspects of the medium through radical delimitation.

[7] In this Part III, I examine evaluative claims about specific films offered by a selection of writers. The evaluative claims were offered in a range of specific institutional, cultural, critical, and categorical contexts, and I do not always have the space to contextualise (and it is often not particularly relevant to the evaluative concept being unfolded). At the same time, I hope I have not misrepresented. An important aspect to Part III, unlike the previous parts of the book, is my own extended examinations of film sequences. The purpose of them is to present a more elaborate exemplification of the aesthetic topics than is often attempted in the philosophy of criticism literature; to show how evaluative claims might be clarified, built upon or tested as part of an ongoing critical discussion; and to model a form of evaluative close reading.

# The aesthetic evaluation of film

**3.1** *My Dinner with André* (Pyramide Distribution, 1981).

succeeds in not disturbing André. (Minor changes and adjustments by the characters are more noticeable within the film's restricted sphere of action.) Or it might *not* because the return to this angle of view will merely appear to be a continuation of a familiar and functional shot/reverse shot scheme, and the gesture of replacement will merely appear to be a perfunctory part of the dinnertime naturalism (while André's storytelling will also be absorbing the attention). The performance of the gesture, the timing of the edit, the context of the editing pattern, and the composition of the shot are essential in creating this subtlety, and they are all quintessentially 'cinematic'[8]. Indeed, film is equally disposed towards the undramatic as to the dramatic, towards quiet disclosure, and an individual film has no requirement to exhibit its wares to prove its medium credentials (Klevan 2000)[9]. Furthermore, the film's continuities of place and time, its unusual

---

[8] How well these devices work over the whole length of the film, their capacity for productive variation, would be a further matter to be examined.
[9] Alain Bergala asks us to beware of films that have 'a rather unpleasant "show off" quality about them. The screenplays must be brilliant, the endings climactic, the storylines convoluted, the camera angles bizarre, the lighting conspicuous, the camera movements virtuosic: each shot seems designed to say, above all: "look what I can

inclusion of activity that other films would omit, and its calm observational acuity would accord with Bazin's conception of cinematic realism. Kawin considers that the film extends the 'possibilities of realism in the narrative film' because it has a 'spatial integrity' that is in fact 'intriguingly cinematic' (1981/2: 61).

One claim for *My Dinner with André* is that it is provocatively experimenting with what is possible in the medium. An arresting fiction film, it proposes, may simply consist of an intellectual dinnertime conversation. Smith argues that whatever one thinks of the film's aesthetic qualities, an acknowledgement of the medium is important to make sense of the project, and recognise the apparent perversity, and challenge, of making a whole film out of unprepossessing subject matter (2006: 145)[10]. For Cavell, it is a merit for a film to not simply accomplish things through the means of the medium, but to interestingly reflect on itself *as a film*: to be self-reflexive. Some films, for example those of director Jean-Luc Godard, are explicitly reflexive by baring devices or disrupting the fiction. Cavell celebrates films from the Hollywood cinema of the 1930s and 1940s that self-effacingly acknowledge and explore the medium without necessarily overtly disturbing the fiction. Sometimes, Cavell implies all films are unavoidably self-reflexive partly because the medium is intrinsically aware of its presentation of reality. Yet, if film as a medium exists in a natural state of reflexivity then it becomes more difficult to ascertain what constitutes a particularly worthwhile instance of it. The difficulty of gauging the aesthetic value is also not helped by the frequent presumption in film literature that self-reflexivity, perhaps because it denotes intelligent self-awareness or perspectival complexity, is an automatic merit.

William Rothman's essay on *The Rules of the Game* (Jean Renoir 1939 France) – 'The Filmmaker in the Film: Octave and the Rules of Renoir's Game' – helps us to see why a particular instance of film reflexivity might be aesthetically worthwhile (1989). Jean Renoir, the director of the film, is also an actor within it playing the character of Octave. Like the director,

---

do"' (2016: 103). He says this is a way of bypassing 'the real difficulties of cinema', and he quotes film director Martin Scorsese: 'What is truly difficult is to make two actors sit face to face, and to make them act out a long dialogue accurately and affectingly' (103).

[10] Smith also suggests that the film has other 'artistic virtues' such as 'its philosophical play with ideas, its love of argument, and perhaps its overall conception' (2006: 146). (See distinction between the artistic and the aesthetic in 1.1: 'The origin and definition of aesthetics'.)

# The aesthetic evaluation of film

**3.2–3.3** *The Rules of the Game* (Janus Films, 1939).

Octave orchestrates many of the events in the fiction and so the film is arranged to reflect upon its own moves[11]. In the final stages, Octave is on the verge of eloping with the Marquis's wife Christine (Marcel Dalio; Nora Gregor). The chambermaid Lisette (Paulette Dubost) chastises him about this plan and presents all the reasons why she considers it a mistake. At this point, the camera pans to André (Roland Toutain), an aviator, former lover of Christine, and friend of Octave (who has brought him to the Chateau after a record-breaking flight) (Fig. 3.2). Reappraising, Octave sends André to meet Christine in his place. Schumacher (Gaston Modot), Lisette's jealous husband, is waiting outside the chateau, with a gun in hand (alongside Marceau (Julien Carette), the poacher turned gamekeeper). Because Christine is wearing Lisette's cloak, Schumacher mistakes her for Lisette, and shoots André with whom he supposes her to be philandering. Effectively, if unwittingly, therefore Octave sends André to his death. According to Rothman, the pan represents a movement from a shot where Octave is the subject to one where he is now absent. The pan occurs at the moment of Octave's realisation, when he 'can no longer fail to recognize himself'; it becomes 'a figure for the achievement of self-knowledge' (121). This self-knowledge leads to Octave banishing himself from the Chateau and so the film narratively confirms his exclusion which was prefigured by the pan. The character 'acknowledges' his responsibility as does the director. Octave – and Renoir – must take responsibility for nothing less than death because the pan represents the moment of replacement that leads to André's demise (121). Although Rothman is concerned to highlight matters of acknowledgement and the consequent ethical value, I would say that his analysis is implicitly recognising the meritorious way in which reflexivity is intricately absorbed within the dramatic progression and presentation. A camera pan that might appear merely functional, therefore, moving from one character to another, is in fact pivotal and permeated[12].

Looking a little closer, there is more evidence to show, in line with Rothman, how the meta-fictional is *involved* in the fictional. Lisette closes her speech by saying, 'Madame will not be happy with you', and Octave finally hears her, and realises. As he looks at himself in the large mirror,

---

[11] There are films where the director is also one of the lead actors that are not necessarily concerned with this manner of self-reflection.

[12] Intricate absorption is not the only way that self-reflexivity can be worthwhile. See analysis of *Vivre sa vie* in 3.8: 'Relation'. I am explaining one way in which self-reflexivity might be of aesthetic merit.

his reflection reveals his eyes staring back accusingly and secretively from behind Lisette's hair (Fig. 3.3). This doubling matches the actor/director duality: as well as Octave chastising Octave, in Rothman's terms, it could be Renoir chastising Renoir (through the character). As he addresses Lisette, Octave is now deflated. André's voice is heard off screen asking, 'Where's Christine?', and it is at this moment that the camera pans quickly leftwards to find him in the corridor. The camera appears to dart away from Octave and Lisette too quickly because it travels a little too far and has to make a slight adjustment to the right. This repositioning is akin to an artful deliberate mistake, betraying the movement as a movement by a camera, and not simply a motion to reveal the questioner. It hints at its handling.

Rothman's singling out of the pan as a figure for 'the achievement of self-knowledge', however, is perhaps not persuasive because it could equally be argued that Octave has still not learnt. Despite realising that his romantic partnership with Christine would be a mistake, Octave is nevertheless crudely and thoughtlessly riding roughshod, trying to force and contrive events, and the hurried pan could be taken to represent his impulsive overreaction and over compensation. It is arguable that his behaviour is somewhat reflex and expedient in response to his exposure by Lisette in front of the mirror (hence the matching character of the camera movement). The pan is indeed preceded by some sort of self-consciousness bordering on embarrassment on Octave's part, but what sort of self-knowledge this amounts to is difficult to say. The film does not specify what type of self-recognition has occurred. Octave's lack of self-knowledge is in accordance with, and is narratively represented by, the limitations in his (general) knowledge. He is not aware of the whole picture that includes the game-keeper waiting outside the chateau armed and dangerous. Renoir, the director and performer, *is* aware. It is the discrepancy between Octave and Renoir's knowledge that leads to a reflection upon the directorial manipulation of the fiction, and provides a doppelgänger tension. Rothman claims that through 'the camera movement ... Renoir acknowledges that he and Octave are one', but the pan plays a different role for each of them (121). The two versions of Renoir are not equivalent: it is the contradiction in Renoir's identity that presses major concerns of the film such as duplicity and infidelity deeply into its fundamental structure. Furthermore, the pan does not straightforwardly represent Octave's exclusion because although he is excluded from the shot for that moment of the pan, the film urgently cuts back to him with barely enough time for the camera to rest on André (and André then walks into this shot *of* Octave). It shows

Octave very much still present as he eagerly chivvies André out of the door, and to his death. The pan is not representative of Octave's later expulsion either because his decision to expunge himself from the chateau comes *only* after he later realises the catastrophic consequences of his meddling (conspicuously immediately after hearing the news of André's death). There is a tragi-comic element to the latter part of the film where characters – Schumacher, Marceau, and Octave – fail to depart when they should, and hang on, and around, the chateau. Rather than representing Octave's exclusion, the pan expresses André's unfortunate and untimely appearance that leads to a hasty and ill-considered substitution. Nevertheless, the spirit of Rothman's account is still alive. Through a thorough internalisation, Renoir nimbly, and troublingly, reflects upon (his) knowledge, control, responsibility, and even his very being, in the medium of film (and beyond).

## 3.2 Constraint

Each medium will come with a variety of constraints: economic (for example, the budget), cultural (censorship), institutional (the producer), technical (microphone placement), logistical (filming at night), temporal (only three weeks to shoot), stylistic (period styles, for example the nouvelle vague), conventional (the happy ending), generic (needing songs in a musical). Any of these types of constraint may enhance or diminish aesthetic achievement. Classic examples: bigger budgets may liberate, or they may indulge; the studio system may facilitate, or it may oppress. Although constraint is sometimes conceived of as negative, because it restricts artistic freedom, all artworks will have, and need, constraints of some sort. A thirty-minute television situation comedy will not be better for being longer as illustrated by the number of failed attempts to extend them to feature film length (Elster 2000: 211). Therefore, although some constraints necessarily must be accepted without choice, perhaps reluctantly, others are chosen, or opportunely embraced. With regard to the latter, Jon Elster writes, 'The creation of a work of art can ... be envisaged as a two-step process: *choice of constraints* followed by *choice within constraints*. The interplay and back-and-forth between these two choices is a central feature of artistic creation' (176, original emphasis). Constraints should be stringent, but not too stringent – 'as in all forms of self-realization, motivation is maximized if the task is neither too easy nor

3.4   *The Immigrant* (Lone Star Corporation, 1917).

too difficult' – and the right level of challenge stimulates, rather than inhibits, inspiration (212)[13].

Within film study, Rudolf Arnheim believes that self-imposed formal limitations are the route to inspiration. He is especially concerned that the camera should not simply adopt the most functional view. He uses an example from the opening of *The Immigrant* (Charles Chaplin 1917 US) where Charlie the Tramp (Charlie Chaplin) is shown hanging over the side of a ship's deck with his body in spasms and his legs twitching (1957: 36) (Fig. 3.4). It appears as if Charlie is vomiting, but he is actually catching

---

[13] Elster makes another useful distinction between creativity which is 'working within constraints' and originality which is 'changing the constraints' (2000: 180). Sometimes 'there is an overvaluation of originality at the expense of creativity' even though both are equally valuable (226). It is worth noting that originality should not be equated with creativity because each film by Yasujiro Ozu may be relatively similar to his previous ones, and therefore not original, but each film is still a creative variation, and of no less value, a priori, than a radical intervention. Ozu's oeuvre as a whole, though, may be considered original. See also Choi (2011: 294).

and wrestling with a fish, something revealed when he turns around to face the camera with fish in hand. Because the camera is directly behind Charlie rather than in front of him, his behaviour misleads. For Arnheim, the gag is created by the position of the camera that restricts access to the necessary information, and the inventiveness stems from the restriction rather than from the subject matter by or in itself. He values constraints that challenge the filmmakers to find less straightforward types of communication, and that in turn challenge a viewer's perception.

Arnheim does not go into detail, but a closer examination of the sequence reveals the inventiveness he valued. It could be argued that the very fact that Charlie's activity is hidden may telegraph a revelatory *turnaround* such that an alternative explanation is already being sought. That is to say, the set-up makes the situation more predictable than Arnheim admits. The predictability is tempered, however, because the film could simply be showing a vulgar gag based on the inference of a disgusting excretion (which it cannot show). This is also encouraged by the context. The preceding shots of the deck show the tilting and swaying of the boat and may induce nausea in a viewer. They are also solemn: first, a mass of huddled bodies, then an intertitle that reads 'A widow and her daughter', and then a daughter cradling and comforting her mother. Charlie's vomiting over the deck would be continuous with the inhospitable conditions while providing a gag that contrasts, tonally and behaviourally, with the gravity. Nevertheless, something fishy may be sensed before the reveal because his movements alter. His spasmodic indications of retching slip into a more vigorous wriggling, and he leans more drastically over the deck. This means, however, the gag is richer than simply seeing one thing (vomiting) and turning out to be another (fishing) because clues that he is fishing are already built into his behaviour. Whether the gag is consciously worked out, or subliminally sensed, before the reveal, or only realised upon it, it has the character of the figure of the duck-rabbit: it appears to be two things at once.

Film is suited, through framing and viewpoint, to delimit the visual field, and therefore to stimulate perception (and Arnheim, as mentioned in the previous section, was trying to discover distinctive opportunities in the medium). Firstly, perception is stimulated because the camera can de-familiarise by giving a 'fresh angle on a thing' (39). Secondly, the unexpected point of view, by drawing attention to the position of the camera and the restricted viewpoint, also encourages an 'awareness *of* [film] form', and this too is to be welcomed for Arnheim because it encourages a bilateral viewing (subject matter *and* form) (Higgins 2011: 7). Thirdly,

Arnheim thinks that a viewer, rather than receiving a clear communication, should be encouraged to decipher a performer's physical behaviour. He celebrates film's ability to express actions and states of mind through the body. Chaplin's physical dexterity achieves this: the way he combines both possibilities, and surreptitiously adjusts his behaviour, before the reveal, without fully transforming it[14].

The features that Arnheim prioritises are important in evaluating films, and remain relevant in less extreme instances: the stringency of viewpoint, the encouragement to engage with the form of the presentation, and the stimulation and revivification of perception. These priorities supersede the stereotypical account of his position: that it is a merit for films to avoid realistic or mimetic representation and instead employ artificial and expressionistic devices. Some of Arnheim's more immoderate views, such as his scepticism about the use of sound, have not helped sustain the relevance of his work[15]. Yet, his worries, which he shared with Chaplin, are part of his philosophy of film evaluation that depends upon limits. It is more fruitful to take his views to be about the achievements that occur from synchronised sound's absence rather than the failures that arise from its presence. For example, the absence of the spoken word required filmmakers to find inventive ways of conveying action and ideas. It means that Chaplin 'does not *say* that he is pleased that some pretty girls are coming to see him, but performs the silent dance, in which two bread rolls stuck on forks act as dancing feet on the table'; and means that he 'avows his love by smiling, swaying his shoulders, and moving his hat'; and means that when 'he is sorry for a poor girl, he stuffs money into her handbag' (Arnheim 1957: 106–7)[16]. Chaplin finds visual representations for pleasure, love, and pity, and the manner of substitution must be appropriately adjusted to suit different situations and moods. Lack of spoken word alone is not enough to 'concentrate … the spectator's attention more closely on the visible aspect of behavior', but it is a possibility that good filmmakers can pursue (110). Even in the sound film, the merits of doing rather than saying remain.

Arnheim's concerns are summarised by Meraj Dhir as the 'aesthetics of "expressive implication"' (2011: 98). Implication, and perhaps, indirection. Indirectness should not be automatically preferred to its opposite as it

---

[14] See 3.5: 'Encouraging perceptual activity'.

[15] See Higgins' edited collection (2011) for an assiduous attempt to revive his reputation.

[16] The sequence with the dancing bread rolls is in *The Gold Rush* (1925 US).

might result in obscurity or evasiveness[17]. Directness is a quality too – especially for film. Because film so often involves recording, or showing, what is in front of the camera, it thrives, naturally, on the direct, the immediate, the material, and the literal. If scenes are too straightforwardly expressed and experienced, however, or too easily 'read' in Arnheim's terms, they become obvious and exhaust as they proceed. Directness and indirectness are often tussling with each other, and a challenge for films is to thrive on this tension, making use of the transparency on offer without surrendering to it.

Chaplin's generic context permits relatively extreme instances of withholding because comedy conventionally uses contrived viewpoints for gag construction. Yet, as discussed in Part II, a precise evaluation cannot be derived from the generic category. A set-up, similar to the vomiting/fishing gag in *The Immigrant*, will make a useful comparison. In *The Idle Class* (Charles Chaplin 1921 US), Charlie, a rich man, stands in front of a desk and opens a letter from his wife announcing that she will not return to live with him until he stops drinking. He turns around to face the desk, picks up and then puts down a framed photograph of her, looks away forlornly, and starts to sob (Fig. 3.5). His convulsing increases, and then he turns towards the camera again which reveals that he is no longer sobbing, but vigorously shaking a cocktail. Arnheim acclaims the 'revelation as especially effective because there has been no obvious concealment beforehand, no artificial suggestion of secrecy' (1957: 51). It is true that Charlie's position in front of the desk looks perfectly natural, and he does not look *initially* to be artificially masking. On the other hand, although there is no 'obvious concealment beforehand' there is an acute awareness of the concealment *afterwards* because the cocktail paraphernalia has been carefully situated so as not to protrude. It is interesting to wonder whether the moment would be of more merit if some indications of the cocktail paraphernalia, if not the cocktail shaker itself, had been made available. I might become aware earlier in the set-up, and so the comedy in the surprise would be less, but so would the contrivance; the gag could rely less on the reveal and the trick, and more on amusement as it proceeds. Even if I do not realise, I might later be amused that I had missed the clue.

Perhaps the contrivance in the similar vomiting/fishing gag appears better justified and motivated, firstly, because it is culturally rooted: it is

---

[17] See Klevan (2014b) for an extended appreciation of indirection in *Trouble in Paradise* (Ernst Lubitsch 1932 US).

# The aesthetic evaluation of film

3.5–3.6  *The Idle Class* (Charles Chaplin Productions, 1921).

reasonable, on grounds of censorship and tact, to imply, but not see, the vomit. Secondly, despite the wilfully restrictive angle and the fact that his makeshift fishing equipment is hidden, the possibility of fishing is available in the visual appearance of the initial set-up (impoverished man reaching overboard into the sea for food). The possibility of the cocktail shaking, although suggested by the narrative scenario, is not suggested in the image, or by the immediate environment. Thirdly, the withholding seems more natural in *The Immigrant* because the fishing gag starts the film, and we join Charlie in *medias res*. Fourthly, during the fishing gag, Charlie is consistently doing one activity which may be misread, and then the truth is revealed; in the shaking gag, Charlie (very) suddenly moves from doing a clearly expressed activity to one that is hidden. Fifthly, the (pretence of) the activity of vomiting smoothly metamorphoses into an activity that more precisely resembles fishing, and some of the latter had already been present in the former. The transition from sobbing to shaking is less smooth because there is an eye-catching gestural shift as Charlie sharply moves his arms from by his side to in front of his stomach (Fig. 3.6). This adjustment appears to service the shaking more than the sobbing, and once adjusted the withdrawn arms are not particularly characteristic of a sobbing motion. Therefore, the two actions are neither as physically continuous as the vomiting and the fishing nor as effectively dovetailed[18].

By mentioning the possibility of 'obvious concealment' and 'artificial suggestion', Arnheim shows that he is concerned that his preferences can result in damaging contrivance. He believes the creation must contribute to the action and emerge from the story world, and not merely be 'ingenious'; the limitations should be set by context and not merely be imposed; and the aim should be for the viewer to be involved in interpretation and not merely to experience 'pictorial surprise' (40). He takes an example from *The Diary of a Lost Girl* (G.W. Pabst 1929 Germany) where the film is showing a pharmacist's assistant kissing his employer's daughter and it cuts from an interior to an exterior shot. Arnheim believes the change in viewpoint to be pointless, 'superficial and decorative', and 'artistically weak' because it is 'insufficiently motivated' and 'signifies nothing' (50)[19].

---

[18] It is possible that I am underrating some of the merits of *The Idle Class* sequence, but an equally important purpose here is to demonstrate an evaluative comparison.
[19] The nature of the critique, including the pejorative use of 'decorative' and the insufficient meaningfulness of the formal choice, prefigures those made by the *Movie* critics.

The aesthetic evaluation of film 137

Interestingly, Arnheim goes on to claim that the shot choice would not be redeemed *even* if it were discovered that someone was watching them from outside. This would 'motivate the sequence through the plot', but would not necessarily lead to 'symbolic depth' (50). This indicates that justification of a formal occurrence needs to go beyond cognitive coherence and continuity: perceptual stimulation rather than perceptual clarity is the goal. The shot from the exterior also contravenes his principle of constraint because the moment needlessly adopts a viewpoint from a place that should have been out of bounds. Luxuriating in too many angles is also his problem with the scenes from *The Passion of Joan of Arc* (Carl Theodor Dreyer 1928 France) where the priests are in discussion with 'the Maid':

> The real interest of these scenes lies in the spoken word. Visually there is little variety to be extracted from the endless confrontations of arguing speakers. The solution of the difficulty is surely to avoid putting scenes like this into a silent film. Carl Dreyer decided otherwise, and mistakenly. He tried to animate these cinematographically uninspiring episodes by variety in form. The camera was most active. It took the Maid's head obliquely from above; then it was aimed diagonally across her chin [and so on] … in short, a bewildering array of magnificent portraits … the spectator is irrelevantly entertained to prevent his being bored. (40–1)

Although good aesthetic reasons might be offered for Dreyer's approach, this passage shows that Arnheim is alert to the problem of what he called '[f]orm for form's sake' (41). Throughout *Film as Art*, one sees him wrestling with the dilemma of how a film might bring out the unusual while it respects the recognisable; how it might lead to a keen interest in the formal qualities of people, objects, places, and situations without violating their integrity; and how it might be inventive without straining to be interesting or intense.

A couple more scenes in films by Charles Chaplin will help explore the regulation of constraint. A sequence in *The Pawnshop* (1916 US) has a unity of purpose and yet a high degree of diversification. A man brings a clock into a pawnshop, and needing to verify that the clock is working, Charlie checks for vital signs by tapping his fingers on it, flicking it, and listening to it with a stethoscope. Then he proceeds to use a wide variety of tools – a hammer, a drill, a can opener, and some pliers – to dismantle the clock. In order to diagnose whether the clock is working properly, Charlie needs to perform more and more invasive and drastic surgery

3.7 *The Pawnshop* (Lone Star Corporation, 1916).

which results in its certain failure to work (or even to exist as a clock). The implements, the range of which would be found in the miscellany of the pawnshop, are put to a perverse and devastating end. Arnheim claims that the 'substance of such a "gag"' is that 'these things are objectively so far apart, but are so ingeniously brought together' (148). This ingenious bringing together of objects and actions creates surreal visual conversions, and correspondences, such that an alarm clock, turned on its side, becomes a food can, and the telephone's earpiece, turned around, becomes an expert watchmaker's magnifying eyepiece (Fig. 3.7). The assortment of the sequence is held together, against all the odds, by the precision of pretence achieved by Chaplin's exceptional talent for mimicry: Charlie executes all the terrible actions with the complete self-assurance and finesse of a professional. The accuracy and fluency of the mannerisms are in tension with the brutality of the outcomes.

In *The Gold Rush* (1925 US), Charlie is living in extreme poverty and desperate for food, he cooks and eats a large boot[20]. The tough boot is

---

[20] Arnheim finds the scene in *The Pawnshop* comic but 'unenlightening' because 'there is no deeper meaning' (1957: 148). The boot sequence in *The Gold Rush* (1925 US)

The aesthetic evaluation of film 139

**3.8** *The Gold Rush* (Charles Chaplin Productions, 1925).

'not quite done yet', and so Charlie gives it a couple more minutes to cook. He wipes specks of dirt off the plate with his sleeve despite the boot's dirtiness (and the sleeve). He ladles several spoons of liquid over the boot to achieve the ideal distribution of gravy. He lifts the laces onto a side plate as if they were unwanted strings from a joint of meat; later they resemble spaghetti. He yanks the top of the shoe off its sole and reveals the nails, thus freeing the meat from bones (Fig. 3.8). He also takes a bite of the sole, chews, and then makes a face that says: 'It's not too bad'. He puts the nails on the side of the plate, but later he chews them and sucks them clean. The poverty in the story world is itself ideal at restricting, and this sequence pushes the motto of 'making the best of what you've got' to a hideous extreme. Charlie converts the boot into a meal, and yet throughout it remains stubbornly and concretely a boot. It is not transformed, and yet it is transfigured. It is rough and dirty, and yet dinnertime

exemplifies the 'deeper meaning' Arnheim thought lacking in *The Pawnshop* as it provides a more 'profoundly human' justification for the comedy (145). It is arguable, however, that there are 'deeper meaning[s]' in *The Pawnshop* sequence, for example, one concerning the dangers of mistaking the façade of professionalism for competence.

formalities and etiquette are impeccably observed. Each action is repulsively incongruous, and yet satisfyingly analogous. In Arnheimian terms, the sequence is inventive because its meanings are situationally constrained and ingrained, and perceptually fascinating because of its both-things-at-once simultaneities.

It is unsurprising that Arnheim is drawn to instances from comedy because one of its modes is to try to squeeze as many gags as possible from apparently very little, for example, from one situation, object, idea, or phrase. The challenge is to extend the point at which the gag might be expected to run out of steam. Both sequences use strategies of inventive variation, but the combination of boot and the culinary situation are more restraining than the clock and the tools. The limited room for manoeuvre with the boot makes the ability to produce the variations resourceful. The variations are closely related and close-knit so there is also the sense of something being satisfactorily filled out (or filled in). The pawnshop scene, on the other hand, while dependent on the clock as the core object and the tools available in the shop, is more extensive than intensive, and centrifugal rather than centripetal. The satisfactions come from the incorporation of the unorthodox and unexpected, and the pushing out to the limit (while also shrewdly pushing out the limits, or re-imagining what they might be). The clock scene risks looseness and arbitrariness. The boot scene risks being too neat and self-contained, but at the same time it must not diverge from the consistency upon which it depends. It also risks taking the one joke too far resulting in diminishing returns *or* not far enough because a fertile set-up may prematurely cease and be insufficiently realised. Both scenes appear to avoid, rather wonderfully, these associated demerits as they differently exploit the bounds of possibility within formal constraint.

*Rope* (Alfred Hitchcock 1948 US) is an example of a film which upholds severe constraints for its entire length (unlike the Chaplin sequences). The film is situated in one city apartment, choosing not to open out the stage play on which it is based. It also takes place in real time, and is filmed in a few long uninterrupted takes, some of which are cunningly, if not always subtly, fused to look even longer. The film's constraints are self-imposed and extreme although they do match the fictional scenario of wilful containment. The film begins with two men, Brandon (John Dall) and Philip (Farley Granger) murdering David. To test their daring and ingenuity, they risk being exposed – while arrogantly believing they will not be – by placing David's corpse in an unlocked chest and then holding a party for friends in their apartment where the chest resides. In one

The aesthetic evaluation of film 141

**3.9** *Rope* (Warner Bros, Transatlantic Pictures, 1948).

sequence, discussed by Perkins, the housekeeper is shown clearing the top of the chest of food, cloth, and candelabras, after which she starts to open the chest to replace some books that are normally kept in it (1972: 124). A fixed angle of viewpoint, from the side, shows her travelling to and from the chest, three times, across the length of the apartment (Fig. 3.9). Dramatic suspense builds because as she clears the chest and brings the books she is on the verge of discovering the body. The single take and fixed camera present the activity in real time. The hosts and the guests are just to the right of this activity, mostly out of shot[21]. The film does not show, because of the restricted viewpoint, whether the hosts can see how close she is getting to this discovery. Might they be distracted? Or might they be ready to intervene and prevent exposure? Given that the aim of the party is for the hosts, especially Brandon, to experience the danger of having the guests gather unknowingly around the corpse, and to revel in omniscience and mastery, they might be allowing the housekeeper to get as close as possible ...

---

[21] I say 'mostly' because half of Rupert's body (James Stewart) is visible. See further discussion of this sequence under 3.4: 'Choice and expectation' below.

The film is open to the accusation that not showing the hosts is simply an expedient and artificial contrivance to generate suspense. How does the film win acceptance for its stubborn immobility? Firstly, Perkins says it does so because 'the position of the guests ... was established naturalistically *before* the housekeeper began her clearing up' (126). Secondly, the guests are so placed in the apartment, in relation to the chest and wall, to make it impossible to show them *and* the housekeeper's back and forth journeying simultaneously. The camera would have to be further back to view the whole width of the apartment, but this would necessitate filming through a wall, or inconspicuously and conveniently pretending, for the sake of this shot, that the wall is no longer there. Films might do this, but it is unlikely that *this film* will do it because the precise space and boundaries of the apartment have been important to the 'reality' of the drama. Perkins writes that 'the camera has explored the apartment so freely in the preceding sequences that ... we have come to accept its reality and the limitations which it imposes' (126). In fact, the walls of the set were on rollers and could be silently adjusted to accommodate the camera, but this does not refute Perkins' claim. The filmmakers would not take advantage of the flexibility of the walls to such an extent that they would spoil the optical illusion of the 'real' space. The skill has been to situate the components of the drama such that even this unnatural viewpoint is accommodated and rendered reasonable.

Another thing the film will not do is use shot/reverse shot to show the housekeeper and then the guests because of its scheme of using continuous shots. (It does have edits, disguised and undisguised, but only at the end of the takes.) Perkins says that films establish their own 'norms' about the story, situation, and presentation (127). These 'norms' might include formal or stylistic rules. Of course, there might be scepticism about a norm if it is perhaps considered insufficiently productive relative to its pronounced severity (and therefore a gimmick or a stunt). If the norm is productive enough, however, then it will be embraced, and any lapse will prompt disappointment[22]. Once accepted a radical deviation or departure will need exceptional justification. Therefore, it is in keeping with *Rope's* design not to 'break' the wall or the take; these would be failures *within its own terms*. Indeed, the scheme legitimates the shot: the restricted viewpoint would be more likely to appear contrived if it were adopted only on this occasion for a one-off effect. This device is part of a

---

[22] See 1.5: 'Aesthetic pleasure'.

well-established scheme of seeing and understanding that is capable of creative and enriching variations.

Although the rule in *Rope* is suitable for the story and drama, an effective film adaptation of the play could sensibly have had more flexibility. Adrian Martin writes about films with a '*dispositif*', or translated, a 'disposition' that are 'intensively rule-bound', and the aim of the filmmakers is to experiment with the rule or rules (2014: 180). An evaluation, therefore, would not only treat form as something devised compliantly to serve the subject matter in a locally effective manner. It would also assess how well the formal rules shape and interpret the subject matter and how well the subject matter shapes and interprets the rules. This is not to say that the subject matter need be randomly chosen or irrelevant; the subject matter should benefit from the rules, and the rules may initially have been conceived with a certain type of subject matter in mind[23]. Some fine filmmakers, such as Yasujiro Ozu, have formal rules that they will obey from film to film, and this constitutes their distinct, individual style. (In addition, Ozu's rules do indeed suit the delivery of his subject matter: undramatic, domestic family stories.) One way of conceiving of a style, individual or group, is as a distinct and compatible collection of formal constraints. Leonard B. Meyer actually defines style as 'a replication of patterning ... that results from a series of choices made within some set of constraints' (1987: 21)[24]. A potential problem for films with a determined style is that they will be too constrained and therefore perhaps monotonous or unresponsive; while a potential problem for films with too little style is that they will permit too much flexibility of form and be lax.

## 3.3 Convention

The formal constraints in *Rope* are not dictated by convention. A convention, according to the dictionary, is 'a way in which something is usually done, especially within a particular area or activity' (Pearsall 1998). *The Film Studies Dictionary* defines it: 'In any art form, a frequently used technique or content that is accepted as standard or typical in that tradition or genre'

---

[23] This is my extension to Martin's idea.
[24] See discussion of style in 1.9: 'Form and style'. Filmmaker Manoel de Oliveira has written: 'The style of a film is not really defined until after having filmed the first dozen shots. We then become prisoners, in a way' (Bergala 2016: 81).

(Blandford *et al.* 2001: 57). There are, for example, conventions of narrative, character, costume, lighting, editing, and they differ depending on styles, periods, genres, and national cinemas. Very basic instances would be the use of low-key lighting in film noir or a black costume for a villain in a Western (57). The entry in *The Film Studies Dictionary* goes on to say that, 'Conventions function as an implied agreement between makers and consumers to accept certain artificialities' (57). They therefore establish some basic ground rules for evaluation because it would be odd to criticise or praise a musical simply because, accompanied by orchestral sound, its characters burst into song. This is accepted as conventionally done in a musical.

Sometimes it is presumed that mainstream, popular, or narrative fiction films are more reliant on conventions than experimental or avant-garde films. This may be because some experimental films are understood to be deliberately avoiding mainstream conventions or undermining them, or functioning in an oppositional way. Yet, all films work with conventions. For example, trance, lyrical, structural, and psycho-geographical films have conventions that recur from film to film (and it is what allows them to be categorised). The avoidance of mainstream conventions is itself a sort of convention or a conventional strategy[25]. There is also osmosis between different cinemas so that, for example, features typical of non-mainstream films are appropriated by the mainstream (and vice-versa). As Andrew Britton writes, 'All styles are "group styles": that is to say, the style of any given artist is a more or less complex, adventurous, and idiosyncratic inflection of conventional cultural materials which, by definition, precede and create the conditions for the artist's work' (2009 [1989]: 433). For Britton, conventions, like formal constraints for Arnheim, are not merely restricting, but enabling.

A film may achieve distinction by noticeably avoiding a typical convention. When Bazin praises films which avoid straightforward analytical editing, it does not necessarily mean that he is against editing in itself, but rather those editing methods that are 'imposed by custom' (1997a [1948]: 12). He feels that it is too often the easy choice: analytical editing will guide a viewer too straightforwardly through the material as if the film is holding their hand. The 'neutrality' he ascribes to the style of director William Wyler specifically refers to 'the advance neutralization of numerous

---

[25] Some blanket negative evaluations of the narrative fiction film may be because the particular conventions it adopts, and their cultural dominance, are disliked rather than because the category is seen as more conventional as such.

film conventions' (12). The style is described as 'neutral' because familiar modes of presentation are not decidedly directing a viewer[26]. When in *The Little Foxes* (1941 US) Wyler refuses to cut to Horace (Herbert Marshall) as he collapses on the stairs behind Regina (Bette Davis) as she remains unmoved, Bazin appreciated the refusal of the obvious choice. In addition, unlike the background figures in *The Best Years of Our Lives* (1946 US), a film by the same director, Horace is a blurry figure rather than sharp and clear. Therefore, Bazin points out that Wyler uses deep focus in different ways in different films because '[e]ach scene had to find its [own] technical solution' (13).

A film may not avoid a convention, but utilise it in such a way that it is not rendered merely conventional. The difficulty for evaluation, however, is to detect the special occasions because they might *appear* to be operating merely conventionally. As George M. Wilson writes, it is important not to 'suppose ... that the customary surface forms and strategies ... define the limits [of a film's] possible concerns and accomplishments' (Wilson 1992: 197; and quoted in Pye 1989: 52)[27]. Douglas Pye takes the example of angle/reverse angle cutting with eye-line match. Although a conventional formal feature in Hollywood cinema, Pye acclaims its placement in the opening of *Strangers on a Train* (Alfred Hitchcock 1951 US) when Guy (Farley Granger) and Bruno (Robert Walker) initially meet. The film concerns the guilty association of these two strangers as they agree to exchange murders (Guy's wife, Bruno's father). Although Guy considers himself more morally upright than Bruno, the film suggests similarities that he would not care to admit. Pye considers that the use of the angle/reverse angle cutting 'self-consciously draws on the full potential of that familiar strategy to embody simultaneous and intermeshed parallelism and contrast' (1989: 48). The technique can even take on 'ironic force' because it insistently parallels the two men even as Guy wishes to assert his difference through 'his blithe dismissal of Bruno's idiosyncrasy'. Crucially for Pye, the convention can be used mechanically in a dialogue sequence, or it can be used as part of a 'self-conscious strategy with a precise and considered place in the systems of the film' (48). For example,

---

[26] This understanding of 'neutrality' partly explains the apparent perversity of the description given Wyler's emphasis on multi-layered, deep focus arrangements that are emphatically composed.

[27] Wilson was writing within what he considered a context of insufficient appreciation for the 'Classical Hollywood Cinema' (whose films were typically conceived as standardised).

the angle/reverse angle of their conversation follows on from the mirroring or paralleling of the men just before their meeting on the train, especially the cross-cutting between their legs (and feet) as they both approach the station and platform. He repeatedly emphasises that 'the status of a formal figure' is acquired through 'context and intention' and '[o]nly in [the] network of dramatic, formal and other decisions ... can the significance and status of the formal decision be weighed'. If a viewer were not alert to this 'network' or the concerns of the film, the distinctive deployment might be overlooked because 'superficially ... [the formal decision] could appear equally conventional' (48).

A film may productively deviate from a familiar convention (*The Little Foxes*) or pertinently deploy it (*Strangers on a Train*). A film may also succeed in boldly embracing and invigorating a convention. This has been claimed for the ending of *It's a Wonderful Life* (Frank Capra 1946 US) where George Bailey, a character who has been unfailingly generous throughout his life, is bailed out of trouble by all the townsfolk of Bedford Falls. George Toles argues that the director Frank Capra uses conventions as a way into a scene or situation, a way of bringing them into 'preliminary focus'; they then 'shed this easy affiliation with the usual setup and become self-sustaining' (2001: 57). The film finds ways of unexpectedly 'sustaining' the convention of a 'happy ending' rather than simply concluding with it. The ending is prolonged and its capacities enlarged. It multiplies connections to the preceding story hence augmenting significance, and varies and layers the sentiment. The film also reflects on matters of revelation and conclusion, by pushing the limits of what is possible with a denouement, and more specifically a 'happy' one. Like *Rules of the Game*, it provides an example of a reflexivity that is complexly integrated and multifaceted, and one that is compatible with the film's evident aim to make its fiction compulsive and affecting[28]. Toles writes, 'What [Frank Capra] consistently strives to distill out of [conventions] is a moment that effectively bursts the bounds of the familiar situation' (57). One way of thinking of this is that the film and its makers are in conversation with the (tradition of the) convention. Cavell thinks of the best films within a genre as 'mounting a critical study of the conventions hitherto seen as definitive of that genre' (Mulhall 2007: 112).

The finality of endings forcefully incites evaluation. Is an ending tying up satisfactorily, or is it too neat? Is it stimulatingly open-ended,

---

[28] See Klevan (2005b) for a fuller, more evidenced account of the ending of *It's a Wonderful Life*.

or frustratingly inconclusive? Is it suitably consistent with what has gone before, or too predictable? Is it perhaps a betrayal?[29] James MacDowell, in his study of the convention of the 'happy ending', takes the example of *All That Heaven Allows* (Douglas Sirk 1955 US). The film concerns the relationship between Cary, a middle-aged widow (Jane Wyman) and Ron, a much younger gardener (Rock Hudson). The relationship is opposed by Cary's children and causes scandal within her community of Stoningham. After feeling pressurised to halt the relationship, she finally returns to Ron. Unfortunately, when eagerly trying to call out to her, he injures himself by tumbling down a snowy incline. The final scene shows him lying on a couch with serious concussion, joined by Cary who desperately hopes for his recovery. They then commit to each other. Behind them is a large window through which a deer can be seen (Fig. 3.10). MacDowell explains how the ending has been judged as 'ringing hollow' because it is implausible, too 'picture perfect', too 'artificial', and *too* happy (2014: 160). In order to be evaluated positively, therefore, the ending has been treated as parodic or ironic. From the ironic point of view, it is deemed deliberately excessive, subversively rupturing. This undermining of the narrative convention is then consistent with the film's exposure of the repressive workings of societal convention. MacDowell, however, convincingly argues against the claims of parody and irony. The ending is consistent with the values of the film: the mill and the deer represent the world of Ron that to all intents and purposes is depicted as desirable, and much more desirable than the world of Stoningham (163). Why, MacDowell asks, would the film want to 'ironise the putative triumph of a mode of living and set of values which [it] has in general ... affirmed' (165)?

---

[29] Endings also highlight the more general matter of resolution. There are internal resolutions, for example, for scenes and sequences, and shots. One interest of a long, continuous take, because it is long, is when and why it ends. When something has been varied or multifaceted, like a dense Charlie Parker saxophone solo, or an involved sentence by Henry James, we might marvel at how they have been satisfactorily *resolved*. On the other hand, many shots or scenes in a film will want to end without resolving, that is without tying disparate elements together. Balancing the resolved and the unresolved in, for example, a film's shots or its plot or its design or its rhythm, is a skill. Resolving something too quickly prematurely relaxes tension, but failing to resolve in good time generates frustration. Each film will establish its own timings and expectations regarding resolution and these would be acknowledged, if not necessarily commended, by an evaluation. See 3.4: 'Choice and expectation' and 3.5: 'Encouraging perceptual activity'.

3.10–3.14  *All That Heaven Allows* (Universal International Pictures, 1955).

# The aesthetic evaluation of film

**3.10–3.14** (Continued)

MacDowell thinks that the faulty evaluation is arising because some critics have a problem accepting the 'happy ending' (as a matter of principle). The first reason is that they see it as a disabling cliché rather than an enabling convention. Cliché is a form of expression that has lost force through overexposure and denotes something 'fixed', 'standardised' and 'mechanistic'; alternatively, a convention, while also subject to repetition at the same time still carries conviction and is alive to creative variation

(9)[30]. The second reason is that the happy ending is considered as '*innately conservative*', and therefore must be subverted (166, original emphasis). The ending is restrictively conceived as a binary choice: either 'unproblematically celebratory or seditiously subversive' (161). Other qualities that the ending exhibits fail to be seen because they disappear in the chasm created by the extremities. For example, MacDowell shows how happiness is not assured in the ending of *All That Heaven Allows* – Ron's sickness 'reinforce[s] symbolically the hardships that this couple will necessarily face in the future' – and he prefers to see the ending as 'tentative[ly] romantic' (162).

A further reason for the faulty evaluation might be that irony and subversion, albeit important evaluative criteria in the appropriate contexts, are being disproportionately valued; there is a bias towards them, and an eagerness to find them. I think this predilection means that the fairy-tale wonder in the ending is overlooked. This wonder would be in keeping with the fantasy the film offers Cary. If the film has a potential problem it is that its drama is too patently diametrical, setting the good Ron against the bad Stoningham, and that neither is sufficiently complicated. It is arguable, however, that this is not a film that depends on the quality of its moral finessing, and it need not be judged by that criterion. Instead, it openly presents Ron as a fantasy figure and then situates Cary's struggle, social and psychological, in relation to it[31]. This fantasy is presented as an invitation to make real an imaginative realm that is not restricted by the worst confinements of her *social* reality (rather than being presented as something that is impossible to achieve). Nevertheless, *realising* it will inevitably be a struggle. Extending MacDowell's observation about the ending being tentative, the wondrous elements are only part of a final scene that is simultaneously imbued with hope and apprehension. The deer in the landscape is offered to Cary, and to a viewer, as magical and conditional; and like a life with Ron, with whom the animal is associated, it is strange and unsettling. These features are not to ironise, undermine, or even compromise the happiness, but rather to enrich a comprehension of what is at stake in it, or its fulfilment.

To adequately reveal the merits of the final scene, it is necessary for me to show how it relates to the previous parts of the film. A fundamental

---

[30] An evaluation will try to recognise a cliché, and differentiate it from a viable convention. It should be noted, however, that even clichés can be deployed advantageously with skilful handling, and may also be revivified.

[31] This is an example of needing to find the right ground on which to build an evaluation.

aspect to point out is that the ending is the culmination of a pattern of scenes that takes place in the location of the old mill, each of which dramatises a significant development in Cary's relationship with Ron[32]. It is the fourth major scene which is set there, and these scenes are evenly spaced throughout – at approximately 20 minutes (18 to be exact), 40 minutes (34), 60 minutes (exactly) and 80 minutes (the ending) – providing a spine for the film. The renovation of the mill is initially prompted by her suggestion that it will make a fine place for him to settle down when he finds the right woman (although she does not at this point admit, or consciously recognise, that she will be this woman). Ron's hard work in renovating the mill comes to represent his commitment to a married life with Cary. The first scene is the excited discovery of the dilapidated mill, the second is after its renovation and includes them making love for the first time, the third is when they break up after she has become convinced that their relationship is untenable in the face of social outcry, and the fourth scene is the 'happy ending'. This ending is permeated with the activity of these previous scenes which strengthens, intensifies, and authenticates its features, especially the deer and the window, rescuing them from accusations of being superficial and stereotypical.

Simplistic and sentimental picture postcard accounts are undermined by the deer's previous appearances. The second mill sequence begins with Ron tenderly feeding the deer as Cary arrives. As they begin to make love, the film returns outside to the deer. It stops eating from the bucket that Ron had left, skittishly leaps through the snow, and exits the frame. The film then dissolves back to Ron and Cary reclining, post-coital. The deer symbolically stands in for the pleasurable lovemaking that is not shown by the film. He is an antlered young buck, and crucially not a fawn or a doe. In this sense, the deer is associated with Ron who, among other things, represents sexual potency. Accounts of the film often maintain that the primary cause of the scandal is anxieties around class: he is a gardener and this is unacceptable in Cary's social circle. This is not the whole story, however, and may be primarily a cover story. Ron's young, handsome presence is threatening – he is much younger than Cary – as is his natural virility (the outdoors, the animals, the *growth* of trees). This is no ethereal or romantic love story; love is conceived sexually, and this is an essential part of the fantasy. Another animal that Cary encounters

---

[32] MacDowell's contestation, aside from mentioning some narrative connections to the final scene, does not mention this formal pattern. The recognition of the pattern, however, cements his claim that the ending is a continuation rather than a departure or a rupture. See also 3.7.

through Ron is the pigeon that they disturb when they first enter the dilapidated mill. Her fear of the bird, which he queries, represents her fear of nature after her cloistered, suburban lifestyle, and the fear of the outside coming inside. The kiss at the end of the scene has a powerful erotic charge for her and she walks off screen dumbfounded. After he follows her out of the shot, the camera stays in place and shows the bird sitting on a stair and looking straight into the camera and cooing. Operating rather like the deer at the end of the film, the situational presence of the bird appears to be artificial and yet at the same time the actual bird looks real and appears to be natural (which, at this early stage in her transformation, Cary fears and then ignores). The film therefore complicates the terms – 'artificial', 'real', and 'natural' – and pre-empts any judgement of the final scene as ersatz[33].

Extending high and low, leaving very little room for the wall, the window reduces the barrier between inside and outside, between the fabricated and the natural world. The large window (twelve panes) is originally not part of the mill, but is put in by Ron during his renovations. On her first sight of the window, Cary walks towards it and says with delight, 'You've put in this big window', and the camera pans right to take in its size and its panorama (Fig. 3.11). This largeness of the window and the pan establish expansiveness – 'You can see for miles', she says – and the window symbolises expanding horizons and transforming views. (It contrasts to the sightless window of her daughter's attic room; it also contrasts to the diminutive frame of the television set that her family wishes to impose on her and which offers views of which she cannot become part.) All fiction films are to some extent symbolic, in that features in the fiction represent or stand for something else, but a heightened symbolism is privileged in the design scheme of *All That Heaven Allows*. In evaluating the film, there is a need to be attuned to a peculiarly symbolic drama[34]. The difficulty of attuning is built into the film. Its symbolic mode does more than colourfully figure and delineate meaning, or provide a suitable way of expressing the fantasy that is presented to Cary. Its flagrancy presses questions of obviousness and thereby tests a viewer's credence

---

[33] Erasing the boundaries between the artificial and the natural is a feature of Douglas Sirk's films. See, for example, *Imitation of Life* (Douglas Sirk 1959 US). This is an example of how extrinsic knowledge – in this case other films by the same director – might help inform, or corroborate, an evaluation of a film. See 2.8: 'Comparison, category, and context'.

[34] This means that the category is respected, not that all aspects of the symbolism are beyond reproach.

# The aesthetic evaluation of film

and acceptance. Cary's difficulties in accepting Ron and his world, therefore, are mirrored by the challenge to a viewer to accept the film. The ending pushes this challenge to the limit, and yet, by this stage, the hope is, no doubt, that a viewer will be sufficiently acclimatised to what is at stake in its style of communication. What might a viewer, like Cary, come to believe is true? Perhaps the wintry blue Christmas card image framed by the window. 'Why it's unbelievable', Cary exclaims when asked whether she likes the window and the view. Far from an ironic treatment, the film wants to see if her utopia, where the unbelievable becomes believable, can be shared. The film takes a chance that it may prompt a snigger so that a viewer might take the far-fetched seriously[35].

Some summary accounts of the closing sequence make it seem as if the first sighting of the window in the scene, and the deer through it, is at its very end[36]. The window, however, is an important part of the choreography of the whole of the final scene; it is arguably its locus. While Ron is still unconscious, Cary comes over to it while Alida (Virginia Grey) is closing the shutters, and looking through the part of the window that is not yet quite closed up, she expresses her cowardice and regret. As she announces that she lets other people make the decisions, and that she lets things come between her and Ron, the view is closed off by Alida. The following morning, the nurse opens the shutters and lets in the light. After the doctor and nurse leave the room, there is a cut to show Cary standing over Ron as he lies with the expanse of the window behind them. It is *at this point*, not at the very end, that the deer makes its entrance. She turns and walks towards the window to look at the deer (Fig. 3.12). He is shown for some time foraging for food and sometimes looking through the window at Cary, and seemingly at Ron, his feeder; in fact, when Cary turns to look towards Ron, the deer's head, in tandem, appears to do the same. This is important because accounts can give the impression that the deer appears suddenly to close the film (as the camera rises to bring in the complete window after Ron awakes and they reconcile). Consequently, there is the implication that the deer is something of a discrete symbolic flourish with which to close the film, presented to a viewer over the heads of the characters. They misleadingly suggest that the animal's appearance is a pointed, and pointing, exclamation (rather than an underscoring).

They also misleadingly suggest that the window, the view through it, and the action in front of it are relatively separate, whereas actually

---

[35] See discussion of aesthetic risk in 3.4: 'Choice and expectation'.
[36] They also sometimes make it sound as if it is their first sighting *in the film*.

they dynamically relate and interrogate each other. Significantly, Cary engages with the deer in the final scene, and her position – her *situation* – chimes with the many other occasions when her view out of the window represents thoughts about the future of her life. On first seeing the window after the renovation, she is drawn towards it with delight. Perturbed after he proposes to her – 'I hadn't thought about marriage' – she also moves over to it. After they have made love for the first time, she gets up from the floor, announces that things will not be easy, and approaches the window once again (and they then both open the shutters) (Fig. 3.13). She is often suspended before the new vistas it offers, caught in a dilemma, not knowing how to move forward. In the third scene in the mill, when Cary suggests they live at her house (not the mill), it is Ron, fearing that her suggested compromises will mean that he is reined in, who walks to the window. On this occasion, Cary joins him, but afterwards pulls away from the direction of the window even though he tries to pull her around (Fig. 3.14). He remains at the window as she decisively breaks off the relationship and walks away. At this moment, she is consumed, incapable of looking out and beyond. It does seem now, at last, in the final scene, as Cary faces the deer, given the animal's connection with Ron, that she is finally recognising her connection to him, bringing what is inside (her) and outside (her) together. Like the deer, Cary can now make the mill and its surrounds her home.

The 'happy ending' is therefore informed by her interactions with the window. The window resonates with occasions that have preceded it and its presence is far more significant than providing a frame for a picture postcard image ('celebratory' or 'subversive'). The implication of both a sentimental thesis and an oppositional rupture thesis is that the 'happy ending' is one-dimensional. The development of the window within the narrative and the characters' involvement with it within individual scenes enables the ending to be multi-dimensional. A film can do much more with a convention than merely support or subvert it: the 'happy ending' in *All That Heaven Allows* is used to amalgamate, distil, evoke, suggest, and suspend.

## 3.4 Choice and expectation

The standard appraisals of *All That Heaven Allows* may not ultimately be justifiable, but it is arguable that the film provokes them. The provocation relates to what Alex Clayton calls 'aesthetic risk taking' (an idea he derives from the criticism of Perkins) (Clayton 2015: 209). This is where a film daringly and precariously risks dangers – for example, incredulity, absurdity, or sentimentality – generating the 'special thrill' from going up to a point and stopping 'short of collapse' (210; quoting Perkins 1996: 226 and 1972: 124). Concomitantly, it risks being misread or mistaken (as being, in the case of *All That Heaven Allows*, mawkish or ironic). The awareness of the danger creates what Perkins labels 'aesthetic suspense' (1996: 226). With narrative or dramatic suspense, a viewer is uncertain about possible development and outcomes in a story or in a scene. With aesthetic suspense, the speculations concern non-fictional outcomes. An example of aesthetic suspense is provided by *Vertigo* (Alfred Hitchcock 1958 US) where two-thirds of the way through the film there is a flashback that reveals the extent of Elster's trickery (Tom Helmore) and the fraudulence of Madeleine (Kim Novak). Robin Wood says that the film is daring at this point because it challenges an expectation: it breaks a 'law of the mystery thriller ... divulge[s] the "surprise" solution' too early, and risks an anti-climactic and a purposeless final section (1989: 120). The flashback does not only provide information about the story, it forces an evaluation of how, when, and where the information has been delivered: it raises the question of the filmmakers' choices. Clayton argues that 'we judge these choices in terms of what they offer, what they refuse, what they claim, and what they betray' (2015: 212). The suspense arises because Clayton's viewer, viewing from an aesthetic point of view, is conscious of 'the ever-present possibility of an aesthetic misstep' (216). Their engagement is with the handling of the fiction as much as it is with the fiction.

For Clayton, the sequence in *Rope*, with the housekeeper and the chest, is aesthetically suspenseful as well as dramatically suspenseful. Even if one accepts Perkins' defence of the sequence, as outlined in section 3.2, it exhibits a contrived use of the continuous take and viewpoint. It audaciously tests the 'pact of tolerance' with the 'self-imposed rule' of the continuous take (211). Rupert (James Stewart) is placed half in the shot and half out of it with his back to the camera, and he is side-on to the chest. Already half-turned, the possibility of him turning around at any moment further adds to the dramatic suspense, as does his conjoining of on-screen and off-screen activity which emphasises the proximity of the group. At the same time, the shot appears to be insistent about its construction to the point of being affectedly mischievous[37]. Rupert's

---

[37] Neither Perkins nor Clayton suggests this interpretation, although it is consistent with their understanding of 'aesthetic suspense'.

hovering on the edge appears awkward, noticeably poised; and his conjoining makes the group absurdly *so* near and yet *so* far. Furthermore, the group's conversation, which is all about the whereabouts of the deceased David, is an emphatic soundtrack to the activity of the housekeeper such that the dramatic ironies are crassly insistent. Even her real-time journeying takes the form of a drawn-out gag without quite becoming one. The sequence verges on the comical without collapsing into it and therefore, as the menace is lightened and the humour is blackened, the tone is complicated.

The concept of 'aesthetic suspense' has wider ramifications because a film need not be risk taking for the viewers (and before them the filmmakers) to be, at any moment, aware of the proximity of other options and outcomes. John Gibbs writes that, 'Every frame, every cut, every element of performance and every note on the soundtrack results from pursuing one option and refusing many others' (2006: 5). When evaluating a film, 'a valuable approach is to identify a decision, or a group of decisions, and ask "what is gained by doing it this way?"' (5). Options are understood as apposite or inapposite, and even damaging[38]. A fine line often divides a good outcome from its opposite. There is a sense of roads not travelled, for better or for worse. A film might have a difficulty or a problem, explicit or implicit, and the achievement is measured in terms of how well the problem has been solved, overcome or negotiated. ('The problem for the film is that it needs to get to x without doing y ... .') A film is tested based on the experience of other films, and other artworks; a store of knowledge is built up about how things are often done and can be done. (We may recall how Bazin praised William Wyler for resisting conventional analytical editing in *The Little Foxes*.) A film also generates its own prospects so it is also tested against the expectations it establishes itself. An initial scenario may end up not delivering the dramatic and thematic complexity it promised, or an apparently unpromising scenario may turn out to be unexpectedly fecund. A formal scheme may be seen through, or it may lapse. Expectations may adjust when the film is viewed in different ways. Some occurrence may prompt disappointment, perhaps the revelatory

---

[38] The vocabulary of 'choice' and 'options' can imply that every detail and achievement of a film is separately and explicitly intended. Criticism can sensibly talk in this way without the implication. Nevertheless, not all the merits of a film, for example those that seem to be against the grain of, or despite, the filmmakers' purpose, are best assessed from within the language of choice. Drawing a line, however, between what is and is not intended is very difficult. See 2.9: 'Intention, achievement, and skill'.

flashback in *Vertigo*, but then later make sense, or fulfil a hitherto unnoticed aspect of the film's design. Although the appearance of the deer through the large window at the culmination of *All That Heaven Allows* is consistent within the design and the meanings of the film, it would be too much to state that it is expected. It makes sense within the bounds of the film's possibilities while it offers a rejuvenating surprise (for a viewer as well as Cary). Creative variations on a scheme are often unforeseen *and* fitting; they may initially appear eccentric and end up being requisite.

A sequence of merit might play subtly with expectations moment-to-moment. Toles closely monitors the progressions in a short scene of approximately one minute and fifteen seconds in *The Shop Around the Corner* (Ernst Lubitsch 1940 US) (2010). The scene in question is the one where Mr Matuschek (Frank Morgan) sacks Alfred Kralik (James Stewart) from his employment in the shop. Matuschek's action is surprising because the two have been close friends and colleagues for many years, and the film withholds the exact reason for his draconian decision. Matuschek has been behaving tetchily towards Kralik for the day and this, in turn, has prompted some insubordination. The expectation is, however, that as he visits Matuschek's office on this occasion the problem will be aired and eradicated. Even though the scene is of conspicuous narrative significance, the many skilful modulations and adjustments it contains, and depends upon for it to be best appreciated, may not be initially recognised. Toles's analysis is a distinguished example of the way close reading in aesthetic criticism can articulate, more deliberately, a series of essential operations by a film. These operations take place too quickly and naturally for explicit acknowledgement during a viewing. Close reading *slows* this down and highlights aspects of the film and the experience of it that may be taken for granted.

*To modulate* is to adjust or regulate the degree of something – in music more specifically adjusting the tone, pitch or volume – and what Toles monitors are the delicate modulations of the sequence that hinder expectations[39]. Firstly, there are generic matters: genres carry expectations about scenarios and situations, and their tonal character. Toles discusses how the film is set up, and has been proceeding, as a light comedy, but then deviates into a territory that is sorrowful. The distinction is that this comedy achieves a tone that, in the context, is unexpectedly serious and disarming, not merely that it has a scene with an unhappy incident or one

---

[39] I am gathering together, categorising, and making explicit the points that speak to the topic of expectation because the topic is not foregrounded by the essay.

that upsets the flow. At the same time, the tonal shift skilfully takes place without compromising the film's prevailing demeanour: it is not radically disruptive or disjunctive. Pauline Kael describes the film as an 'airy wonder' with 'steel underpinnings' (quoted in Toles 2010: 1). In that vein, Toles writes that it contains 'painful struggle' and the 'prospect of tragedy' without 'souring its delight' or 'vanquishing its core tranquillity' (1). The film fuses these seemingly incompatible qualities, or more accurately, it embeds the former in the latter. This also creates what he calls 'a shadow line': a zone which is generically and tonally less distinct and where expectations are less secure (1).

Secondly, related to genre, is characterisation: in character (and performance), Matuschek looks to be a straightforward comic type. Although such a character is expected to be somewhat peripheral, to be exempt from more profound developments in the drama, and to have a limited set of repeated traits – 'reliable quirks, attitudes, and ailments' – the scene discloses 'a more demanding character psychology' (3–4).

Thirdly, there is the interrelated movement of performer and camera: Toles notes the elaborate tracking shot that films James Stewart's eager and energetic approach to Matuschek's office. The shot shows an unusual 'virtuosity' for a 'stylistically self-effacing film' which when combined with Stewart's presence creates a momentum that seems to promise their reconciliation (4). He writes of 'James Stewart expanding within the frame to his full height and claiming the prerogatives of star magnetism and amplified focus with every step he takes … As he advances directly toward the camera (and us) he seems to draw all the best parts of his physical personality together in pursuit of a single worthy aim'; in light of this, 'How might such a beautifully enlivened presence be turned down for anything?' (4). Simultaneously though, 'lofty sureness … often (in drama)' prompts the intuition that the character is 'headed for a fall' (4). Because the movement holds both outcomes in balance – it does not undermine the confident approach by clearly signalling that it is misguided – it makes the 'thought … switch on the instant' (4).

Fourthly, there is the timing and tone of the performances of Morgan and Stewart. Near the end of the conversation, Toles notes a slight but significant change from the script – 'Well, we might as well say goodbye' changes to 'I guess we might just as well say goodbye' – which provides the 'extra few words [which] allow Morgan to stretch the build up to an anticipated show of feeling that, distressingly, fails to materialise' (7). More generally, Morgan performs 'flickering intimations' of Matuschek's familiar behavioural traits, for example, his distractedness and hesitancy, which suggest that the conversation might proceed towards reconciliation (4). This 'flickering' is important: if Morgan discards familiar traits then he risks his character appearing too fundamentally altered while overemphasising them will risk his character appearing too similar to before. Morgan also uses the familiar traits 'tactically' to deceive: his character seems to be heading in one direction while going in another (4). This also deepens the dejection, for Kralik and for Toles, because traits associated with avuncular friendliness and a bumbling lack of ruthlessness are the same ones Matuschek deploys to smooth the passage to a decisive divorce (Fig. 3.15). Similarly, when Matuschek suggests that Kralik would be happier elsewhere Kralik replies, 'Well I guess there is nothing more to be said' and there is 'not a whisper of retaliatory coldness in Stewart's delivery' despite his feelings of frustration, bewilderment, and hurt (5). 'Retaliatory coldness' would be a sensible expectation and this shows how the effect of the delivery achieves distinction in light of probable options. Kralik's response also enhances the understanding of their *particular* relationship (and a certain type of interaction). Indeed, Toles explains how, ironically, it is at this occasion of severance, partly because of Kralik's dignified and considerate behaviour, that their bond can be seen and felt most

**3.15** *The Shop Around the Corner* (MGM, 1940).

clearly. This exemplifies that an aspect can be clear and clearly felt when it emerges indirectly on an unexpected occasion out of apparently contrary matters.

## 3.5 Encouraging perceptual activity

The scene between Matuschek and Kralik does not convey the strength of their bond directly through displays of obvious amity or harmony. The disadvantage of direct expression is that although its immediacy may be affecting, it may also be insufficiently occupying. To encourage perceptual activity, and along with it cognitive and imaginative activity, artworks often try to suggest or imply[40]. In Part I, we saw how aesthetic pleasure was yielded by the imagination being stimulated to make sense of the arrangement of the artwork; and Malcolm Budd claimed that the 'form must not offer too little perceptual contemplation or exploration' (2008: 15–16). Arnheim thinks that good works of art should have some 'cognitive difficulty' requiring a viewer 'to actively marshal their hermeneutic resources in order to comprehend the work's sophisticated and subtle shades of meaning' (Dhir 2011: 93). The work should find ways of leaving 'gaps' that a viewer fills by searching for clues in the visual and aural presentation (97)[41]. Equally, Bazin discourages a form of presentation that thoroughly clarifies, and which too specifically directs perception. Consequently, he favours the continuous take and multifaceted composition because he considers them less determining. The freedom for a viewer that he advocates arises because the image is released from the requirements of easy telling or 'efficient representation' to become fruitfully indefinite (Andrew 2005: xx; see also Cardullo 1997: xiii–xiv).

This freedom does not simply refer, as is commonly iterated, to the ability to liberally scan the frame. Nevertheless, because the image has multiple components, it may profitably distribute attention. A scene, which contains deep focus compositions, from *The Best Years of Our Lives* is exemplary for Bazin. Three soldiers – Al (Frederic March), Fred (Dana Andrews), and Homer (Harold Russell) – return to their hometown after the Second World War. Fred's marriage has disintegrated and he has fallen in love with Peggy (Theresa Wright) who is the daughter of Al. The scene

---

[40] 'Perceptual' includes the aural.
[41] Arnheim does not advocate overtly puzzling films and he dislikes formal strategies that aggressively 'thwart ... interpretive activity' (Dhir 2011: 93).

The aesthetic evaluation of film 161

**3.16** *The Best Years of Our Lives* (Samuel Goldwyn Company, 1946).

takes place in Butch's bar, a location associated with the veterans' unity – it is where they agree to meet after returning home – and now becomes a place of division. Al expresses to Fred his disapproval of the relationship with his daughter and requests that he break off contact. After the conversation, Fred walks to the back of the shot (which is the front of the bar by its entrance) to make his call to Peggy in a telephone box. The telephone box, within which Fred is shown making the call, remains a small element in the background of subsequent shots, and the film never cuts into the box to listen to Fred or the conversation. At this point, Homer enters the bar. Seriously injured in the war, Homer has two false forearms with metal hooks (substituting for his hands). He now wants to show off his piano prowess to Al, so he plays a duet with Butch (Hoagy Carmichael), the owner of the bar. They play in the right foreground of the shot while Al stands, also to the right, in the middle ground, looking over the piano. All the while Fred remains in the booth at the back left (Fig. 3.16).

I imagine there are a number of meritorious features in this set-up for Bazin[42]. The multiple planes and points of the composition are ideal

---

[42] Bazin does not himself precisely delineate them.

for expressing distances and divisions in a film exploring the reintegration of soldiers with family and friends. However, they are not simply of expressive significance because the composition also invites a dynamic involvement by wrestling with a viewer's attention. Al is the pivotal figure in the composition, and *his* attention is divided between Fred's conversation – he anxiously turns his head round to look – and Homer's performance. The opportunity is presented for a viewer's attention to be divided between these two ongoing activities, while in addition watching Al's awareness of both[43]. To the left middle of the shot, two anonymous customers enjoy watching the playing so when Al too is watching Homer most of the eye-lines point towards the piano. The composition is therefore biased such that when Al shifts his look around towards Fred at the back of the bar there is an affective pull away from this weighted foreground. The image and the attention to it are also prevented from settling by the uncertainty surrounding each of the points of activity. The film omits to show the exchange between Fred and Peggy, and instead leaves it to the imagination (and Bazin explicitly emphasises this aspect (1997a [1948]: 15)). Al's consternated behaviour is also not clarified: is he anxious to see that the relationship has been promptly terminated, worrying about the consequences for his friendship and his daughter, or regretting his demand? Even Homer's piano playing, despite its confident and vigorous execution, is fraught with the prospect of failure (increased by the desire for it to succeed).

The sequence is compositionally dense and complex[44]. Bazin thought perceptual activity could *also* be encouraged by loosening the composition (and drama, and narrative). He acclaims a sequence from the end of *Boudu Saved From Drowning* (Jean Renoir 1932 France). Boudu (Michel Simon), a tramp, is rescued (from drowning) by Edouard Lestingois (Charles Granville). Lestingois takes him into his household where Boudu causes much havoc. He is to marry the maid (Séverine Lerczinska), but during his wedding day celebrations he capsizes a rowing boat and swims away

---

[43] The shot showing all of the points of activity is twice interrupted by a closer shot that shows Al looking round towards the phone booth and excludes the piano playing. Although he does not explicitly state it, Bazin is at best ambivalent, and at worst disappointed, by these interpolations because they narrow the scope of the viewpoint hence the relational intricacy. Bazin suggests that Wyler cautiously includes what he calls these 'safety shots' to reroute a viewer's eyes in case he or she has become too absorbed in the piano playing (1997a [1948]: 16).

[44] The sequence is also open to negative appraisal. I return to it in 3.6: 'Prominence'.

from them, and drifts back to his former life. What sort of features might Bazin have admired[45]? Firstly, regarding performance, Simon's presentation of a tramp, unlike for example Chaplin's, is not pointedly parodic or satisfyingly inventive. Nor does it invite appreciation of its cleverness, its good timing, or its multi-dimensionality. His movements and expressions, like the wafting of his arms, his lopsided, stumbling walk, and his grotesquely grimacing face, are all exaggerated and uncoordinated, and are not well formed or formulated into a routine. Secondly, regarding composition, there is no sense of careful arrangement. On the contrary, some of the shots – one of the riverbank is out of focus and only becomes clear when Boudu comes into shot – might appear crude and amateurish. Thirdly, regarding duration, Boudu's actions are followed in something like real time and this following is mainly, if not wholly, without narrative propulsion. Despite moving towards its conclusion, the film adopts a more leisurely pace. Fourthly, regarding continuity, the editing and camera movement do not straightforwardly focus or direct the attention. For example, as Boudu floats away on his back, he is filmed as if just sighted, in the distance, through some trees. He is drifting away, not only from the wedding party, but also from the film's grasp. When the film does cut to a closer shot, it is abrupt because of the sudden change in angle and distance; and when it cuts again to yet another perspective, there seems to be no clear logic to the shot progression. Fifthly, regarding narrative, the ending is not clearly marked. The film could end with Boudu simply floating away. However, it does not: some time passes as he climbs out of the river, changes clothes, takes some bread from a couple … It is unclear how long he will drift, and as the film continues in this semi-picaresque way, the place where it will end becomes ever more optional, perhaps even whimsical.

The final stages of the sequence exemplify the protraction. As he sits on the bank, Boudu discards his bowler hat. (Until this point, he has held on to his hat despite his long float down the river and the exchange of his wet wedding clothes for those of the scarecrow.) Given that this is the last vestige of his temporary bourgeois existence, it might be appropriate for the film to leave him at this point. Yet, it seems not to want to deliver a dénouement too symbolically neat. Although the film does eventually leave Boudu to follow the hat, it does not cut to it immediately after he throws it into the water. Instead, the camera continues to observe him

---

[45] Once again, Bazin does not analyse this sequence in detail, but he praises similar features in other contexts.

chewing his food and singing (at the same time!), and even pans in the opposite direction to accommodate him as he lies back upon the ground facing the sky. Only *then* does the camera reverse its direction and bumpily move away from him in a hurry as if the film now realises, a little too late, that it is time to leave the tramp and chase after the hat. This is one of a few features of the sequence that contribute to an unevenness of rhythm (another is his gruff, grating singing which accompanies the image). Will the film now end? Not quite. As the hat bumps into a post, the camera rises to take in the expanse of the river with its anonymous rowers, and the story of the tramp is now absorbed into a generalised image of river life. This is The Bigger Picture, and another possibility for a perfect conclusion, which is why the film might not want to end at this point either. Instead, it cuts back to the wedding party, sitting on the bank, drying out further up the river, pondering Boudu's disappearance, and *then* cuts to a low angled shot of men parading and singing in town. Finally, it ends.

The sequence has a witty tension: despite being an ending, it is opening up and out. Christian Keathley refers to 'the 'open' work', a phrase coined by Noël Burch, where a film is open to the intrusion of natural contingencies (2006: 79). It may then capture the in-between and transient material that would be cut out in a film that was more stringent and composed. Many commentators have noted that the medium, because of its history of recording material reality, has been particularly suited to this mode. Although the final sequence of *Boudu* is notably impressionistic, the contingent inevitably intrudes even in more controlled sequences. From an evaluative point of view, the risks for the 'open work' are that it will become, for example, careless or sloppy, too diffuse and vague, or too beholden to the prospect of an interesting contingency (that might fail to materialise). I.A. Richards writes that one cause of 'badness in poetry' – a chapter title in his *Principles of Literary Criticism* – is that the work 'is not sufficiently specific' (2001 [1924]: 185–6). A good poem should make a 'demand' upon the reader, 'but the demand made must be proportional to the poet's own contribution' (186). If the reader must supply too much of the poem, then the perceptual activity will be of the wrong sort, and the relationship between reader and work will be tenuous[46].

Why might the *Boudu* sequence avoid these risks? One answer is that despite having the quality of being *unfinished* it is not careless or sloppy:

---

[46] Once again, rather than simply acclaiming a category (for example, 'the open film'), an evaluation attempts to ascertain the merit of any work within the category.

many different areas of filmmaking (temporal, compositional, performative, and narrative) are contributing, in different ways, to a purpose, and this indicates a thoroughgoing and well-achieved design. One purpose of its form is to be in tune with its wayward hero, so for example, when the film cannot find the *right* angle to film Boudu perhaps it is because he disallows a settled view. The sequence seems also to be inviting the viewer to be in tune with him and his attitudes. Simon's performance might test some viewers' patience because it refuses – like Boudu in society – easy acceptance or assimilation, but the proposition is to relinquish (bourgeois) control and relish the unpredictability (Fig. 3.17). The sequence's lack of tidiness – rejecting another bourgeois value – is also fitting.

Despite achieving an appropriate form for its content and intent, however, there may also be limited rewards: the film needs to offer a worthwhile perceptual experience. Keathley, explaining Bazin's preferences, writes about the perceptual opportunities offered by 'the sketched film' (2006: 73). In a sketch, unlike a well-formed painting, the whole picture is not provided, and much remains implicit. '[B]y sketching in only a sufficient amount', Keathley writes, 'the viewer will be encouraged to actively

**3.17** *Boudu Saved from Drowning* (Les Établissements Jacques Haïk, Les Productions Michel Simon, Crédit Cinématographique Français (CCF), 1932).

engage with what she's watching, and will have the satisfaction of *coming to an understanding* rather than being explicitly told' (79; my emphasis). In addition, an active viewer may discover details in the image and they feel 'revelatory' because they are not pointed out (79). With regard to the *Boudu* sequence, Bazin acclaims the way the looser filmmaking releases the sensuous qualities of the environment so that he can newly appreciate them (1992 [1971]: 85–6). He writes, for example, about the camera picking up 'a bit of grass where, in close-up, one can see distinctly the white dust that the heat and the wind have lifted from the path' (86). He goes on to say that '[o]ne can almost feel it between one's fingers' (86). Sadly, I cannot even see the white dust on the Criterion copy I am working from[47]. Although it is difficult to judge when viewing less than pristine prints, I think Bazin might be overstating the sensuous affect[48]. It is fair to claim, however, that 'the scene … becomes … the spectacle of [Boudu's] pleasure' (85). And he is certainly right to emphasise the greater prominence of the environmental qualities as the narrative and dramatic logic become less compelling. Indeed, another merit of the final stages of the film is the seamless transition from primarily presenting a fictional scenario to what appears to be impromptu documenting, unfolding naturally, spontaneously even. The film consequently stealthily shifts its mode to one that is primarily ontological, where film and viewer watch Boudu's existence in the world and his interactions with it (the river, the scarecrow, the couple, the goat, the bank). The variety and specificity of the interactions during the final stages also guards against the vague. Furthermore, the film unwinds without becoming too diffuse. Indeed, I consider one of the main achievements to be the way its form relaxes, and expresses relaxation, and relief. The film is roguishly amusing as it eases the tramp back into his leisurely liberty, luxuriously indulging him while inspiring a less targeted and urgent viewing. In summary, the form of the sequence,

---

[47] I also cannot locate the 'extraordinary slow 360-degree pan' that Bazin says occurs when Boudu comes up on the bank (85).

[48] I also think Bazin understates the role of meaning in the scene. Keathley writes that Bazin resists focusing 'on what is interpretable or translatable', arguing that 'such 'meaning' is precisely *not* what makes this scene effective' (66). Bazin is right to recognise that the merit of the scene does not depend on, for example, complexity, profundity or incremental progression of meaning, and that merit need not depend on qualities related to these sorts of achievements in meaning. However, the scene's motions and emotions, mood and attitude, are expressively related to meaningful behaviours and mentalities, for example those associated with class.

as well as loosening, has design, purpose, suitability, specificity, and an agile control of time, pace and mood, all of which encourage perceptual realignment.

*The Best Years of Our Lives* and *Boudu* sequences, although different in style, are not evidently *pointing* out one thing, or pointing out one thing at a time in case something is missed. Nor are they point-making. Gibbs explains, in his history of British film criticism, that the critics working at the journal *Movie* disliked 'point-making' in films because it made matters too easy for a viewer. 'The central characteristic of "point-making"', according to Gibbs, is that the decisions the filmmakers have made 'serve ... *only* the end that is the "point"' (2013: 177). These critics celebrate directorial styles that have pronounced features, which both the sequences just examined also contain, so they do not only value subtlety or discretion. Rather they desire that the filmmakers' decisions 'fulfil a number of functions simultaneously' (177). They warn against one-note effects that disallow 'complexity of texture' and, consequently, 'complexity of response' (180)[49].

Therefore, claims for merit cannot depend on a tight fit between a device and its meaning or effect. A much deployed simplistic example: a shot from a low angle in *Citizen Kane* (Orson Welles 1941 US) is claimed to be of merit because it is effective at making Charles Foster Kane look overbearing. It is a simple equation: the low angle = overbearing = good. The evaluation rests on one device succesfully producing the one effect or the one point. The shot may well be of merit for reasons that pertain to Kane's domineering stature, but for the *Movie* critics an evaluative claim could not rest on this simple equation alone. Therefore, evaluative claims based only on the communicative efficacy of a device, for example in successfully conveying a meaning, are insufficient because the effect might be limited[50]. The *Movie* critics scolded Ernest Lindgren who they believe falls into this trap in his book *The Art of Film*. He thought that achievement rested on an 'uncomplicated process of communication between filmmaker and audience' so that 'the director's task is to choose precisely [the viewpoint] which will be most effective for his purpose'

---

[49] Quoted phrases are taken from an interview with one of the *Movie* critics, Charles Barr, conducted by John Gibbs (19 June 1997).
[50] There may be instances of effects which despite being relatively one-note have other merits. They might have been difficult to achieve, or the experience might be unusual or unconventional.

(Gibbs 2013: 180; then Lindgren quoted in Gibbs 2013: 180)[51]. The *Movie* critics, on the contrary, encouraged a complicated process of communication; they looked for 'the qualification or shading that a figure of style will receive from its context' (180). In the poetic context, Richards discusses the problem of devices that are too decisive: a 'heavy regular rhythm', 'the triteness of the close', the 'dead stamp' of a rhyme, or 'the obviousness of the descriptions' (2001 [1924]: 187). All of them 'accentuate the impression of conclusiveness' (187).

There is a range of ways a feature might be obvious: it may be insufficiently complicated or suggestive, over familiar (a cliché), overstated, conceptually limited, inadequately integrated, or prematurely crystallised[52]. Many critics have been attracted to states – suspension, uncertainty, poise, paradox, ambiguity, ambivalence – that prevent a straightforward reception of the work. These states are admired because they honestly reveal or reflect complication; because interest is sustained if the work does not settle; because they often entail elements mutually informing, or interrogating, each other; because unusual connections can be forged especially when the elements are apparently contradictory; and because it is an achievement to hold alternative elements advantageously in play, and make them cohere rather than clash. Empson refers to the need for a 'logical disorder' in the work that will prevent it from being a 'simple statement' (2004 [1930]: 48, 7; quoted in Olson 1976: 119). Unless a film holds, or suspends, two or more different things intriguingly in balance, there will be too much of one thing and not enough of another. Having said this, a work may be suspended such that it is indecisive and irresolute, neither one thing nor another. This is the sort of fine distinction that an evaluation investigates and articulates in relation to particular works. Furthermore, as the literary New Critics argue, balance and tension should not simply be resolved or tidied up in critical accounts. They should be honoured in a close reading that faithfully records the complexity of perceptual activity engendered by the works.

Ambiguity is a complicating feature that has been particularly valued (for example by Bazin). For Empson, the great chronicler of literary ambiguity, it refers to 'richness and variety of meaning' as well as uncertainty

---

[51] The problems in merely acclaiming the communicative efficacy of a device are similar to the problems in acclaiming the fulfilment of a filmmaker's intention. See 2.9: 'Intention, achievement, and skill' for a fuller discussion.

[52] Interpretative and evaluative claims can be obvious for all the same reasons, and consequently will not be sufficient to adjust perception or to persuade.

(Righter 1963: 101). It is any element that 'strike[s] the reader in more than one way', and 'gives room for alternative reactions' (100–1). In his later writing, he developed the idea of a 'complex word' which is a word that changes complexion as the reader sees it fitting into the work in different ways (Fuller 2006: 157). This idea can be transferred to film, for example to images or sounds which change their aspect when they are perceived as part of an alternative structure or pattern of the work[53]. From an evaluative point of view, what is at stake is not simply the possession of a double meaning because one can have an 'obvious pun' or a 'patent irony' (Olson 1976: 119). For Empson, in these cases there is 'no room for puzzling', and there is no 'pleasure derived from ... mental activity' (and he would not regard them as ambiguous) (Empson 2004 [1930]: x; Olson 1976: 121).

The worry for Elder Olson is that critical activity might end up being like solving a riddle or conundrum about which we are emotionally indifferent. Empson's method, where more and more meanings are extracted from words, was described by Richards as producing 'an endless swarm of lively rabbits' and was categorised by T.S. Eliot as 'the lemon-squeezer school of criticism' (Watson 1963: 208, 206). Even if the countless rabbits genuinely live in the warren of the work, it is possible for a work to be too abundant. Multiplicity is not always a merit. Nevertheless, Empson's multitudinous revelations from his close attention warn against premature and definitive assessment. Although attending to literature, his work also encourages film criticism to be alive to the multiple implications and stimulations of images and sounds especially in films that may not declare their density.

For Olson, ambiguities should be well regulated and well situated, in terms of character and circumstance; they should have a human dimension, and be insightful (1976: 129). A pertinent example of ambiguity in this regard is given by Perkins from the beginning of *In a Lonely Place* (Nicholas Ray 1950 US) where the director gives 'the same gesture to three different characters within the ... space of the scene that establishes the film's Hollywood setting' (Figs 3.18–3.20):

> [E]ach of them approaches another character from behind and grasps his shoulders with both hands. The first time, it is a perfunctory and patronizing greeting whose pretense of warmth is a bare cover for the assertion of superiority. Then, between the hero and an old friend, it conveys intimacy and genuine regard. Finally, when a large-mouthed

---

[53] See the account of George M. Wilson's work in 3.7: 'Pattern'.

**3.18–3.21** *In a Lonely Place* (Columbia Pictures Corporation, Santana Pictures Corporation, 1950).

# The aesthetic evaluation of film

3.18–3.21 (Continued)

producer uses the shoulders of the hero himself as a rostrum from which to publicize his latest triumph, it is seen as oppressive and openly slighting. These moments are significant in their own right, but their deeper purpose is – in a perfectly ordinary context – to dramatize the ambiguity of gesture itself. (1981: 1144)

The 'ambiguity of gesture' occurs because the first and the third gestures are both greetings *and* something else, and because all three taken together show how a similar category of gesture, customary and apparently insignificant, can take on a range of meanings[54].

### 3.6 Prominence

As *In a Lonely Place* continues, ambiguities regarding gestures of grasping or gripping become more visible and grave. The three gestures at the beginning of the film, highlighted by Perkins, act as an undramatic overture. It is likely that these preliminary gestures will not be properly registered, or only sensed subliminally. This has been true for many students with whom I have watched the film. Even if they register the gestures, they do not acknowledge their significance. The gestures may be seen because they are reasonably prominent in the image (the second and third instances), and even emphatic, but as Sherlock Holmes might say, they are not necessarily properly observed. Why is this so?

It is because they are ingeniously and dextrously immersed, and I think there are a few aspects which help explain how this is achieved. It is the beginning of the film so a viewer would not yet be oriented to its concerns, and the gestures are subordinated to a primary engagement with the commencement of the story. They could exist simply to establish the film's world, add local colour, and contribute to the credibility and fluency of the fictional realism. It is also, as Perkins says, 'a perfectly ordinary context', and the gestures signify customary male engagement and rapport. Equally, as one thing runs into another, they are carried along in the dramatic flow. The first gesture, by Lloyd Barnes (Morris Ankrum), is filmed from a reasonable distance and takes place in a cluster

---

[54] I would argue the second greeting also contains a dual meaning and is less innocent than Perkins suggests. The 'old friend' is a once famous, but now aged, 'washed-up' actor consoling himself in drink, and he is abusively dismissed by the 'large-mouthed producer'. As well as conveying 'intimacy and genuine regard', the greeting signifies that the 'hero' tends to, and perhaps needs to, legitimise, identify with, and emotionally invest in, the excluded and marginalised male figure.

of activity including children requesting an autograph from lead protagonist Dix Steele (Humphrey Bogart), and a greeting by Dix's friend and agent Mel (Art Smith). Before dominating the image, the second gesture is first shown from side-on and is contradicted by yet another gesture of the same type – one that Perkins does not mention – again by Lloyd who grasps Dix to pull him away from Charlie (Robert Warwick) in the opposite direction (Fig. 3.21). The specificity of Dix's embrace is partly absorbed therefore into the assertion of his commitment, physical and verbal, to place himself alongside Charlie ('What's wrong with right here?'). The overriding thrust of Dix's motion and attitude – and Bogart's extraordinary, charismatic star presence – attract attention and set a momentum that discourages a viewer from focusing on the ordinary gesture. The attraction of his non-conformism and his contempt for the conventional may also overshadow it. Similarly, although the third gesture is actually held for twenty seconds, it is the producer's abusive proclamations, and the tension they cause, that dominate. The film also cuts away during the first and third gestures and this further distracts, and in the first instance obscures. Furthermore, the gestures and their significance are recessive because they are unlikely at first to be seen as part of a pattern that would bring them to greater prominence. The gestures are each a minute apart with much banter and activity in between, and the sequence they appear in, although continuous, plays out as a number of discrete short scenes. It moves from outside to inside and passes through different sections of the restaurant with various encounters and interventions. This separates the gestures and situates them in different contexts.

The sequence shows the power dynamics in ordinary gestures without proclaiming them. It therefore remains faithful to the way ordinary gestures incorporate power and obscure the dynamics. One important evaluative issue here is that, in *Movie* terms, this sequence is not insisting on making the point. Perkins' example indicates the difference between prominence and significance: some features may have low prominence and be highly significant while some may be highly prominent and have low significance. Once a feature's significance is recognised, perhaps with the help of alert criticism, it appears as revelatory. Films often reveal by paying attention (to something), and an important capacity of film is to direct attention through editing, to focus on one thing while excluding others. This also means, however, that it can be too easy for the medium simply to point things out. The *In a Lonely Place* example shows how a film can also reveal by not drawing attention; it can disclose the overlooked (the neglected) by not overlooking (looking too hard).

Perkins writes that *In a Lonely Place* reconciles 'clarity with depth of suggestion' (1994: 231). The gestures are clearly shown and available to view, but they are weighted in relation to a range of other features such that their prominence is reduced. Perkins elsewhere writes that '[f]ilmmakers continuously develop the repertoire of devices through which to adjust the prominence with which they present an item of information' (1990: 5). Recognising the weighting of elements in a work is another task for aesthetic evaluation. According to Perkins, a repeated feature (like the shoulder grasps) may be 'acknowledged or ignored or vaguely apprehended' and '[s]uch shadings are not easy to achieve' (2000: 41). Of the film *Letter from an Unknown Woman* (Max Ophüls 1948 US), he claims that the 'eloquence of its effects … depend[s] on its capacity to stir our recall, with *varying degrees of definition*, of moments and patterns that we have seen before' (45; my emphasis). Attention to prominence is more commonplace in arts such as music and poetry where the stressed and the unstressed, of notes and syllables, are at the forefront of creation and appreciation. Although traditionally less articulated in relation to film (and other dramatic arts), sensitivity to emphasis enables a monitoring of when, how, and how well aspects are disclosed.

In his major work on aesthetic evaluation, *Film as Film*, Perkins argues for the embedding of meaning and significance. For example, the meaningfulness of an object should be a consequence of its secure place in the progression of the story and action. In *Johnny Guitar* (Nicholas Ray 1954 US), therefore, a hat has 'expressive value only as the hat of a particular woman at a given point in a specific story' (1972: 79). Equally, formal features, for example the perspective of the camera, or the arrangement of the shot, should reveal the significance of what is happening as a natural consequence of showing what is happening. The assertion of a commentary, even the presence of one, should not be felt. Meaning should be 'contained', rather than 'imposed' and '[t]he meanings which are contained most securely … are those formed at the deepest level of interrelation and synthesis' (119; 117). Perkins is not alone in desiring this type of presentation. His 'containment' resembles some aspects of Leavis's 'concretisation'[55].

---

[55] Perkins' work is also similar to Leavis's in believing that emotion and feelings, as well as meaning and significance, should be embedded, but this is implicit rather than explicit in *Film as Film*. For Leavis, if emotion is not concretely actualised and realised in dramatic specificity it will be too sentimental, insistent, and vague. It should not detach from precise reference or fictional context that particularises, modulates, and qualifies (see Casey 2011 [1966]: 160–3). 'Concretisation' is used flexibly

Similarly, Bazin thought that *Seven Men From Now* (Budd Boetticher 1956 US) was the 'best western [he had] seen since the war' because its significance emerged as if spontaneously, even unconsciously, out of 'the intelligence of the scenario' (1985 [1957]: 169–70). He thought that too many Westerns were being reinforced with social and philosophical theses and with Western mythology too consciously treated as the subject (170)[56]. Perkins' recommendation of integration has a few evaluative consequences. It draws attention to films that might be undervalued because they are self-effacing and reticent about claiming significance (especially if they are of a 'lowbrow' generic form – melodramas, thrillers, musicals, and Westerns). Similarly, it warns against overvaluing films with explicitly 'interesting' subject matter or a fascinating concept. More generally, it shows that rather than simply pointing out subject matter or meanings, aesthetic evaluation depends on assessing *how* they manifest. It also encourages scepticism about devices, albeit captivating or emotionally affecting, that are too blatant in their expressive capacity.

A sequence from *River of No Return* (Otto Preminger 1954 US) has been much cited in relation to integration of meaning. It concerns Matt Calder (Robert Mitcham) and his son Mark (Tommy Rettig) helping engaged couple Harry Weston, a gambler (Rory Calhoun), and Kay Weston, a salon hall singer (Marilyn Monroe), when they lose control of their raft on the river near his farm. While the rescue is taking place, Kay's suitcase falls into the water and drifts down river. For Perkins, the disappearing case is symbolic: 'The loss of the bag is the first in a series of events which ... strip the heroine of the physical tokens of her former way of life' (1972: 129). The crucial point for Perkins is that 'the symbolism is so completely absorbed into the action' such that 'it may easily pass unnoticed' (128). This claim is different although related to a claim that Charles Barr makes, in a pioneering work on the evaluation of widescreen composition, that

---

by Leavis to capture a variety of aspects relating to the *living* quality of the work, for example, vividness, real-life responsiveness, and the organic aliveness created by interacting elements. These are also qualities which are valued in *Film as Film*.

[56] Bazin claims *Seven Men From Now* to be intelligent rather than intellectual (1985 [1957]: 170). This distinction helps illuminate an ideological reason for why Perkins advocated the form and films he did: he considers them to be, in spirit, democratic and egalitarian (see also Gibbs 2013: 186). They are not esoteric, and do not appeal to an elite or a 'club' requiring specialist cultural capital. The significance they promise is accessible in the ordinary lucidity of figurative drama. (A leftist case can also be made, and is commonly made, for more intellectual, esoteric or abstruse forms.)

the case itself may go unnoticed. He writes that 'the spectator is "free" to notice the bundle' and calls it a 'detail' which 'an alert spectator will notice' (1963: 11).

In fact, a relatively oblivious spectator would probably notice it, as it is far from a 'detail' in the scene. It is a notable, and noted, presence[57]. To begin with, the dropping and disappearance of the case are marked by musical expression. Harry picks Kay up, and she clings round his neck with her right arm, also holding a guitar and a shoe bag (containing her red high-heeled shoes), while the left arm picks up her bulky case. The strings and trombones are strenuously ascending on the soundtrack as he steps into the water (and moves towards the river bank and the camera). The trombones drop significantly in pitch and prominence as his knees buckle whereupon Kay instinctively reacts by dropping the case and throwing her left arm around his neck. At the exact moment the case drops, the music adjusts again as the violins and flutes begin playing a single high note; this tremolo accompanies the case as it floats rightwards off-screen and ends with a snapped flourish as it exits the frame[58]. The trombones become prominent once again as Harry moves forward towards the bank. The changes on the soundtrack precisely pocket the case's rush along the current and along the widescreen frame. The dialogue is even more pointed than the music. Just before the case disappears off-screen, Kay releases her left arm from Harry's neck and reaches for it while shouting 'My things!' (to which he exclaims 'Let it go!') (Fig. 3.22)

The case's departure is emphatic. How far the symbolic meaning is emphasised is a different question. Barr claims that a close-up of the departing case would point out that it is symbolically significant, and the

---

[57] I should offer the suggestion that Barr may be referring to later appearances of the case when it moves further into the distance. This is because he writes about the case in the 'background'. However, he does not discuss the case's striking earlier appearance in the action which affects its status during the later stages of the sequence. It is important to note at this point that much of the criticism from this period was written without the benefit of video or DVD playback. Accounts will have relied on seeing the film once or more in the cinema, and taking notes in those real-time screenings. (In some cases it is possible that the film may have been available for close viewing on a Steenbeck editing table.) Given this, the accounts are remarkably alert and sensitive, and although sometimes inaccurate in detail they often latch on to a crucial aesthetic issue.

[58] David Bordwell also refutes the claims for subtlety concerning the case's presentation. He writes that 'a chord sounds on the musical track' and he is probably referring to the change in the music (i.e. either to the dropping trombones or to the tremolo) (1985: 23).

film wisely avoids this more demonstrative option (11)[59]. It is not self-evidently clear, however, why a close-up would point out the significance because adopting a close-up does not necessarily equate to the act of pointing out significance. A close-up may be deployed for affective purposes, rather than purposes of designation; a close-up may also express a different significance, rather than express the same significance more emphatically. The stripping of the 'physical tokens' of Kay's former life is probably *less* apparent in a close-up than it is in a wider shot that shows the trajectory of the case as it horizontally rushes across, and out of, the frame, away from her, and then shows it, as the shot continues, drifting ever further away in the distance.

It can be reasonably argued that the case's symbolic meaning is not presented to pass unnoticed, or it is, at least, relatively available. Making claims about prominence, especially those relating to meaning, can be a slippery business because they are affected by, among other things, a viewer's predisposition. For example, the presence of meaning can vary on different viewings as perception re-orientates[60]. Nevertheless, Perkins appears to overstate the subtlety of the case's significance when he claims that the symbolism he attributes 'would seem an absurd and pretentious exercise in "reading-in"' (1972: 129). His more moderate claim, however, that the loss of the case '*could* [merely] be seen ... as a demonstration of the dangerous power of the current' is applicable (129; my emphasis). Or it could be seen as 'a demonstration of the dangerous power of the current' *at the same time* (and this would be in keeping with the overarching aesthetic thesis of *Film as Film*). However more or less apparent the significance of the case's departure is taken to be, it makes sense in the specific setting of the rushing river and as a natural consequence of the unfolding situation and action[61]. The merit of the sequence, therefore, is not necessarily only,

---

[59] He makes this claim within the context of an essay that is justifiably arguing for the merits made possible by the large CinemaScope frame. In particular, he shows that the apparent grandiosity of the widescreen is capable of subtle compositional relationships.

[60] In Perkins' interpretation of the case's disappearance, he adds that the process of stripping 'the heroine of the physical tokens of her former way of life ... parallels the character's moral development from fatalistic acceptance towards a degree of self-conscious decision' (1972: 129). This adjoining interpretative claim is more recessive because it is part of a larger pattern yet to unfold and can only be accessed retroactively. See also discussion of George M. Wilson's work in 3.7: 'Pattern'.

[61] Perkins writes with regard to the use of car headlights which become floodlights to theatricalise the chicken run in *Rebel Without a Cause* (Nicholas Ray 1955 US) that the achievement is to make 'the desirable look unavoidable' and 'to take what is available and make it meaningful' (1972: 84).

3.22–3.24  *River of No Return* (Twentieth Century Fox Film Corporation, 1954).

if at all, one of understatement. It is to particularise, concretise, and energise the meanings. The meanings present themselves from within a persuasively dynamic dramatic context. This suggests that a meaning can be relatively to the fore and still have meritorious qualities, for example, being ideally situated or vividly realised. Indeed, it may be the aptness of the dramatisation that gives the impression that the symbolism of the dropped case is more discrete than it actually is. It is perhaps worthwhile distinguishing

The aesthetic evaluation of film    179

between the indicated and the integrated. Some features of a film might be relatively prominent or pointed out (indicated) and still be tightly and effectively contained (integrated). Something can stand out in certain respects and, at the same time, in other respects, be settled in.

Kay's case is a crucial component of a dynamic continuous take that progresses through various stages. The shifting composition encourages vacillations in attention. My eye is drawn from the foreground to the background, towards the case and away from it; it reaches out to the case, clings on to it and lets it go (like Kay). I think that the sequence is less about the failure to notice the case or the failure to notice its significance, and more about this push and pull facilitated by the lateral movement of frame, object, and performers[62]. As Harry carries Kay and stumbles forward, he moves towards the right and as he does so the camera accommodates, bringing the case into shot again in the middle distance (Fig. 3.23). Although the couple are central and most prominent, the case is noticeable especially in the context of its recent loss: ah look, it has reappeared in the vicinity. Also, it has now opened, revealing her belongings – in particular, what appears to be the emerald evening dress that she wore earlier when she sang by the piano in the makeshift saloon – materially actualising, and poignantly specifying, the loss. Although the dress is discreetly shown – the green occupies a very small portion of the screen – it is magnified by the memory. (Attention to the case is not necessarily related to the amount of the screen it occupies.) Very soon, as they reach the bank, Matt once again enters the frame, and he draws them, and the eye, to the left against the direction of the current and the case. This is physically enacting the shift that takes place in the story as Kay is drawn from Harry to Matt. In Perkinsesque terms, this wider significance is 'contained' within the

---

[62] The section of the film that immediately precedes Harry and Kay arriving on the raft also prepares a viewer to be alert to activity taking place in the background of the shot. Matt is teaching Mark how to shoot, and this section too revolves around things in the distance: first a branch at which they aim, then smoke coming from the top of one hill, then, much further still, smoke from another hill. Mark then asks his father to turn when he spots something else in the far distance, barely visible, this time on the river. The concern is continued ironically. 'Can you make them out?', Matt asks his son who replies, 'It looks like a couple of men'. One of the men is, of course, Marilyn Monroe. These orientations are predisposing to the subsequent continuous take. This shows how one part of a film, while appearing to be occupied with its own distinct dramatic concerns and subject matter, can condition a viewer perceptually for a forthcoming part. (The final image of the continuous take, as the small figures of Kay and Mark are seen running towards the house, caps the compositional scheme of objects and people moving in the distance.)

immediate necessity of bringing the couple to safety, and is appropriately subdued at this early point in the story[63]. The three adults speak towards the left/centre of the frame, and at just the moment the action of the men shaking hands catches the eye, the case once again drifts off screen (right). As it disappears, Mark enters the shot (from the right) and fills the space in the composition – now four figures are evenly distributed across the frame – replacing the case as the newly important object of Kay's interest. She affectionately pulls the boy towards her and they both run off together. Consequently, the river is again more visible in the right hand side of the frame. When Matt moves rightwards across the foreground of the frame and Harry follows him, the case once again comes into shot although it is now much smaller because it is some way down the river in the distance, the figures are more dominating near the camera (waist-up rather than full), and Matt's purposeful walk draws the attention (Fig. 3.24). As they move towards the right, and the camera moves with them, the case moves to the left of the composition, against the grain of their movement and its own typically rightwards trajectory. It eventually disappears for the last time from the left hand side of the frame.

The relationship of the case to the figures is shifting throughout the stages of the shot. Speaking in terms of stages, however, risks making the compositional adjustments sound too marked and distinct (as does the analysis). The relationship of camera to soundtrack to figure to action to conversation to environment is deftly orchestrated so the shot proceeds, like the river, fluently and naturally. Indeed, the sequence has a number of aesthetic qualities: fluent movement, compositional agility, perceptual challenge, vivid articulation, concrete realisation, internal tension and dynamism, intelligent shape, and some subtlety of meaning (although the latter may not be primary)[64].

As well as being concerned with the prominence of formal device, shot content, and meaning, therefore, I think aesthetic evaluation *also* needs to be concerned with the difficult process of weighing the relative importance of qualities and criteria. It is arguable, for example, that despite the qualities of density, complexity, and ambiguity that Bazin claims for

---

[63] Indeed, this may be more subdued than the symbolism of the departing case. During a class on the sequence, one of my graduate students pointed out the subtle irony that although Harry looks to be carrying Kay 'over a threshold' (it evokes such an occasion), he is in fact carrying her away from their 'marriage' and towards a new relationship (with Matt). The urgent necessity of Harry's actions improves the insinuation of the irony.

[64] For more on the internal dynamism of this shot see 3.8: 'Relation'.

the bar sequence in *The Best Years of Our Lives*, the organisation of the frame is too posed, the positioning of the figures is too overt, and their interaction too laborious. Consequently, the qualities (of density, complexity, and ambiguity) are present, but too demonstrated, and compromised by the exaggeration. In addition, the depth of focus offered by the technique is too accentuated (worryingly close to *trompe-l'œil* kitsch), and too heavy and unwieldy (given the subject matter and concerns, and in the context of a procedural docu-drama which in many respects, other than compositionally, is relatively naturalistic). Perhaps a problem may be that the depth of focus is indeed offered as a technique, and is imposed rather than growing out of the material. It looks like the use of a technique – 'look this technique is being used' – rather than an expression that emerges out of a vision of the world or out of the film's world (out of its very being)[65]. Although the technique is used on many different occasions, and is not simply expedient, each time it is isolated. It forces an obvious visual depth rather than coming from a deep place: despite the visual depth provided by the technique, the technique itself is not deeply embedded, and therefore remains on the surface of the film.

Historically, film evaluation has wrestled with the question of whether elements are inappropriately obtrusive. Arnheim is concerned that if an element draws too much attention then it will 'sever' itself from the body of the work, and kill the organism (Dhir 2011: 98). How then might elements and techniques that are frequently deployed in films, which are not understated, for example those that are demonstrative, exaggerated, or simply protrude, be positively evaluated? Posed composition, overt positioning of figures, and laborious interaction are not in themselves a problem because some films render them ideal (although because they are common demerits, it is a particular challenge to turn them into merits)[66]. Nor is singular or uncharacteristic deployment necessarily a problem because films can advantageously break from their familiar patterns. In his essay on *The Shop Around the Corner*, Toles discusses a pronounced shot which closes the sequence concerning the termination of Kralik's employment (discussed in section 3.4, 'Choice and expectation'). It is one of few shots that stand out because the film is primarily self-effacing. The

---

[65] As distinct from the technique's integral place in *Citizen Kane*. For more on the importance of 'world' see 3.7: 'Pattern' and 3.8: 'Relation'.
[66] Celebrated meritorious examples would be *The Bitter Tears of Petra von Kant* (Rainer Werner Fassbinder 1972 West Germany), *Playtime* (Jacques Tati 1967 France), and *Ordet* (Carl Theodor Dreyer 1955 Denmark).

shot is a relatively artificial tableau that shows the shop workers, standing still like statues with their backs to the camera, watching Kralik exit the front door of the shop after his sacking (Fig. 3.25). In *The Best Years of Our Lives*, a film that frequently stages performers conspicuously, the shot would be less noteworthy. How well does the 'intensely theatrical device of the tableau' work in this context (2010: 9)? Toles writes that its explicitness might be continuous with the character of Vadas (Joseph Schildkraut), the one colleague who does not shed a tear for Kralik, and who adopts 'studied poses of theatricality', pretends regret and makes a 'showy, rhetorical farewell' (8–9). The difference is that Vadas always has an audience present in his mind whereas his colleagues are not performing their sadness. The sincerity of the 'group goodbye chastens and corrects Vadas's spurious theatricality without directly acknowledging it … and unself-consciously purifies it' (9). Consequently, this self-conscious shot provides an image of the unaffected; and although it appears unnatural in the stylistic scheme, in contrasting and cancelling Vadas' fakery, it expresses authenticity. According to Toles, it makes 'a form of visible artifice real', and becomes 'expressive of genuine loss' (9).

**3.25** *The Shop Around the Corner* (MGM, 1940).

Despite the image being asserted and conclusive, and gathering and channelling emotions, it does not simply or straightforwardly present the characters' sadness. As well as their sombre restraint, the viewpoint from behind them means that they are granted some sort of privacy because a viewer is not privy to facial expressions of sorrow. Furthermore, it conjoins their individual states into a ceremonial communion of which they are unaware. The unwitting ritualisation provides another layer of pathos in its encompassing perspective. A viewer could 'grasp the value of ... [their] togetherness' – the sense of their 'solidarity' – even if the group cannot (9). The populated nature of the shot also evokes the cosy company of the shop that contrasts to the isolation and anonymity of the street, of the world – somewhere out there – into which Kralik has now walked (9). The solidarity, though, because it is accidental and unknowing, is 'easily breakable' creating a fragility that counterbalances the solidity and stillness of the composition (9). Finally, and implicit in Toles's account, the break in the familiar form of the film reflects a break in the shop's routine. Indeed, the shot marks the end of a critical section of the film concerning Kralik's dismissal. It appears as the final *stage* of a momentous Act. However, rather than simply functioning as a reaction to, or a summarising formulation of, something already well understood, the marking encourages a viewer to catch up with the unhappy significance of an event that occurred quickly and unexpectedly[67]. All these aspects gnaw away at the shot's set arrangement, and its status as sentimental statement.

Even an instance in a film such as *Written on the Wind* (Douglas Sirk 1956 US) which is characteristically formally strident and gaudy may seem *too* obtrusive. One example is when Kyle Hadley (Robert Stack) meets his doctor (Edward Platt) in a drugstore and receives news that, because of a 'weakness', he will be unlikely to father children. Distraught at the thought of his sterility, the camera shows Kyle rising from his chair and walking out of the store as the extra-diegetic music crescendoes. The camera pulls back, bringing into view, by the drugstore entrance, a young boy vigorously riding on a rocking horse (Fig. 3.28). Kyle stares at the boy as he departs, and the boy gleefully stares back. In a short piece evaluating the traits of Hollywood melodrama, Wood discusses, and defends, what he calls this 'very loaded, obtrusive shot' (1998 [1974]: 24)[68]. For Wood,

---

[67] Pinpointing exactly at which point a feature occurs, rather than simply pointing out that it does occur, is important in an aesthetic evaluation.
[68] Wood mentions three contexts that help understand the shot. Firstly, he says it can be understood within its generic category of melodrama. This deals with extreme

the obtrusiveness is 'perhaps' justified in terms of 'density of meaning' (25). He writes: 'the boy represents the son [Kyle] has just learnt he will probably never have; second, the violent rocking-riding motion carries strong sexual overtones, and in [Kyle's] mind the idea of sterility is clearly not distinct from that of impotence; third, the child takes up the recurrent idea of the characters' yearning for lost innocence – and for the unreflecting spontaneity and vitality that went with it – a central theme in the film' (24–5). The Symbolic insistence of these meanings (for example, '*strong sexual overtones*') could be seen as part of the problem; however, it is all three taken together, and the 'density' accrued, rather than any meaning taken alone that Wood claims as the justification. Aside from the quality of 'density of meaning', a defence may also lie in the execution. Wood notes that 'uniting them in the frame', instead of cutting to the boy – as Kyle approaches the door, the boy is brought into the shot as the camera recedes – 'stress[es] the connection (both psychological and symbolic)' between them (24). It will be useful to see if there is more to the shot, however, because it is the *stressing* of this 'connection' that could also be regarded as a problem (for anyone struggling with the obtrusiveness).

A crucial feature of the scene is the suddenness with which the boy appears in front of Kyle. The boy has not hitherto appeared in the scene and seems to appear out of nowhere. The rocking horse is shown earlier, but could easily be missed. At the beginning of the scene, when the doctor entered the drugstore, the top of the rocking horse is in the lower foreground of the frame, with no one upon it. Despite the horse's presence, the doctor's passage into the drugstore is the most prominent activity, and the horse is insignificant street furniture associated with a drugstore. The film also distracts attention from it by simultaneously having two women greet the doctor in passing. (Their presence and address, in the context of the scene, implies the doctor's sexually attractive authority and potency.) When the rocking horse is shown with the boy upon it at the end of the scene, it appears to be closer to the drugstore. It blocks Kyle's passage and

emotions, reduces to essentials, and reveals 'fundamental human drives in the most intense way possible' (1998 [1974]: 24). Secondly, the director Douglas Sirk admired and collaborated with Bertolt Brecht. The moment is deliberately disruptive, in a Brechtian sense: the enclosed flow of the fiction is interrupted to be commented upon. The third context is German Expressionism, which also influenced Sirk. Here 'the central aim was the projection of emotional states by means of imagery' (24). Illuminating as these contexts are, and helpful if they suggest comparisons, they cannot form the core of an evaluation – and Wood does not suggest otherwise – because they also provide the contexts for moments of less interest and merit.

# The aesthetic evaluation of film

3.26–3.28  *Written on the Wind* (Universal International Pictures, 1956).

is something to get around. Nevertheless, its presence earlier, although fleeting, allows Kyle's experience to be understood as a transformation of a pre-existing environment without undermining the predominantly intrusive effect. Another significant factor in the presentation is that the boy, after appearing suddenly, is only on screen for approximately five seconds at which point Kyle moves around him and the scene ends. He bursts into the film and soon disappears. The obtrusive therefore actively services something eruptive.

The surprise when the boy comes into the shot is also created by a manipulation of spatial awareness. At the close of their conversation, the camera, filming from a place outside the door of the drugstore, looks to be in the space where the boy and the rocking horse turn out to be. Kyle's eye-line is also an important factor. When he gets up from his chair and walks towards the camera he is in shock; his eyes stare intensely into the near distance as if in a trance (Fig. 3.26). There is a shift in the direction of his gaze from (his) left to his right and then, as he reaches the step at the entrance to the drugstore, downwards (Fig. 3.27). In hindsight, when the boy comes into view, it is clear that Kyle had turned his gaze towards the boy. Before the reveal, however, his wide-eyed movements, shifting one way then the other, and then downcast, without exterior focus, seem only to express the intensification of brooding preoccupation. The same manner of gaze represents his self-absorption *and* his attention towards the boy while the continuous shot, which reveals the boy at a late stage, helps run them into each other. The boy on the horse is rendered a product of Kyle's consciousness because he materialises out of an expression that appears lost in thought. The occurrence is not severed from the drama as Arnheim fears because the protuberance is also a projection.

Part of the obtrusiveness is down to crudity which in this instance is a merit rather than a flaw because it is apt. One definition of crude is to be stark or blunt, and it is apt that the moment is flagrant and abrupt with nothing to soften the blow. The occurrence is suitably jolting in accord with Kyle's shocking news and his stunned reaction. Another definition refers to the natural or unrefined, like crude oil, and it is apt that the moment is not sophisticated or elegantly straightened out. The moment exists in some uncivilised, pre-conscious state and is in tune with the film's Freudian psychodrama about a dysfunctional family. The occurrence is an expressionistic condensation and distortion, the 'dream-work' of Kyle's disordered mind. As the boy pounds the horse, there is peculiar compression in the image that disturbingly includes intercourse, impotence, and self-abuse. These sexual connotations evoke a further definition which is to lack refinement or tact, like a crude joke, and in a film that charts the disintegration of old-fashioned, southern state good manners – as represented by Jasper Hadley (Robert Keith) the 'civilised' Texan patriarch – it is also apt that this is another moment which challenges that propriety.

The confusion of connotation means potency is complicated by indeterminacy (of meaning). The difficulty in separating and pinning down the connotations is exacerbated by being hastily confronted with the imagery. The effect is similar to another scene in the film that Wood understands as having a 'complex significance (a significance *felt*, perhaps, rather than consciously apprehended, as we might experience effects in music)' (25). Furthermore, if imagined outside of the sequence's concerns and Kyle's projection his movements look reasonably innocent. As Wood writes, 'The child's expression and actions are very precisely judged; we see him as enjoying himself, yet we also see how, to [Kyle], his smile appears malicious, taunting' (25). Similarly, a viewer may be led by the sexualised context to transform the sight, and thereby be implicated in the obtrusiveness. In summary, the moment is complicated and demanding, and it is far from straightforward despite being exceptionally prominent.

## 3.7 Pattern

Although the examination of local detail and moment-by-moment execution are essential to aesthetic evaluation, it is also important to look at a film as a whole. In order to make claims for the culmination of *All that Heaven Allows* (in 3.3: 'Convention'), a series of related scenes from across the film were examined. The merit of the part was illuminated by its place within an evolving pattern built around scenes set in the mill. A work's patterned arrangement of similar and corresponding parts and its *prevailing* characteristics, qualities, attributes, traits, and themes are particularly important in establishing its wholeness[69]. Aesthetic evaluation is interested

---

[69] Another holistic concern is structure. For example, are a film and its internal sections of the right duration; and how is material advantageously introduced and developed, or withheld and released, over its length? Kenneth Burke encourages responsiveness to the structuring, and the formal movement, of material across a work, to the production of 'crescendo, contrast, comparison, balance, repetition, disclosure, reversal, contraction, expansion, [and] magnification' (quoted in Booth 1975: 226).

in how the work 'deals with the problem of … [the] repeat': how it 'move[s] and spread[s] in a continuous and longer composition over the whole surface which is covered by the pattern' (J.W. Mackail quoted in Osborne 1955: 279).

A fine example of a holistic aesthetic evaluation, rather than one based on the close examination of a part, is Michele Piso's examination of *Marnie* (Alfred Hitchcock 1964 US). The film concerns Marnie (Tippi Hedren), a kleptomaniac who disguises her identity and steals from businesses. Her secret is discovered by Mark (Sean Connery) who becomes attached to her, and they marry. The film ends ostensibly revealing the traumatic underpinnings from her childhood that have determined her character and behaviour. At first, Piso establishes, at a general level, what she considers the concerns of the film, and shows how this focuses its form, warding off redundancy. In films that do not know what they are about form can flounder. While films might avoid point making, and pointing, they still need to be pointful. She calls the film, 'one of America's most rigorously beautiful studies of communal alienation and lost rapport' (2009 [1986]: 283). Rather than working through sequences, she offers an enormous range of distilled descriptions, a method that might appear cursory if they did not so vividly come together, like a jigsaw with hundreds of interlocking pieces, to reveal the big picture. She writes, for example, about 'domestic spaces … marred by violence and transgression: the bedroom where Marnie has nightmares, the deep-freeze kitchen where she is slapped by her mother, the living room where the child-Marnie murders the sailor, the boat bedroom where Mark … rapes her. Marnie's mother's home has a depressed, banal atmosphere; Mark's mansion is materially bloated, emotionally empty, the site of the father's inertia and Lil's frustrated desire … the aristocratic "home" is a showcase, a display, a façade' (284). In this way, Piso maps the film's physical world, and the pattern of action and motif across it. She also establishes the fundamental tenor, atmosphere, and feeling of its world by illuminating general characteristics of its appearance: for example, 'denaturalized purism', 'geometrics', 'cropped chasteness', 'angularity', 'austerity', and 'shallow surface[s]' (284).

It is a merit for a film to find ways of purposefully connecting seemingly disparate or disconnected elements across its running time, not only ones that are adjacent or simultaneous. Familiar figures and forms may become suffused with the mood of a film, or the identity of a character, or the style of a filmmaker. A comprehensive characterisation of a film is important for understanding, and hence evaluating, features and events within it.

For Piso, the film's artificial occurrences (such as the rear projections or exaggerated painterly sets), which some viewers find to be defective anomalies, are consistent. Rather than 'careless flaws', they are 'hollow fabrications ... defiantly airless inventions that underscore and condemn the unnatural quality of the film's depicted world' (284). Sometimes a feature that in one film may appear limited, in another film appears not only to fit in, but to be complexly integrated because of the developing patterns which inform it (and which it in turn develops).

The essay reveals the thoroughness with which the design of the film is imbued with significance. For example, *'Marnie* is an intricate design of barriers and enclosures, stressing a theme of secrecy' (286). Then there is a 'hostile penetration of the hidden and covert' which means different occasions in the film – theft, staring, interrogations, eavesdropping, and rape – meaningfully relate (286). This is in turn linked to the 'hostile clarity' which is achieved by 'planar lighting' and 'modern fluorescence' at the racetrack, the office, and the Rutland home, which limit Marnie's 'physical and psychological independence' and lead to humiliating exposure (285). As the essay continues, thematic subdivisions proliferate: economic circulation, possession, belonging, domination, desensitisation, denaturalisation, enclosure, secrecy, visibility, exposure, violation, and invasion. They are folded into each other thus avoiding a cluttered film juggling too many concerns. Each forms its own strand while informing and transforming the others. The strands are extensive, variegated, and nuanced. The symbolism is symbiotic, goes deep and wide, and this symbolic scheme finds its apotheosis when Marnie is raped by Mark on their honeymoon. It is the point where the sub-themes meet in a scene that is grave, disturbing, and morally challenging. For Piso, the scene is ethically justified when viewed from within these understandings[70].

Each detail of the rape sequence fits into the network that the film has organised and that Piso articulates. I think therefore the scene could be described accurately using the language that Piso uses to encapsulate other aspects of the film (and in the forthcoming description I have italicised the references to her language). Mark *controls* the conversations, speaking at her, in a montage showing the preceding evenings. He *stares* aggressively over his book into the *enclosure* of the bedroom barely restraining his

---

[70] This justification is implicit in the essay rather than explicitly stated. Piso's analysis provides worthwhile instruction for the aesthetic evaluation of ethically challenging occasions. Nevertheless, the scene might be objected to on other grounds, including aesthetic ones.

3.29  *Marnie* (Universal Pictures, Alfred J. Hitchcock Productions, Geoffrey Stanley, 1964).

sexual frustration. To be less *visible* she further *encloses* herself by shutting the door while explaining that the *light* bothers her. She asks if they may go home, and he is sarcastic about the pleasures of the trip. He storms through the door, *invades* her room, and she reiterates her dislike of the light. He slams the door and dismisses her concerns. She screams a high pitched 'No' and this rhymes with her response to a previous *violation* when the sailor gets far too close to her as a young girl. Mark rips off her clothes in frustration. She *freezes*. He apologises, and wraps his dressing gown around her, but his apology indicates no change in behaviour as his ostensibly chivalric protection allows him to move closer, *encircle* her (more *enclosure*), and take advantage. She remains *frozen* as he caresses her. There is a close-up of her *blankly staring* face, and *desensitised* she robotically tilts back onto the bed (Fig. 3.29). The *abstracting dehumanising* continues: the close-up of Mark's face which moves ever closer to his eyes *staring* harshly as he moves to *dominate* and *possess* her, breaking perhaps the most profound *boundary* and *barrier* of all, her face still *inert*, and then the pan to the *cold, metallic, geometric figure* of the porthole. The next morning she is lying face down in the swimming pool having attempted suicide. He implies it is not a genuine attempt, simply a 'cry for help'.

Piso values the character of Mark as an integral part of the bleak world that is presented. She does not value him because she likes him, or because he is an antidote to that bleak world (or Marnie's saviour).

Wood, in contrast, values Mark for being 'the one most in charge of situations, most completely master of himself and his environment, most decisive and active and purposive' (1989: 186). This mastery is of value, for Wood, because it carries 'great moral force' and 'embodies a powerful and mature life quality' (and as a consequence, the rape shows 'sexual tenderness') (186, 189). Alternative ways of reading and evaluating the film, based on different patterns, may well be available, including ones that justify Wood's point of view. As it stands, however, it is not clear from Wood's account of the film that it values Mark's mastery in the way that Wood does, and if it does why this would be meritorious in this context[71]. In contrast, Piso does give an account of how Mark's mastery may be understood, and valued, within an elaborate set of stylistic, thematic, and tonal patterns. Gibbs and Pye note that the illumination of pattern is important not only to reveal the aesthetic value of a film, but also to 'critical method': 'the degree to which [a critical argument] can identify significant patterns which give credence to the understanding of the part advanced ... [is a] major factor ... determining how persuasive it may be' (2005: 11).

Wood's own moral views appear to be presiding: he is valuing a masterly male character independently of the film and in advance. Sometimes sentimental attachment to a single element, for example, to a character or to an actor, obscures formal pattern. In a later essay, he returns to the film and accepts Mark is a more ambivalent figure than he had previously acknowledged, and that he has some flaws in his character (2002). Nonetheless, he still holds Mark as a sympathetic character in his *treatment* of Marnie (indeed, in his view, Mark provides a necessary and successful therapy). The interest of the claim is not simply whether this is correct or not, but the insistent *need* for it to be correct. For Wood, the merit of the film depends upon it. He claims that if one accepts an interpretation like Piso's (although he does not mention her account explicitly) then, for example, 'we read Marnie as simply choosing one prison over another' (2002: 392). It is not clear why this would constitute a failure of the film if it makes sense, and is insightful, within the patterns of the film (and

---

[71] Robin Wood's book *Hitchcock's Films* was a pioneering study of Hitchcock's films and of film evaluation, and it still contains, after decades of voluminous criticism on the director, penetrating and relevant discussion. Here I want to challenge one of his claims about *Marnie*, which I do not think is well substantiated, in order to illuminate a particular critical point, rather than wanting to invalidate the study's significant contribution to criticism.

the patterns of life). Once again, what constitutes a good conclusion, like what constitutes a *good* character, is apparently being asserted independently and in advance. 'We' might want to congratulate the film on its clear-eyed dramatisation of a dilemma; actually, it presents the sort of formal and thematic double bind that the literary New Critics might have admired. The evaluation of characters (or events) need not be based on whether a film elicits identification with them (or whether a viewer likes, sympathises, or empathises with them). Some films will require evaluation on this basis, but often the interest and merit of a character (or an event) will need to be judged by their suitability as a component of the film's complex. A film may invite an engagement with the film's world, and, through that, with the characters (and not vice-versa). Wood also claims that '[t]hose who can't accept Mark on any terms will, I'm afraid, have to abandon the film on the grounds of its sexual politics' (393). Yet, this depends on what is meant by 'accept'. One might 'accept' Mark, without being sympathetic to him, 'on the grounds' that he is a well-conceived and performed character – Sean Connery is *perfectly*, handsomely hard and cold – in a film that is painstakingly designed to explore 'sexual politics'[72]. One might even be sympathetic to him as a product of an ideology and culture (rather than for his treatment of Marnie). According to Tania Modleski, Piso exhibits an understanding of Mark as a man unable 'to free himself from the constraining ideology of his wealth' and 'from the authority and certainty it confers' (2005: 128; Piso 2009: 287). For Piso, the film presents a densely realised and penetrating perspective on social and sexual dynamics *of which Mark is a compelling part*.

According to Piso, the film deliberately masquerades as a psychological story, and this may mask another story about money, class, gender, and exploitation. The psychological story is about 'a woman who compensates for a traumatic past and need for her mother's love by stealing but is brought to a breakthrough by a man who helps her confront her past and unlock the repressed truth' (292). A viewer may be seduced with this redemptive, even romantic, psychological story with its 'revelation' of the repressed murder, and seduced, or mastered even, by the suave and charismatic Mark. There is another thread, however, that is less straightforwardly prominent in the storytelling: there is 'not the single trauma of the murdered sailor, but the several wounds of a mother and daughter oppressed by poverty and violated in prostitution and marital rape, of the

---

[72] For this to be true, the filmmakers need not have conceived the film from within the discourse of 'sexual politics'.

female body drawn into the categories of illegitimacy and frigidity and supposedly reconstituted in marriage' (293). This story is revealed by the formal patterns that Piso identifies. The temptation to mistake the identity of the film arguably has the merit of implicating a viewer in a (Hitchcockian) deception, thus reproducing the common experience of overlooking less apparent explanations. Indeed, in Piso's terms, that would make the film faithful to the Marxist argument which is that the underlying, or 'base', structural causes of problems, the fundamental and comprehensive explanatory patterns, are too often occluded by an investment in individualised instance as manifested, for example, in personal psychology (making the film structurally, as well as thematically, Marxist)[73]. Furthermore, this understanding answers some of the charges brought against *Marnie* – the psychology is too determined, the repressions and displacements too stark, the cure too neat and the 'revelation' trite – because the film is not relying on the psychological story alone.

Piso does not simply give an alternative reading of the film, she shows how the coexistence of the alternatives is part of the film's achievement. The socio-economic story enriches the psychological story. Her Marxist and feminist evaluation is also an aesthetic one because she believes the film has patterns that can reorient perception to reveal a better film[74]. In this respect her evaluation joins hands with the work of George M. Wilson who writes that 'factors that either appear on the screen or are implied

---

[73] This does not mean that Hitchcock consciously intended to make a Marxist film. This is similar to the point made about sexual politics in n. 73. See also 2.9: 'Intention, achievement, and skill'.
[74] Piso's essay is a good example of how ideological and ethical concerns, of film and critic, in this case specifically Marxist and feminist, are compatible with aesthetic evaluation. There are two things I wish to note here: one about external application of the critic's concerns and one about all-encompassing critique as distinct from criticism. Firstly, Piso allows the ideological concerns to inform and illuminate an understanding of the form of the film. These ideological concerns may well be constant concerns for her – and most critics have ongoing concerns, ideological or otherwise, dear to them – but the question is how far we perceive them to be relevant to an evaluation in any particular case. There is a balance to be maintained between the extrinsic and intrinsic, and it is a matter of judgement whether they seem imposed or germane. Secondly, her ideological concerns do not lead to the sort of ideological critique that would, for example, dismiss all Hollywood films as patriarchal and as serving the wishes of capitalism (which they may well be). In criticism, the political value of the film's form is judged on a case by case basis. In this case, *Marnie* is shown to be offering its *own* critique of economic and gender relationships. See the work of Andrew Britton (2009) for criticism that works in this vein.

but not shown in the film ... may be assigned a weight in the narration in such a way that the chief issues raised by the drama come to be modified, displaced, or otherwise reappraised ... when this counternarrative weighting is apprehended, the whole gestalt of the film often seems to shift' (1992: 10). Such patterns, however, may only be experienced in a 'fragmentary way', especially if they are 'subtly weighted', 'so the problem for a viewer ... is to locate a 'centred position' from which the oblique strands of narrational strategy can come together in a configuration that reorganizes his or her perception and comprehension of the fictional events' (11).

Wilson's most telling exemplification of this is his examination of *You Only Live Once* (Fritz Lang 1937 US). He makes the case that the film has greater structural complexity than had hitherto been acknowledged. Such an acknowledgement means that segments, such as the ending, that had seemed 'seriously flawed' can be seen in a more 'satisfactory light' (16). The plot concerns whether Eddie (Henry Fonda), an ex-con, has committed a bank heist. He is arrested for the heist and imprisoned once again. His devoted fiancée Joan (Sylvia Sidney) believes in his innocence. Wilson argues that there is a common reading of the film – he calls it the 'standard' reading – that shares Joan's belief. This standard reading takes the film to be dramatising a miscarriage of justice, and expectations are influenced by what looks to be its generic category: the 'social consciousness' film, especially prevalent in the 1930s, which told sombre stories of social hardship during the Great Depression. Another component of this standard reading is that the film explores the harsh workings of fate: given his disadvantaged place in society, Eddie cannot escape the social forces that inevitably lead to his demise. Wilson argues, however, that the film is not a socio-economic fable. It does not confirm whether Eddie is involved in the crime or not, and is about ambiguity, rather than an unequivocal injustice. The film shows the problem of holding a single perspective on the action.

According to Wilson, the film contains segments which taken narrowly could mean one thing, but when seen within the wider context come to mean another. Firstly, there is the robbery itself which suggests, without confirming, Eddie's guilt. Immediately prior to it, Eddie is sacked from his job; frustrated and violent, he announces that his only option now is to return to crime. His hat, with the embossed initials E.T. (Eddie Taylor), is shown in the car, as is what appears to be his suitcase that Joan had gifted him earlier in the film. A pair of eyes stare out, through the back window of the car, and look sideways in a manner repeated twice after the robbery – first in Eddie's prison interview and then just before he escapes from his cell – and therefore seem to implicate him. A viewer and the police are led to believe that Eddie is guilty. It is possible, *however*, that his criminal associate Monk (Walter De Palma) is responsible. Eddie had been meeting with him earlier and Monk had easy access to his hat, and perhaps his case. Indeed, much later in the film, the police find the armoured truck with Monk's drowned body. At this point, they conclude that Eddie is innocent. It could be, *however*, that both were involved in the crime. Torrential rain, gas (and gas masks), and selective camera angles all obscure the truth. A viewer only hears, rather than sees, the armoured truck career off the road in the dreadful weather. Eddie might well have escaped from it (19–20).

Wilson analyses two other sequences that reveal that the film is concerned to expose the ambiguity of facts, to highlight the difficulties of seeing clearly, and to mock the way people make 'brusque pronouncements' in the face of circumstantial evidence (21). The first is after Eddie has been sacked from his job just prior to the robbery being committed. It starts with a shot of a bedside table showing Eddie's initialled hat. The camera then pans leftwards to show a picture of his fiancée Joan. It continues panning to a bed on top of which Monk is lying despite the film leading a viewer to think, after showing the hat and the photograph of Joan, that it would be Eddie. There is then a cut to a more expansive shot of the room which shows Eddie standing looking out of the window (Figs 3.30–3.33). This, according to Wilson, is exactly the pattern of inference that may be associated with the robbery: it looks as if it will be Eddie, but it turns out to be Monk. However, both might be present, with Eddie ... looking out of a back window. A similar pattern is repeated in a sequence during his trial. First, the film shows a close-up of a newspaper announcing his innocence, and so it appears that he has been acquitted. The camera then pans left to show another front page headlining that the jury is deadlocked. Finally, when the film cuts back to a broader perspective, it now includes a front page announcing the guilty verdict. The film shows that all three front pages have been prepared, each one announcing a different possible result of the trial. At first, Eddie is definitely one thing, then definitely another, but then it appears that all options are possible. All three sequences – robbery, bedroom, newspapers – intelligently *rhyme* with each other, rhyme being a 'subsidiary device of patterning' (Osborne 1955: 279). Recognising the rhyme is not straightforward because the sequences are separated and different in kind – the rhyming is 'imperfect' in the poetic sense – but once recognised each instance is given a meaning, weight, and relevance they do not have alone.

3.30–3.33   *You Only Live Once* (Walter Wanger Productions, 1937).

# The aesthetic evaluation of film

3.30–3.33 (Continued)

Wilson's account claims *You Only Live Once* implicates a viewer by 'leading [their] perception ... astray', so that the concerns are not simply comprehended, but experienced (1992: 38). For Wilson, the film is about the failure of characters 'to grasp the underlying significance of what they see', but crucially, this theme is only revealed when viewers of the film grasp the underlying significance of what *they* see (37). Wilson provides a host of examples of characters appearing in frames, and understood within the standard reading of the film these would be images of entrapment, or *framing* (by the law, or by fate). When re-orientated, however, to the film's more subtle concern of 'our perception of other human beings ... schematized into a crude mode of picturing them', these more obvious meanings are finessed (23). Characters have a duck-rabbit status making them difficult to read, which makes for a perceptually more mysterious film: is Eddie an innocent victim or is he fundamentally weak and dishonest (or both); does Joan have a privileged insight into Eddie or does her loving devotion render her dangerously blind (or both) (28–9). The standard reading of the ending, where Eddie, escaping with Joan, is shot by the police, has also encouraged the judgement that it is a 'disastrously maudlin lapse' (16). The film is thought to be soft-soaping a viewer with some form of redemption and release: the forest is miraculously brightened by heavenly rays of light, there is an angelic choir on the soundtrack, and Father Dolan's voice announces that Eddie is free. Alternatively, Wilson's essay shows that, if suitably orientated, a pattern can be observed of characters projecting their vision sentimentally to distort the truth. Eddie's 'dying vision', therefore, may be 'the ultimate misperception that culminates the vast chain of misperceptions' (36). Wilson writes that, '[Eddie's vision] may be genuine or it may be horribly false, but we surely cannot accept without question a heavenly promise of life after death in a film whose title is, after all, *You Only Live Once*' (37). A film that appeared at first sight, and for many years (until Wilson's essay), to be conventionally about fate and destiny becomes a fine-grained exploration of perception and misperception, pictures and picturing, and failures of vision (17). Wilson draws attention to the 'subtly weighted patterns' that lead away from taking the film at first appearances[75].

---

[75] Patterns need not be subtly recessive, as in the Wilson example, to be worthwhile. They may be advantageously foregrounded. Patterns, however, are not in themselves of merit: they may be, for example, too regimented or irrelevantly decorative.

## 3.8 Relation

Relation is the most fundamental concern of aesthetic evaluation (and pattern is a type of relation). How do the internal parts of a film satisfactorily relate: for example, character, performer, dramatic action, and setting; one character, or performer, to another; one scene to another; a shot to the one before it and the one after, or to one much earlier; the components of a shot; the image to the sound; the style, tone, pace or rhythm to the subject matter? How does a feature, for example a scene, contribute to the overall structure; and in what way is its appearance now, at just this point in the layout, advantageous (or not)? How does it beneficially affect what went before, and what is yet to come; would it have benefited from coming earlier or later? The quality of transitions is of associated importance: how does a film move from one shot to another (cut, fade, dissolve), one place to another, one person to another, or one tone to another. So much of the aesthetic evaluation of film is the appraisal of how elements relate[76]. To recognise this is not to prescribe a particular type of relationship – although some critics like Perkins do – because, as in life, there are many types of successful relationship. Furthermore, although it is the particular arrangement of a film's features that are of primary concern, this does not entail severing it from other films or the world outside; aesthetic evaluations also assess a film's relationship with external content, category, and convention.

I return to Perkins' *Film as Film* as the pioneering intervention on the topic of internal rapport. In the book, he writes that the 'understanding and judgement of a movie … will depend largely on the attempt to comprehend the nature and assess the quality of its created relationships' (1972: 118). Perkins emphasises that one cannot take any element of technique, or feature of the medium, for example editing, and separate it from other elements, for example, the movement of the actors, or the camera, or the setting, or the lighting because 'each of them derives its value from its relationship with the others' (23). Consequently, isolated components should never form the basis of an evaluation. The same applies to the

---

[76] Even something as apparently discrete as a performer's successful delivery of a line is based on relation: the relationship between each of the words (pace, rhythm, flow) *and* the relationship between the words and the manner in which they are said (intonation, quality, tone) *and* the relationship between their delivery and other aspects of the performer's behaviour and being (position, movement, posture, gesture, expression).

contents of the drama. Perkins would therefore not necessarily harshly judge crude or overused features, which might in themselves be banal, clichéd, or stereotypical. Indeed, he thinks that films of merit, especially those in popular cinemas, such as Hollywood, do contain such infelicities. Part of their achievement is to create qualities and significance out of the organisation of unprepossessing elements. A more moderate example would be a feature that is unimpressive or unexceptional taken alone, but is ideal for the fictional environment within which it becomes notable. Equally, components, for example subject matter, which are regarded as intelligent, worthwhile, emotionally affecting, ethically principled, politically relevant, or simply interesting should not automatically receive approval in an aesthetic evaluation. Perkins does not evaluate by way of criteria that frequently lead to films receiving acclaim in cultural discourse (such as in newspaper reviews): for example, characters or scenarios 'the viewer can relate to', exciting plots, sophisticated dialogue, beautiful imagery, sociological and cultural relevance, or realistic portrayal. The independent value of these features is not decisive and may be deleterious. Throughout the book, using words such as synthesis, interaction, and interrelationship, the principle is continuously affirmed.

Perkins celebrates those films whose elements are integrated as well as interrelated, and harmonised to result in a coherent whole. His initial claim for the importance of coherence as an evaluative criterion is based in his understanding of the medium. He proposes that the best fiction films will combine the medium's recording aspects (emphasised by theorists such as Bazin) with its creative aspects (emphasised by theorists such as Arnheim), 'photographic realism' together with 'dramatic illusion', and films that push to either extreme will be imbalanced (61). However, Perkins' advocacy of coherence is not only, if at all, medium dependent; this is unsurprising given that philosophers of criticism attending to other arts, such as Monroe Beardsley, have also esteemed the criterion. He also understands coherence as 'the prerequisite of *contained* significance' (as discussed in section 3.6: 'Prominence') (117). He goes on to add that '[t]he meanings which are contained most securely ... are those formed at the deepest level of interrelation and synthesis' (117). This is not only to value subtlety. I think Perkins desires this for a more fundamental aesthetic reason: he is interested to see how eloquently films can express themselves by *using their formal arrangements*. In addition, the more a film locks in its meanings, then the more perceptually and cognitively stimulating it will be for an aesthetically oriented viewer to release them.

Furthermore, Perkins celebrates films where the formal elements, not only meaning and significance, fit and fuse, tightly and productively. (Perceptual and cognitive stimulation is again an important reason because an aesthetically oriented viewer will be aroused by registering the multiple connections.) If the elements of the organism do not grow strongly together, performances will look bereft, characters unmotivated, events contrived or opportunistic, and so on. An unsecured individual element might be of merit, but the interest is likely to be momentary or isolated. When enmeshed, the element will feel essential and inextricable, and will benefit from the film's lifeblood.

For Perkins, if techniques and features are not incongruous, or intrusively over-asserting themselves, or inorganically and expediently extracted from elsewhere, or opportunistically endeavouring to achieve a local effect at the expense of the whole, then the film will create an integrated world. By showing how a whole range of aspects of *Marnie* coherently enmeshed, Piso revealed it to have such a world. The film is not only a linear entity, a progression of events in a narrative; it has dimensionality, and this is bestowed upon it by the multi-directional interconnectedness. Richard Rushton understands Bazin's desire for realism as a desire for films to present an authentic sense of the existence of *a* world rather than a representation of *the* world, or for verisimilitude (2011). Sometimes a film creates a world so internalised that it *appears* to exist, and proceed, without recourse to its viewer (and that is a fine achievement too in a medium that is necessarily displaying). Rushton's discussion derives from Michael Fried, which is in turn derived from Denis Diderot, who contrasts this mode of absorption with a mode of theatricality (71–8; see also Klevan 2000: 53–7). In real life, theatricality carried negative connotations for Diderot. Theatrical people are trying to attract attention and impress, and people, like art, should act without the need for an audience. In fact, many of the films that Bazin praised, such as those made by Orson Welles and William Wyler, show high degrees of theatricality as well as absorption, and ultimately, an evaluation would assess in what ways a film's inward and outward looking directions beneficially relate[77].

---

[77] An example of when the outward overrides the inward in a film is when, during a conversation, one character says things to another character that they would obviously know and not need to hear (in the fictional world). The film is using the conversation as merely a vehicle to inform a viewer.

Perkins believes a viewer should not 'observe ... a disproportion between the effect produced and the means employed to produce it' (1972: 87). Means and effect should be in a balanced and proportional relationship. He explains that if he says little (in *Film as Film*) about 'traditional qualities' such as 'inventiveness, wit and economy' or about 'traditional failings' such as 'vacuity, sentimentality or pretension' it is not because he thinks them unimportant, but because he sees them as by-products of relational balance and imbalance (132). He continues:

> What, after all, is sentimentality, if not a failure of emphasis, a disproportion between pathos asserted (in music, say, or image or gesture) and pathos achieved, in the action? What is pretension other than an unwarranted claim to significance, meaning insecurely attached to matter? And what [is] inventiveness, but the ability to create the most telling relationships within the given material? (132)

Beardsley similarly believes that 'attitude' and 'situation' need to be in proportion: the situation should warrant the attitude and not 'fall ... short of what seems fitting' within the context (1970: 102). A lack of proportion between attitude and situation may, for example, result in an inflated monumentality. David Thomson refers to the late work of David Lean: '*Lawrence* [*of Arabia*][1962 UK/US], [*Doctor*] *Zhivago* [1965 US/Italy/UK], and *Ryan's Daughter* [1970 UK] ... seem to me to be examples of size and 'the visual' eclipsing sense' (1995 [1975]: 428). Manny Farber labelled films that he considered guilty of stylistic inflation 'white elephant art', examples of which are the early films of director François Truffaut who fills 'every pore of a work with glinting, darting Style and creative Vivacity' (1998 [1962]: 140)[78]. If style outweighs content then a film may end up being decorative, ornamental, embellished, ostentatious, or pictorial[79]. The films that Thomson and Farber cite are not in their eyes sufficiently economical: they do not achieve an orderly interplay between their parts and they are,

---

[78] Form and subject matter may also contradict. Ian Cameron not only accuses *The Guns of Navarone* (J. Lee Thompson 1961 US) of didacticism when it proclaims an anti-war message in dialogue meditations, but of hypocrisy when it then presents war, in its action sequences, as 'enjoyable' (Gibbs 2013: 129).

[79] These were core critical words for the *Movie* group. See Gibbs (2013) for a full account of the history. One might want to argue over whether a film is, for example, pictorial or ostentatious. The style of director Max Ophüls was once regarded as decorative 'window-dressing' and later became the exemplar of form-content fusion. Alternatively, these properties might be valued for other aesthetic reasons. Nevertheless, the relationship between form and content is an inescapable concern for the aesthetic evaluation of film.

The aesthetic evaluation of film    203

as a consequence, inefficient, failing to avoid unnecessary waste. Economy, like balance and proportion, has traditionally been a highly valued criterion in aesthetic evaluation. A film, like most artworks, is already, necessarily, a condensation and it requires that material is successfully concentrated (even in a film with a lengthy running time). J. Middleton Murry emphasises the art of 'crystallization', and this would apply not only to imagery or images, but also to scenarios, stories, situations, scenes, actions, and gestures (1965 [1922]: 80). Economy leads to qualities of precision, density, trenchancy, richness, and comprehensiveness, the 'power to discern [the general] in the particular, and to make the particular a symbol of [the general]' (84). It guards against exaggeration, dilution, and pointless accumulation[80].

One of the reasons Bazin lauds continuous takes and deep focus compositions is that they bestow on the image complex relational schemes that can produce an 'internal dynamism' (1997b [1947]: 234). The continuous take in *River of No Return*, discussed in section 3.6, contains many currents and crosscurrents, literally and metaphorically. The shot begins with a rope, raft, river, and the line of the bank all horizontally congruent with the slim CinemaScope shape. Any inert neatness in the correspondences is offset by Matt, and his horse, pulling a rope (attached to the raft) against the grain of the current. The struggle appears as a tug of war across the frame[81]. Compositional parallels are continuous with antagonistic movements in the action. The shot has a number of changes in direction, by camera and figures, mostly in relation to the current of the river, that create strain and friction. Harry cuts across the current while carrying Kay, and comes towards the camera, while the dropped case travels along the current, and horizontally along the widescreen. (Kay's posture, because she is being carried, brings her more in line with river and frame, as does her outstretched arm reaching for the dropped case.) When they reach the bank, Matt makes them turn towards the left of the frame, and soon after Mark and Kay head off towards the right. As the case finally drifts off to the left of the screen, and the river too disappears, the camera swivels round in a clockwise direction to follow Matt and Harry as they walk up the bank. Harry is led towards the farmhouse by Matt, against the direction he ultimately wants to go in and was going

---

[80] Worthwhile though the appreciation of economy is, it should not mask achievements arising from looser forms, for example, those in *Boudu* or *Vivre sa vie* (which is discussed below).

[81] Note how this evaluation, as well as being derived from compositional relationships, is also medium oriented by drawing attention to an effective use of the widescreen technology.

(on the raft, to find gold, downriver). The continuous take culminates with Matt and Harry turning inland towards the house where their direction of travel falls into line with Kay and Mark who are running eagerly in the distance in front of them. They all head in the same direction, but away from the river; and during the approximately two-minute shot the camera has gradually moved around 180 degrees to face away from it. Yet, even though the river has visually disappeared, the sound of the rushing water keeps it a salient presence – behind them. The sound of the river allows a viewer to imagine the case still being carried away, and so there is one more tension: between the case being pulled *down* the river in one direction and Kay running *up* to the farmhouse in the opposite direction.

Bazin also hails the currents and energies (included those that are blocked), the attractions and repulsions, that are created within the dramatic space, and more specifically within an image. He gives an example of a shot, which is also one short, whole scene, from *Citizen Kane*. In the extreme foreground, a glass with a spoon in it, and a medicine bottle loom large upon a bedside table; in the less extreme foreground, by the table, Susan Alexander (Dorothy Comingore), Kane's wife, is a black shadow, lying in bed, breathing stertorously. In the background, Kane (Orson Welles) and servant are trying to enter the room, insistently banging on a closed door. (The middle ground is almost non-existent because of a foreshortening.) For some time – twenty seconds from the first knock – the sound of Susan's breathing continues in the foreground while the sound of Kane's knocking, banging, and struggling with the door continues in the background (Fig. 3.34). Bazin claims that the image is stretched between foreground and background. When Kane eventually enters the room, and comes to the bed in the foreground, the 'tension … dissolves' (234).

There is even more in the shot to support Bazin's appreciation. When Kane initially bursts through the door, he stays at the back of the frame, stopped in his tracks; his momentum and energy are momentarily halted, and the quietness is stark after his noisy efforts to intrude. Kane then moves from the light at the back of the shot, produced by the opened door, towards the darkness that envelops Susan. Although his face is lit, his dark suit conjoins with her shadow; and the *movement* into the darkness continues as he kneels at the bed and the image starts to fade slowly[82] (Fig. 3.35). The fade stalls for just a second – again a slight

---

[82] Before the fade, he raises Susan's head, which remains shrouded in darkness, and instructs the servant to get the doctor.

# The aesthetic evaluation of film

**3.34–3.35** *Citizen Kane* (RKO Radio Productions, Mercury Productions, 1941).

retardation – that occasions a gloomy and pitiful moment of stasis as he says 'Susan' before the image then extinguishes. The scene comes and goes more quickly than expected, snuffed out before it has had time to come to life. It began by slowly emerging out of darkness, as if brought into being, if not to life, by Susan's strained heavy breathing, and it remains in a fragile state of low energy, for its perilously short existence[83]. Susan may not be physically dead, but there is nowhere for the scene, or for them, to go. The characters' collapse in the narrative is matched by the premature collapse of the image. Through the combination of frame, figure, space, light, and sound, the shot/scene manages to channel and impede. As well as the precisely regulated contribution of individual features, such as the lighting, the mood of deflation and decline is created by excellent *timing*. In assessing relation, aesthetic evaluation seeks to ascertain how well elements move *in time* together *over time*. Both the shots in *River of No Return* and *Citizen Kane* also have a rhythm: they both use movement, duration and accent to give them a pulse and a flow. While not needing to be tightly regulated or overtly musical, the achievement of a rhythm within shots and between them is an important part of the art of film direction[84].

Perkins writes that 'attention must be paid to the whole content of shot, sequence and film. *The extent to which a movie rewards this complete attention is an index of its achievement*' (1972: 79; my emphasis). This is why, reiterating a point, close reading is essential to aesthetic evaluation because it endeavours to reflect and transcribe this 'complete attention' in order to articulate the achievement. A film that is exemplary in rewarding this 'complete attention', and is the object of repeated close study for Perkins, is *Letter from an Unknown Woman*. It concerns a young girl, Lisa (Joan Fontaine), who falls in love with a pianist, Stefan Brand (Louis Jourdan), but her love is complicatedly unrequited. Two of his essays on the film are pinnacles – and not only in Film Studies – of aesthetic evaluation rooted in close reading. The first is a long, meticulous piece on a short scene that is a test case for Perkins because the scene is marginal

---

[83] 48 seconds to be exact.

[84] Situations of slow or minimal movement also require evaluations of their timing and rhythm. There is a fine tradition of restraining movement in film. See Klevan (2000). See also the scholarship around 'Slow Cinema', for example, de Luca and Jorge (2016). On rhythm see Yvette Bíro's study *Turbulence and Flow in Film: The Rhythmic Design* (2008).

The aesthetic evaluation of film 207

(1982)[85]. It is one of the few scenes in the film not to be set in a fictional Vienna (it is set in Linz) and it is stylistically and tonally distinct. It also appears, unlike so many of the other remarkable scenes, 'effective without being astonishing' (61). For an aesthetic evaluation, an apparently inconsistent feature compels a judgement about whether it is reconcilable. What Perkins shows is that despite being relatively modest, the scene's internal elements are intricately unified. More importantly, despite being uncharacteristic, it ties into the patterns and themes of the rest of the film. The scene works to provide a reverse perspective, or a photographic negative. Matters of destiny, freedom, fantasy, love, marriage, independence, society, and gender that are elsewhere presented with an intensity that is sometimes grave take on a semi-comic form in the Linz sequence. Yet, they are enriched and even crystallised. By the end of his essay, the scene is shown to be an essential part of the film's scheme, while not losing its status as peripheral and odd.

In his companion essay, Perkins considers that *Letter from an Unknown Woman* has a number of inconsistent features that are nonetheless made to cohere, and beguilingly. The film is narrated by Lisa by way of a letter written at the end of her life, now being read by Stefan, and this results in moments that defy 'narrative logic' (2000: 42). Perkins claims the reason for this is 'to ensure that we cannot come to feel that there is a real world within the fiction where Lisa's writing of the letter can merge with Stefan's reading. Their coming together occurs only in and through the artifice of the film' (42). For example, Lisa works in a dress shop, Madame Spitzer's, that is also surreptitiously and informally an escort agency. Lisa is modelling a dress and an elderly army officer moves over to Madame Spitzer to inquire about her availability. Madame Spitzer explains, 'she is not like the others', and always goes 'straight home'. The film emphasises that Lisa would be highly unlikely to hear Madame Spitzer's words at this point: Lisa is occupied with her modelling for an elderly woman, presumably the officer's wife, who similarly must not hear the illicit inquiry; the camera follows the officer as he moves towards Madame Spitzer, taking Lisa out of shot, and he directs his question in the opposite direction from Lisa, quietly over a handrail; finally, Madame Spitzer replies in a collected and dispassionate manner while taking care not to break her clerical activity (Fig. 3.36). As Perkins writes, 'the words [are] … conspicuously withheld

---

[85] An essay all of its own would be required to do justice to the moment-by-moment intricacy of Perkins' analysis of the formal arrangement of the scene. I attempt here only to encapsulate its evaluative purpose.

3.36  *Letter from an Unknown Woman* (Rampart Productions, 1948).

from [Lisa]' (43). Nevertheless, as the film dissolves to show the shop workers departing into a snowy street, Lisa's voice comes on the soundtrack 'Madame Spitzer spoke the truth. I was not like the others … '. His evaluative claim for this moment is that '[b]oldness is balanced with delicacy in the achievement of this impossible continuity' (43).

The moment is 'bold' because the film has 'conspicuously' prepared the ground for the impossibility. At the same time, it has 'delicacy' because the rupture in the fictional reality is conjoined with a smooth verbal continuity: Lisa's words follow almost immediately after Madame Spitzer's statement on the soundtrack as if she were responding directly to her. In general, her narration in the film operates like a to-the-moment voiceover and this contrasts to the original short novella where it is provided by a woman on the verge of collapse at the end of her life. Therefore, her words in this instance are part of a narration that may well be incredible, but operate consistently, and pertinently, in tone and purpose, to give the sense of Lisa 'seeing the past now as Stefan reads about it, and offering her response to its sights and statements' (43). In addition, her words, despite the aural continuity, are 'subtly' positioned 'beyond any real time and place' (43). They come after the dissolve at a later time (end of the day) and at a different location (outside rather than inside the shop). They are removed to become a traditional form of omniscient commentary that further offsets the impossibility (without neutralising it). The merit is not that the impossibility is cleverly masked, but that it is 'conspicuously' emphasised *and* faultlessly incorporated.

Throughout the essay, Perkins shows how *Letter from an Unknown Woman* defies narrative logic and is yet one of the most securely unified of films. 'No rational time-scale or system of subjectivities holds the key elements in harmony' and yet it 'arrive[s] at a persuasive form' (41). This means that the film 'arrive[s] at order and comprehensibility without falling into an impoverishing neatness' (41). What he and others admire in the film is the way that its different 'subjectivities' or points of view – for example, old Lisa, young Lisa, Stefan, Ophüls, the film – are compatibly and compactly folded together while maintaining their differences[86]. Coherence alone in a work is never enough because it can result merely in lazy conformity or stale repetition arising, perhaps, from a restricted palette. Coherence should not equate to uniformity. Weak films are as likely to be strongly coherent, but with limited merits, as they are to be without clear design. As Meyer Schapiro writes, in one of the finest essays on the topic of coherence, 'orders' can be 'dull', 'banal' and 'pedestrian', and 'incompleteness and inconsistency' might be signs of 'serious and daring' works (1966: 3, 5)[87]. Some 'orders', while appearing satisfactorily coherent, are without distinction because they are straightforwardly inherited from period styles (10). Even an individual style, while its features speak together with a unanimous voice, may be more consistent than capable. Wood writes that '[the] notion of coherence is only meaningful in conjunction with concepts like "complexity," "density," "inner tensions"; it can never be an absolute criterion' (2006: 28). Indeed, this is instructive because it is often the particular 'conjunction' or interaction of aesthetic qualities and/or criteria that needs to be assessed. Therefore, it is not only the relationship between formal elements that is under scrutiny, but also the relationship between qualities and/or criteria (coherence *and* density *and* inner tension). For example, the sequence from *Written on the Wind* is crude and obtrusive, but it is also precise (in terms of performance and

---

[86] This perspectival layering occurs within individual shots. See Wilson (1992: 103–8) and Perez (1998: 75–8).

[87] By 'orders', Schapiro is referring to 'the arrangement or disposition of people or things in relation to each other according to a particular sequence, pattern, or method' (Pearsall 1998).

camera perspective) *and* apt (in accord with the film's world and narrative) *and* complex (in its significance). It is the peculiar interaction of qualities that constitute the merit[88].

In *Film as Film*, Perkins criticises coherent oppositions such as palaces/slums or battlefields/stock markets because they are basic binaries. They may understandably be part of an 'initial scheme', but they will need to be 'refined by the pattern of detail built over and around them' (1972: 119). He says that relationships should 'complicate' as well as 'clarify', and that the 'formal disciplines of balance and coherence embrace the effort to maintain the various elements in productive tension and neither to push them into symmetrical alignment (repetition) nor to let them fall into blank contradiction' (119–20). His essay on the logical illogicality of *Letter* is his most developed and meticulous appreciation of the tensions within unity. He writes: 'Ophüls unites precision of form with openness to possibility rather than making it serve the definition of a thesis' (2000: 45).

One of the things to learn from Perkins' essay is that there are many orders within a film – for example, narrative, dramatic, syntactical, spatial, graphic, aural, and tonal – cooperating, counteracting, counterpointing, compensating, and perhaps contradicting. There can be a 'pressure on a critic', especially when attending to a work which is for the most part admired, to find persuasive explanations for a genuine deficiency or a damaging incoherence: to fit them into a 'coherent interpretation' (Radford and Minogue 1981: 36). As many examples in this part of the book have shown, however, certain important orders and patterns may not be immediately recognisable. Something may seem ill-fitting, and turn out to have surprising consonance. There are questions of how long to trust the work, and how long to wait to see if deviant features can be brought into the fold.

Despite the logical breaches that Perkins observes in *Letter from an Unknown Woman*, its elements lock together, and it is formally all of a piece. Adrian Martin asks about those works that appear radically to repudiate the sort of coherence lauded by Perkins especially those that disrupt the contained integrity of their fictional world (2014). He suggests *Vivre sa vie* (Jean-Luc Godard 1962 France) as a notable achievement in this vein. The challenges presented by the film are also usefully discussed

---

[88] As previously noted, weighing criteria is an associated concern: for example, in *The Best Years of Our Lives*' sequence does the demonstration (of technique) outweigh the complexity and density?

## The aesthetic evaluation of film 211

in a round-table discussion held by the *Movie* critics (Editors of *Movie* 1963)[89]. With the exception of Paul Mayersberg, all of the contributors to the discussion, including Perkins, are unhappy with the film. They focus on the first scene of the film where Nana (Anna Karina) and her estranged boyfriend Paul (André S. Labarthe) converse while at a bar in a cafe. The most notable feature of the sequence is that the camera films Nana and Paul from behind such that their faces are largely hidden from view as they speak. This registers as a striking denial because the sequence is over four minutes long, and it greatly troubled the *Movie* critics[90].

I do not share the unhappiness, so in the spirit of the original round-table discussion, and as a way of dramatising the evaluative process (as Part III and the book come to conclusion), I will list each of the charges against the scene, and respond accordingly in order to suggest alternative forms of relational merit:

(1) *Charge*: Hiding the characters' faces in the first scene of the film is wrong because a viewer has not yet had the chance to see them. It is irritating to prevent a viewer from knowing what they look like[91] (Fig. 3.37).

*Defence*: The question is whether there is rhyme or reason in the scene's perversity. *Access* to Nana, in a range of senses, is going to be an important concern for the film, and this is signalled in the first scene. Because the first scene of a film is just when a viewer hopes to be invited in, it might be a good time to hold them off. Rather than straightforwardly identifying Nana, or encouraging an identification with her, the scene is concerned with, and for, her identity. The assertion of distance and its repellent quality are also appropriate for a scene about two former lovers who are irreconcilable, and for a film about depersonalisation.

This is not, as implied in the charge, the first sighting of Nana; the film has given ample time to see her. This is because the credit sequence has already shown her head, albeit shadowed, in different close-ups, facing to the left, to the front and then to the right, as if she is being scientifically observed, criminally catalogued or studied for a sculptural bust

---

[89] Their discussion is a fascinating model of a format that is too rare: a published conversation between critics motivated by aesthetic evaluation.
[90] The scene does cut between the characters, but not in a shot/reverse shot fashion. The camera stays behind her for a period, and then it adopts a position behind him.
[91] Strictly speaking, the charge is based on inaccurate observation because the film shows the reflection of Nana's face, albeit in the distance, in a mirror opposite. It is truer for Paul because his reflection is not seen until later in the scene, and it is then only barely distinguishable.

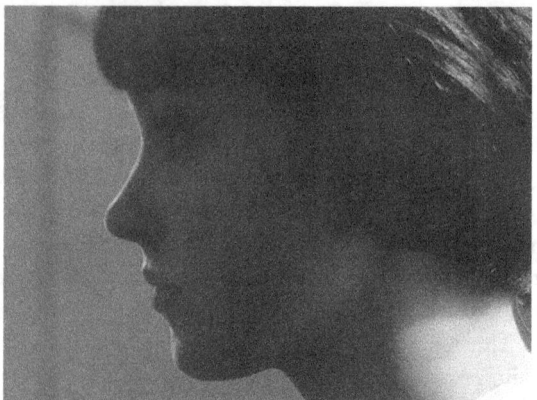

3.37–3.41  *Vivre sa vie* (Les Films de la Pléiade, Pathé Consortium Cinéma, 1962).

(Figs 3.38–3.40). Therefore, the first 'proper' scene of the film is already in a position of contrast (and even completion because it shows the fourth remaining side of her that is not shown in the credit sequence). It partly works as a facetious antithesis to the credit sequence, at the same time as initiating serious questions for the film about *how we see* Nana which

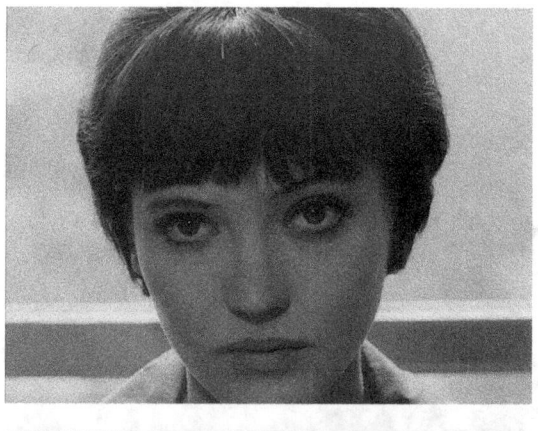

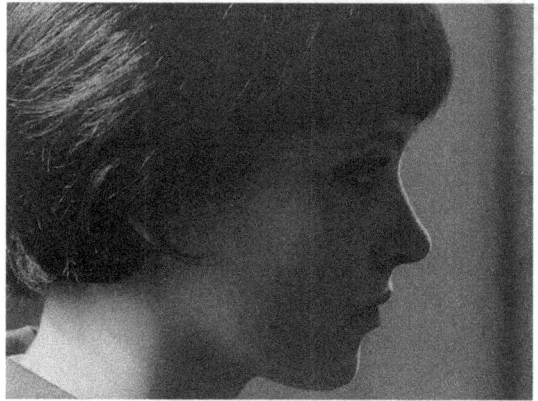

3.37–3.41 (Continued)

correspond to how she sees herself (and during the sequence she does indeed watch herself in the mirror).

It is common to see credits play over the fiction, but because Nana/Karina's head is abstracted from context and environment, it is not clear if the images are part of the fiction, or say, test shots of the actor. It is also common for a character to be simultaneously an actor on film, indeed, it is practically a condition of live-action fiction, but it is much more unusual to be uncertain about whether they are one *or* the other. This uncertainty is especially marked within a credit sequence that is customarily the place for revealing the people, albeit more usually in text, that create the fiction. Are we looking at Anna Karina or the character she plays? Her face is asserted in extreme close-up and from several perspectives and yet little

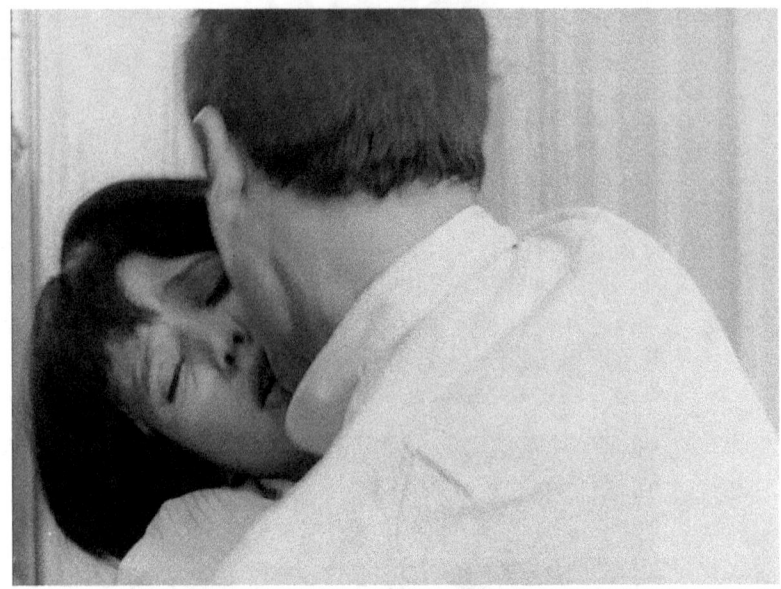

3.37–3.41 (Continued)

can be gleaned about who it is we are looking at. A character may be recessive, obscure or multiple within a fiction, but the questions that this film poses about her identity are not only those which are concerned with her as a fictional character. Martin explains how she functions as a composite, an 'unstable creation', made up of different figures – Karina, Actress, Nana, Character, Female Image (Godard's) Wife – rather than a character traditionally conceived (2015)[92]. I think an evaluation needs to assess the merit or demerit in this cross-category cohabitation (instead of simply bemoaning the fictional fracture).

(2)  *Charge*: The director regards his attitude as more important than the event he is portraying[93]. Perkins says there is an 'unwillingness to allow the movie the degree of anonymity that a fully coherent work assumes' (1969: 39).

---

[92] This instability is evoked through her depiction, in the profiling credit sequence, as a shadowy figure.

[93] Attitude is a concern for evaluation. A film will have an attitude towards its material that may be, for example, serious, sensitive, illuminating, or generous, or it may be frivolous, insensitive, ignorant, or supercilious. It will also have an attitude towards its viewers. It may, for example, trust their intelligence, or underestimate it; it may flatter, or patronise.

*Defence*: Rather than the director's attitude being more important than the event, his attitude is part of the event he is portraying, and constructed to explore his attitude. In particular, he is exploring, via the camera, his *relationship* to Karina. The film is explicitly building into its structure the questions: 'how am I to frame or *regard* (in the double sense of that word) what I am seeing before me, what position am I to take up in relation to it?' (Martin 2014: 37)[94]. It is true that the director's persona is overt, although it is not clear that it is any less so than a director such as Alfred Hitchcock, whose films Perkins admires, and who is a potent (absent) presence. Arguably, however, Hitchcock is still at the service of a tightly formed fictional world. Godard, however, wishes to dissolve the boundaries that demarcate the inside and the outside of the fiction, so his presence is of a different order.

(3)   *Charge*: Given the extremity of the device, the means and end are out of proportion. The scene could express itself more economically.

*Defence*: The scene wants laboriously to play out, like the demise of their relationship, and to render their estrangement undramatically. Because the scene is flat, it equalises much of what they say to each other regardless of import, and it reflects the dispirited, even depressed, mood. Significant information, for example about the wellbeing of their son, becomes just another part of the extended and unvaried mix, and the faceless scheme. The news of him is nearly lost in the blank presentation, as he is to Nana. The means are therefore not out of proportion with the end, and economy would not achieve the same strained effect. Laborious, flat, unvaried, faceless, and blank are in this context productive qualities and not demerits. Gilberto Perez writes that the film achieves a 'dispassionate intensity' (1998: 352). Despite de-dramatising and withholding, the scene is expressive; and despite affectedly underdetermining elements of the fiction, the scene does not undermine them. Although it would be fair to dispute these claims, or perhaps argue that the scene should be *more* economical than it is, it is not fair to insist on the criterion in advance of seeing whether it is applicable.

---

[94] This carries risks of self-indulgence, solipsism, or unproductive obsession. It is arguable that on occasions during the film, the close-ups of her face are so persistent that they are oppressive: this woman exists only for his gaze. The shots reveal little more than a male director who thinks that if he stares long enough through the lens at the beautiful female then he will find the underlying cause of his attraction and perplexity. As with all matters for aesthetic evaluation, the relationship between the interventionist director and the material will need to be evaluated on a case-by-case basis *even within the one film*.

(4) *Charge*: The director is preoccupied with the device at the expense of the meaning.

*Defence*: The device is not only used to express a meaning or create a feeling. It must attract attention because it is itself under scrutiny. Rather than simply presenting Nana/Karina, the film is concerned, self-consciously, with the form and manner of her presentation. Therefore, evaluating how the meta-fictional interrelates with the fictional is as important as evaluating intra-fictional elements. Martin says the film takes place on a number of levels, and Wood argues that the 'development of relationships in traditional naturalistic terms' is only one level (1969: 66). For example, the film is simultaneously a fiction and a documentary about Nana and a fiction and documentary about Karina (Perez 1998: 345). In the credit sequence, a lamenting refrain intermittently punctures silence: when the music is present, the image of her addresses like a fiction, and when it is not, it addresses like a documentary. The first scene is part dramatisation, and with its one awkward viewpoint, as if imposed out of necessity, part rudimentary, parodic documentation. Nana says 'What do you care?' four times consecutively, each in a different manner. This might be the *performer* rehearsing the various ways her character might say the line or providing the director with different options when he comes to edit. Alternatively, it might also be the *character* exhibiting a lack of self-assurance in expression, or being volatile and slippery (with Paul). The perceptual stimulation comes from not easily being able to distinguish.

This might amount to merely clever-clever game playing which could well be a legitimate charge to bring against some occasions in Godard's work. According to Wood, however, the levels can combine to produce a 'delicate and responsive awareness', and meta-fictional 'distanciation' can produce a 'multi-dimensional density' (1969: 67). *Vivre sa vie*'s non-naturalistic presentation produces, in Wood's terms, an 'awareness' of *real* connotations, and complications. At the end of the sequence, while the camera is placed behind Paul, Nana's hand and forearm enter the frame from off-screen left (where she is sitting) to stroke the back of his head sympathetically. Although it follows on from her stating that she does not wish to quarrel again, the gesture nevertheless feels inserted, detached, and oddly discrete. There is no reason why a more affectionate mood should suddenly rupture the impasse. It is unexpected in terms of the general thrust of the scene (and the scheme). The two characters have hitherto remained in separate zones; her forearm now protrudes into his frame and is severed from the rest of her body. The gesture is abruptly

The aesthetic evaluation of film 217

asserted, slightly stiff and halting, and curtailed as it merely strokes a small area of his hair before the arm quickly withdraws from the frame. (Only after this does the film show that she is in effect bringing their exchange to an end, getting up, and moving away.) It genuinely signifies tenderness, but it does not quite achieve or effect it[95]. It is not fulfilled. It is partly naturalistically generated by the character and partly artificially imposed on her by the film. Although it does not only emerge out of the character, it nevertheless offers insights into her character. Fundamentally, there is a sense of it being real and abstract, of Nana enacting it and not enacting it – rather like her life, which may, or more likely may not, be hers to live[96].

A merit of the film, like most of the films discussed in this part of the book, is that it finds forms which relate meaningfully to situations, thoughts, ideas, and feelings in real life. Despite the importance of internal relation for aesthetic evaluation, relevant correspondence to a reality outside the film, even in abstract or non-figurative works, is also important[97]. There is aesthetic merit in mimetic imitation because reproduction in another form – for example when performers capture recognisable human behaviours – takes skill to observe and execute correctly, and may be revelatory, evocative, and perceptually intriguing. Yet, equally, a film may relate to life without needing to be mimetic; and aesthetic evaluation assesses the capacity of film form to investigate, reveal, illuminate, intensify, transform, and transfigure reality through analogy, typification, metaphor, symbolism, and substitution[98].

Sometimes the dogged insistence of a non-naturalistic device reveals a truth, or a true feeling, just as effectively as a naturalistic device that is concretely integrated. Later in *Vivre sa vie*, once Nana has become a prostitute, a client moves to kiss her on the mouth, and she resists by diverting him. He repeatedly persists, and she repeatedly rolls her head back and forth in avoidance (Fig. 3.41). This goes on and on – on my counting eighteen of his attempts to kiss her are shown – as she becomes ever more distressed to the point of petrified catatonia. This is continuing even as the scene fades to black which enhances its never-ending quality;

---

[95] Perez's chapter on Godard in *The Material Ghost* is entitled 'The Signifiers of Tenderness' (1998).
[96] The English language title of the film is *My Life to Live*.
[97] As mentioned in Part II, 'relevance' to life is an important criterion for Leavis in judging form.
[98] Some works may not ostensibly correspond to real life, but relate to it by contributing to it, or penetrating it.

despite her increasing petrification, they are seemingly caught for eternity in this horrible repetition. The number of his attempts and her evasions goes way beyond what is credible behaviour (both in reality and in a fiction). However, by pushing to an extreme, it lays bare the reality of the situation. One forced kiss and one withdrawal, and then success for either party, would not convey, nor provide the occasion for a viewer to suffer, the sense of man and woman locked into an unstoppable, damaging dynamic. The moment *draws out* what is repetitive and compulsive in human connection. (At the same time, this is in tension with the rapid performance of their actions, and this rapidity is partly what generates an automatic quality.) More specifically, it exposes the mechanisation of prostitution, and the demanding nature of male sexual desire, never finding satisfaction. Given that the moment has gone beyond the bounds of the naturalistic or credible to achieve these effects and meanings, how is a judgement made about how long it should be drawn out? This evaluative question, like so many, applies equally to the maker as it does to a viewer. This viewer would want to argue, and try to show, that the moment lasts long enough to emphasise the sad absurdity without being prolonged to such an extent that it exhausts her distress or his lust and entitlement. Once again we are in the territory of aesthetic risk-taking: the risk is that it becomes inappropriately risible, reducing the urgency, the consideration, and the real-life relevance.

In Part III of the book, I have highlighted concerns that have been, and will continue to be, central to the aesthetic evaluation of films. Although subject to modification and diversification, one or more of these concerns will figure: the employment of the medium, the discipline of constraint, the negotiation of convention, the determination of choices, the engagement of perception, the weighting of features, the character of recurrence, and the state of relationships.

# A note on pedagogy

The book has aimed to give a perspicacious account of the theory and practice of aesthetic evaluation particularly as it relates to film. It hopes to encourage the development of new generative avenues for pursuing appraisals; further the exploration of concepts and criteria; and lead to the refinement of process and procedure. Because the strength of any discipline is maintained by good pedagogy, providing some guidance pertaining to this matter is worthwhile. To help students orientate their work towards evaluation, Richard Foster offers the following recommendations, admonitions even, in his essay 'Reflections on Teaching Criticism' (1968). (These recommendations only apply to aesthetic evaluation, and would be inapplicable to other teaching aims and subject areas.) The students' work would start with the principle that the value of the artwork was primary (so that knowledge, information, and skills should serve this principle, and not 'seem ends in themselves') (138). It would be framed so that a viewer's perception of the value was 'sharpened' and 'widened', and their judgement might be 'altered' (142). It would be free to use anything to inform and illuminate, but avoid applying or becoming preoccupied with a pre-existing formulation, theorisation, or intellectual territory that might hamper disinterested 'regard' for aesthetic value (141, 138). It would compare and contrast evaluative statements, and test those statements against the detail of the work as experienced (138). It would question conventional estimations of 'classics', not merely to challenge or debunk – one would want to avoid authorising 'intemperate splurges of critical iconoclasm' – but to reappraise, refresh and revive (142). It would promote neglected or new works from a diversity of categories, places, and personnel. Crucially, the work would not simply exist as a 'study' or an exploration of a topic, a theme, or even formal features (141). It would be focused on *evaluating* the formal expression. Building an evaluative component into essay titles would help maintain this focus (for example, 'Is the perversity of *Vivre sa vie* purposeful?', 'Is the ending of *All That Heaven Allows* damagingly sentimental?', 'Discuss inventiveness in the films of Charlie Chaplin', or 'Discuss the qualities of the continuous take in *River of No Return*'). The questions could be set in advance or better still, because it respects the openness of the evaluative process, constructed and adjusted by the students while they are thinking and writing (in accordance with their critical appraisal of the work). Another productive possibility, suggested by Colin Lyas, would be to start the process with an 'attempt to grasp' an aesthetic quality of the work (2002a: 361). The student could then illuminate how it manifests through close attention to relevant detail.

The methodological enumeration set out in this concluding note also resembles a brief résumé of the book. This is because the recommendations would be equally helpful for more advanced work that sought to enlarge and enrich a domain dedicated to evaluating the form of individual films.

# Bibliography

Andrew, D. (2005) 'Foreword to the 2004 Edition' in A. Bazin and H. Gray (eds), *What is Cinema? Volume 1*, Oakland, CA: University of California Press, ix–xxiv.
Arnheim, R. (1957) *Film as Art*, Berkeley and Los Angeles, CA: University of California Press.
Baldick, C. (1996) *Criticism and Literary Theory 1890 to the Present*, London and New York: Longman.
Barr, C. (1963) 'CinemaScope: Before and After', *Film Quarterly*, vol. 16, no. 4, 4–24.
Barthes, R. (2004; first published 1966) *Criticism and Truth*, K. Pilcher Keuneman (trans.), London and New York: Continuum.
Bawden, T. (2015) 'Male Nightingales Sing Complex Songs to Show Females They Will Be Good Fathers, Say Scientists', *The Independent*, Thursday 18 June, www.independent.co.uk/environment/nature/male-nightingales-sing-complex-songs-to-show-females-they-will-be-good-fathers-say-scientists-10327130.html, accessed 30 January 2017.
Bazin, A. (1985; first published 1957) 'An Exemplary Western' in J. Hillier (ed.), *Cahiers du Cinéma: The 1950s–Neo-Realism, Hollywood, New Wave*, Cambridge, MA: Harvard University Press, 169–72.
Bazin, A. (1992; first published 1971) *Jean Renoir*, François Truffaut (ed.), New York: Da Capo Press.
Bazin, A. (1997a; first published 1948) 'William Wyler, or the Jansenist of Directing' in B. Cardullo (ed.), *Bazin at Work: Major Essays & Reviews from the Forties & Fifties*, New York and London: Routledge, 1–22.

Bazin, A. (1997b; first published 1947) 'The Technique of *Citizen Kane*' in B. Cardullo (ed.), *Bazin at Work: Major Essays & Reviews from the Forties & Fifties*, New York and London: Routledge, 231–9.

Beardsley, M.C. (1970) *The Possibility of Criticism*, Detroit: Wayne State University Press.

Beardsley, M.C. (1981a; first published 1958) *Aesthetics: Problems in the Philosophy of Criticism*, Indianapolis: Hackett.

Beardsley, M.C. (1981b) 'The Name and Nature of Criticism' in P. Hernadi (ed.), *What is Criticism?*, Bloomington: Indiana University Press, 151–61.

Beardsley, M.C. (1982) *The Aesthetic Point of View: Selected Essays*, M. J. Wreen and D.M. Callen (eds), Ithaca, NY: Cornell University Press.

Bell, C. (1913) *Art*, London: Chatto & Windus.

Bell, M. (1988) *F.R. Leavis*, London and New York: Routledge.

Bergala, A. (2016) *The Cinema Hypothesis: Teaching Cinema in the Classroom and Beyond*, Madeline Whittle (trans.), Vienna: Austrian Film Museum and Synema.

Beugnet, M. (2007) *Cinema and Sensation: French Film and the Art of Transgression*, Edinburgh: Edinburgh University Press.

Bíro, Y. (2008) *Turbulence and Flow in Film: The Rhythmic Design*, Bloomington and Indiana: Indiana University Press.

Black, M. (1966) '"Perfection" as a Term in Aesthetics', in S. Hook (ed.), *Art and Philosophy: A Symposium*, New York: New York University Press, 32–5.

Blandford, S., B.K. Grant, and J. Hillier (2001) *The Film Studies Dictionary*, London: Arnold.

Bloom, H. (1981) 'Interview: the Art of Criticism No.1', *The Paris Review*, issue 118, www.theparisreview.org/interviews/2225/the-art-of-criticism-no-1-harold-bloom, accessed 21 December 2016.

Booth, W.C. (1975) *A Rhetoric of Irony*, Chicago and London: University of Chicago Press.

Booth, W.C. (1988) *The Company We Keep: An Ethics of Fiction*, Berkeley and Los Angeles: University of California Press.

Bordwell, D. (1985) 'Widescreen Aesthetics and Mise en Scene Criticism', *The Velvet Light Trap*, no. 21, 18–25.

Bordwell, D., J. Staiger, and K. Thompson (1988) *The Classical Hollywood Cinema: Film Style & Mode of Production to 1960*, London: Methuen.

Britton, A. (2009) *Britton on Film: The Complete Film Criticism of Andrew Britton*, B.K. Grant (ed.), Detroit: Wayne State University Press.

Britton, A. (2009; originally 1989) 'The Philosophy of the Pigeonhole: Wisconsin Formalism and "The Classical Style"', in B.K. Grant (ed.), *Britton on Film: The Complete Film Criticism of Andrew Britton*, Detroit: Wayne State University Press, 425–7.
Brooks, C. (1975; first published 1947) *The Well Wrought Urn*, New York: Harcourt.
Brooks, C. and R.P. Warren (1976; first published 1938) *Understanding Poetry*, Boston: Wadsworth.
Budd, M. (2008) *Aesthetic Essays*, Oxford: Oxford University Press.
Bullough, E. (1912) "Psychical Distance' as a Factor in Art and as an Aesthetic Principle', *British Journal of Psychology*, vol. 5, 87–117; http://web.csulb.edu/~jvancamp/361_r9.html, accessed 21 March 2017.
Byrne, P. (1979) 'Leavis, Literary Criticism and Philosophy', *The British Journal of Aesthetics*, vol. 19, no. 3, 263–73.
Callahan, D. (2012) *Barbara Stanwyck: The Miracle Woman*, Jackson, MS: University Press of Mississippi.
Cardullo, B. (1997) 'Introduction' in B. Cardullo (ed.), *Bazin at Work: Major Essays & Reviews from the Forties & Fifties*, New York and London: Routledge, ix–xvi.
Carroll, N. (2000) 'Introducing Film Evaluation' in C. Gledhill and L. Williams (eds), *Reinventing Film Studies*, London: Arnold, 265–78.
Carroll, N. (2002) *Philosophy of Art: A Contemporary Introduction*, London and New York: Routledge.
Carroll, N. (2009) *On Criticism*, New York and London: Routledge.
Carroll, N. (2016) 'Art Appreciation', *The Journal of Aesthetic Education*, vol. 50, no.4, 1–14.
Casey, J. (2011; first published 1966) *The Language of Criticism*, London: Methuen.
Cavell, S. (1979) *The World Viewed: Reflections on the Ontology of Film* (enlarged edn), Cambridge, MA and London: Harvard University Press.
Cavell, S. (1981) *Pursuits of Happiness: The Hollywood Comedy of Remarriage*, Cambridge, MA and London: Harvard University Press.
Cavell, S. (1996) *Contesting Tears: The Hollywood Melodrama of the Unknown Woman*, Chicago and London: University of Chicago Press.
Cavell, S. (1999; first published 1979) *The Claim of Reason: Wittgenstein, Skepticism, Morality, and Tragedy*, New York and Oxford: Oxford University Press.
Cavell, S. (2002; first published 1969) *Must We Mean What We Say?*, Cambridge: Cambridge University Press.

Cavell, S. (2005a) *Philosophy the Day after Tomorrow*, Cambridge, MA and London: Belknap Press.

Cavell, S. (2005b) '"What Becomes of Thinking on Film?" (Stanley Cavell in conversation with Andrew Klevan)' in R. Read and J. Goodenough (eds), *Film as Philosophy: Essays on Cinema After Wittgenstein and Cavell*, New York and Basingstoke: Palgrave Macmillan, 167–209.

Choi, J. (2011) 'Rudolph Arnheim' in P. Livingston and C. Plantinga (eds), *The Routledge Companion to Philosophy and Film*, London and New York: Routledge, 291–300.

Chojna, W. (2005) 'Roman Ingarden' in D. Cooper (ed.), *A Companion to Aesthetics*, Oxford: Blackwell, 225–7.

Clayton, A. (2012) 'The Texture of Performance in *Psycho* and its Remake', *Movie: a Journal of Film Criticism*, no. 3, 73–9, www2.warwick.ac.uk/fac/arts/film/movie/contents/psycho_clayton.pdf accessed 12 April 2017.

Clayton, A. (2015) 'V.F. Perkins: Aesthetic Suspense' in M. Pomerance and R. Barton Palmer (eds), *Thinking in the Dark: Cinema, Theory, Practice*, New Brunswick and London: Rutgers University Press, 208–16.

Clayton, A. and A. Klevan (eds) (2011) *The Language and Style of Film Criticism*, London and New York: Routledge.

Collings, M. (2009) *What is Beauty?*, BBC Television, www.telegraph.co.uk/culture/culturepicturegalleries/6545910/What-is-beauty-the-10-qualities-that-make-art-beautiful.html, accessed 1 December 2016.

Collinson, D. (2002) 'Aesthetic Experience', in O. Hanfling (ed.), *Philosophical Aesthetics: An Introduction*, Oxford: Blackwell, 111–78.

Costello, D. (2006) 'Overcoming Postmodernism' in J. Elkins (ed.), *Art History versus Aesthetics*, New York and Oxford: Routledge, 92–8.

Costelloe, T.M. (2013) *The British Aesthetic Tradition: From Shaftesbury to Wittgenstein*, Cambridge: Cambridge University Press.

Crowther, P. (2010) *The Kantian Aesthetic: From Knowledge to the Avant-Garde*, Oxford: Oxford University Press.

Daiches, D. (1969) 'Literary Evaluation' in J.P. Strelka (ed.), *Problems of Literary Evaluation*, University Park and London: Pennsylvania State University Press, 163–81.

Davidson, H.M. (1968) 'The Critical Position of Roland Barthes' in L.S. Dembo (ed.), *Criticism: Speculative and Analytical Essays*, Madison, WI and London: University of Wisconsin Press, 93–102.

Davies, S. (2010) *Philosophical Perspectives on Art*, Oxford: Oxford University Press.

Davis, G. (2008) 'Introduction' in G. Davis (ed.), *Praising it New: The Best of the New Criticism*, Athens, OH: Swallow Press/Ohio University Press, xxi–xxviii.

Day, G. (2006) 'F.R. Leavis: Criticism and Culture' in P. Waugh (ed.), *Literary Theory and Criticism: An Oxford Guide*, Oxford: Oxford University Press, 130–9.

Day, G. (2010) *Literary Criticism: A New History*, Edinburgh: Edinburgh University Press.

de Luca, T. and Jorge, N.B. (eds)(2016) *Slow Cinema*, Edinburgh: Edinburgh University Press.

Dewey, J. (2005; first published 1934) *Art as Experience*, New York: Perigee, Penguin.

Dhir, M. (2011) 'A Gestalt Approach to Film Analysis' in S. Higgins (ed.), *Arnheim for Film and Media Studies*, New York and Oxford: Routledge, 89–106.

Dickie, G. (1988) *Evaluating Art*, Philadelphia: Temple University Press.

Donaghue, D. (1998) *The Practice of Reading*, New Haven, CT and London: Yale University Press.

Doorly, P. (2013) *The Truth about Art: Reclaiming Quality*, Winchester and Washington: Zero Books.

Durgnat, R. (1976) *Durgnat on Film*, London: Faber and Faber.

Dyer, R. (2007) *Pastiche*, Abingdon and New York: Routledge.

Dziemidok, B. (1983) 'Aesthetic Experience and Evaluation' in J. Fisher (ed.), *Essays on Aesthetics: Perspectives on the Work of Monroe Beardsley*, Philadelphia: Temple University Press, 53–68.

Editors of *Movie* (1963) 'Movie Differences', *Movie*, no.8, 20–4.

Eldridge, R. (2005) 'Form' in D. Cooper (ed.), *A Companion to Aesthetics*, Oxford: Blackwell, 158–62.

Ellis, J.M. (1981) 'The Logic of the Question "What is Criticism?"' in P. Hernadi (ed.), *What is Criticism?*, Bloomington: Indiana University Press, 15–29.

Elster, J. (2000) *Ulysses Unbound: Studies in Rationality, Precommitment, and Constraints*, Cambridge: Cambridge University Press.

Empson, W. (1995; first published 1951) *The Structure of Complex Words*, Harmondsworth: Penguin.

Empson, W. (2004; first published 1930; third and final revised edn 1953) *Seven Types of Ambiguity*, London: Pimlico.

Farber, M. (1998; first published 1962) 'White Elephant Art vs. Termite Art', *Negative Space: Manny Farber on the Movies*, New York: Da Capo Press, 134–44.

Foster, R. (1968) 'Reflections on Teaching Criticism' in L.S. Dembo (ed.), *Criticism: Speculative and Analytical Essays*, Madison, Milwaukee and London: University of Wisconsin Press, 132–44.
Fuller, D. (2006) 'William Empson: from verbal analysis to cultural criticism' in P. Waugh (ed.) *Literary Theory and Criticism: An Oxford Guide*, Oxford: Oxford University Press, 152–65.
Fuller, G. and T. Eagleton (1983) 'The Question of Value: A Discussion', *New Left Review*, no. I/142, 76–90.
Gaut, B. (2012) *A Philosophy of Cinematic Art*, Cambridge: Cambridge University Press.
Gibbs, J. (2006) 'Filmmakers' Choices' in J. Gibbs and D. Pye (eds), *Close-Up 01*, London and New York: Wallflower, 1–87.
Gibbs, J. (2013) *The Life of Mise-en-Scène: Visual Style and British Film Criticism, 1946–78*, Manchester: Manchester University Press.
Gibbs, J. and D. Pye (2005) 'Introduction' in J. Gibbs and D. Pye (eds), *Style and Meaning: Studies in the Detailed Analysis of Film*, Manchester and New York: Manchester University Press, 1–15.
Goldman, A.H. (1998) *Aesthetic Value*, Boulder, CO: Westview Press.
Goldman, A.H. (2004) 'Evaluating Art', in P. Kivy (ed.), *The Blackwell Guide to Aesthetics*, Oxford: Blackwell, 93–108.
Gombrich, E.H. (1978) 'A Historical Hypothesis' in T.F. Rugh and E.R. Silva (eds), *History as a Tool in Critical Interpretation*, Provo, UT: Brigham Young University Press, 39–42.
Grant, J. (2013) *The Critical Imagination*, Oxford: Oxford University Press.
Guter, E. (2010) *Aesthetics A–Z*, Edinburgh: Edinburgh University Press.
Guyer, P. (1998) 'Baumgarten, Alexander Gottlieb' in M. Kelly (ed.), *Encyclopaedia of Aesthetics*, *Oxford Art Online*, Oxford University Press, www.oxfordartonline.com/subscriber/article/opr/t234/e0066, accessed 22 December 2015.
Guyer, P. (2014) *A History of Modern Aesthetics Volumes 1–3*, Cambridge: Cambridge University Press. [Volumes 1, 2 and 3 referenced as (a) (b) and (c) in the text.]
Hanich, J. (2014) 'Complex Staging: The Hidden Dimensions of Roy Andersson's Aesthetics', *Movie: A Journal of Film Criticism*, no. 5, 37–50, www2.warwick.ac.uk/fac/arts/film/movie/contents/complex_ staging_the_hidden_dimensions_of_roy_anderssons_aesthetics. pdf, accessed 12 April 2017.
Harrison, A. (2005) 'Style' in D. Cooper (ed.), *A Companion to Aesthetics*, Oxford: Blackwell, 403–6.

Hepburn, R.W. (2005) 'Clive Bell' in D. Cooper (ed.), *A Companion to Aesthetics*, Oxford: Blackwell, 51–3.

Herrnstein Smith, B. (1983) 'Contingencies of Value', *Critical Inquiry*, vol. 10, no. 1, 1–35.

Herrnstein Smith, B. (1998) 'Cultural Evaluation' in M. Kelly (ed.), *Encyclopaedia of Aesthetics, Oxford Art Online*, Oxford: Oxford University Press, www.oxfordartonline.com/subscriber/article/opr/t234/e0200, accessed 17 December 2015.

Higgins, S. (2011) 'Introduction' in S. Higgins (ed.), *Arnheim for Film and Media Studies*, New York and Oxford: Routledge, 1–17.

Hinderer, W. (1969) 'Literary Value Judgments and Value Cognition' in J.P. Strelka (ed.), *Problems of Literary Evaluation*, University Park and London: Pennsylvania State University Press, 54–79.

Horowitz, G.M. (2006) 'Aesthetic Knowing and Historical Knowing' in J. Elkins (ed.), *Art History Versus Aesthetics*, New York and Oxford: Routledge, 211–20.

Hough, G. (1966) *An Essay on Criticism*, London: Duckworth & Company.

Hume, D. (2008; first published 1757) 'Of the Standard of Taste' in S.M. Cahn and A. Meskin (eds), *Aesthetics: A Comprehensive Anthology*, Oxford: Blackwell, 103–12.

Ingarden, R. (1973) *The Literary Work of Art*, G.G. Grabowicz (trans.), Evanston, IL: Northwestern University Press.

Iseminger, G. (2004) *The Aesthetic Function of Art*, Ithaca, New York and London: Cornell University Press.

Isenberg, A. (1973) *Aesthetics and the Theory of Criticism*, W. Callaghan, L. Cauman, C. Hempel, S. Morgenbesser, M. Mothersill, E. Nagel, and T. Norman (eds), Chicago: University of Chicago Press.

Jacoby, M. (1969) 'The Analytical Psychology of C.G. Jung and the Problem of Literary Evaluation' in J.P. Strelka (ed.), *Problems of Literary Evaluation*, University Park and London: Pennsylvania State University Press, 99–128.

Johnson, J. (1998) 'New Criticism' in M. Kelly (ed.), *Encyclopaedia of Aesthetics, Oxford Art Online*, Oxford: Oxford University Press, www.oxfordartonline.com/subscriber/article/opr/t234/e0374, accessed 18 December 2015.

Kant, I. (1987; first published 1790) *Critique of Judgment*, W.S. Pluhar (trans.), Indianapolis and Cambridge: Hackett. [Citations by section numbers, noted with §.]

Kawin, B. (1981/2) 'My Dinner with André', *Film Quarterly*, vol. 35, no. 2, 61–3.

Keathley, C. (2006) *Cinephilia and History, or The Wind in the Trees*, Bloomington and Indianapolis: Indiana University Press.

Klevan, A. (2000) *Disclosure of the Everyday: Undramatic Achievement in Narrative Film*, Wiltshire: Flicks Books.

Klevan, A. (2003) 'The Purpose of Plot and the Place of Joan Bennett in Fritz Lang's *The Woman in the Window*', *Cineaction*, issue 62, 15–21.

Klevan, A. (2005a) *Film Performance: From Achievement to Appreciation*, London: Wallflower.

Klevan, A. (2005b) 'Guessing the Unseen from the Seen: Stanley Cavell and Film Interpretation' in R.B. Goodman (ed.), *Contending with Stanley Cavell*, Oxford: Oxford University Press, 118–39.

Klevan, A. (2011a) 'Notes on Stanley Cavell and Philosophical Film Criticism' in H. Carel and G. Tuck (eds), *New Takes in Film-Philosophy*, Basingstoke: Palgrave Macmillan, 48–64.

Klevan, A. (2011b) 'Expressing the In-Between', *Lola*, no. 1, www.lolajournal.com/1/in_between.html, accessed 25 January 2017.

Klevan, A. (2011c) 'Description' in A. Clayton and A. Klevan (eds), *The Language and Style of Film Criticism*, London and New York: Routledge, 70–86.

Klevan, A. (2012) 'Living Meaning: The Fluency of Film Performance' in A. Taylor (ed.), *Theorizing Film Acting*, New York and Abingdon: Routledge, 33–46.

Klevan, A. (2013) *Barbara Stanwyck*, London: British Film Institute.

Klevan, A. (2014a) '*Vertigo* and the Spectator of Film Analysis', *Film-Philosophy*, no. 18, 147–71, www.film-philosophy.com/index.php/f-p/article/view/1079/908, accessed 17 January 2017.

Klevan, A. (2014b) 'The Art of Indirection in *Trouble in Paradise*', *Movie: a Journal of Film Criticism*, no. 5, 1–14, www2.warwick.ac.uk/fac/arts/film/movie/contents/the_art_of_indirection_in_trouble_in_paradise.pdf, accessed 22 November 2017.

Koren, L. (2010) *Which 'Aesthetics' Do You Mean? Ten Definitions*, Point Reyes, CA: Imperfect Publishing.

Krieger, M. (1968) 'Literary Analysis and Evaluation – and the Ambidextrous Critic' in L.S. Dembo (ed.), *Criticism: Speculative and Analytical Essays*, Madison, WI: University of Wisconsin Press, 16–36.

Kuhns, R. (1966) 'The Abiding Values of Art', in S. Hook (ed.), *Art and Philosophy: A Symposium*, New York: New York University Press, 42–8.

Kupperman, J.J. (1966) 'Reasons in Support of Evaluations of Works of Art', *The Monist*, vol. 50, issue 2, 222–36.

Laetz, B. (2010) 'Kendall Walton's "Categories of Art": A Critical Commentary', *British Journal of Aesthetics*, vol. 50, no. 3, 287–306.

Leavis, F.R. (1943) *Education and the University: A Sketch for an 'English School'*, London: Chatto and Windus.

Leavis, F.R. (1972; first published 1936) *Revaluation*, Middlesex: Penguin/Pelican.

Leavis, F.R. (1984; first published 1952) *The Common Pursuit*, London: Hogarth.

Leavis, F.R. (1986; essays first published 1929–72) *Valuation in Criticism and Other Essays*, G. Singh (ed.), Cambridge: Cambridge University Press.

Levinson, J. (2005) 'Aesthetic Pleasure' in D. Cooper (ed.), *A Companion to Aesthetics*, Oxford: Blackwell, 330–5.

Levinson, J. (2010) 'Artistic Worth and Personal Taste', *The Journal of Aesthetics and Art Criticism*, vol. 68, no. 3, 225–33.

Lindgren, E. (1948) *The Art of the Film*, London: George Allen & Unwin.

Logan, W. (2008) 'Forward into the Past: Reading the New Critics' in G. Davis (ed.), *Praising it New: The Best of the New Criticism*, Athens, OH: Swallow Press/Ohio University Press, ix–xvi.

Lyas, C. (2002a) 'The Evaluation of Art' in O. Hanfling (ed.), *Philosophical Aesthetics: An Introduction*, Oxford: Blackwell, 349–80.

Lyas, C. (2002b) 'Criticism and Interpretation' in O. Hanfling (ed.), *Philosophical Aesthetics: An Introduction*, Oxford: Blackwell, 381–403.

Macdonald, M. (1965; first published 1949) 'Some Distinctive Features of Arguments Used in Criticism of the Arts' in J. Stolnitz (ed.), *Aesthetics*, New York and London: Macmillan, 98–112.

McDonald, R. (2007), *The Death of the Critic*, London and New York: Continuum.

MacDowell, J. (2014) *Happy Endings in Hollywood Cinema: Cliché, Convention and the Final Couple*, Edinburgh: Edinburgh University Press.

McFee, G. (1998) 'Dance Criticism' in M Kelly (ed.), *Encyclopaedia of Aesthetics*, Oxford Art Online, Oxford University Press, www.oxfordartonline.com/subscriber/article/opr/t234/e0138, accessed 18 December 2016.

McFee, G. (2011) *Artistic Judgement: A Framework for Philosophical Aesthetics*, Heidelberg, London and New York: Springer.

Martin, A. (2014) *Mise en Scène and Film Style: From Classical Hollywood to New Media Art*, Basingstoke: Palgrave Macmillan.

Martin, A. (2015) *'VIVRE SA VIE'*, DVD commentary, London: British Film Institute.

Meskin, A. (2005) 'Style' in B. Gaut and D.M. Lopes (eds), *The Routledge Companion to Aesthetics* (second edn), London and New York: Routledge, 489–500.
Meyer, L.B. (1987) 'Toward a Theory of Style' in B. Lang (ed.), *The Concept of Style*, Ithaca, NY and London: Cornell University Press, 21–71.
Middleton Murry, J. (1965; first published 1922) *The Problem of Style*, Oxford: Oxford University Press.
Mitias, M.H. (1988) 'Locus of Aesthetic Quality' in M.H. Mitias (ed.), *Aesthetic Quality and Aesthetic Experience*, Amsterdam: Elementa, 25–44.
Modleski, T. (2005) *The Women Who Knew Too Much: Hitchcock and Feminist Theory* (second edn), New York and London: Routledge.
Mulhall, S. (2007) 'Stanley Cavell' in D. Costello and J. Vickery (eds), *Art: Key Contemporary Thinkers*, Oxford and New York: Berg, 110–13.
Nehamas, A. (2007) *Only a Promise of Happiness: The Place of Beauty in a World of Art*, Princeton and Oxford: Princeton University Press.
Norris, C. (1988) 'Editor's Foreword' in M. Bell, *F.R. Leavis*, London and New York: Routledge, vii–xv.
Olsen, S.H. (1987) *The End of Literary Theory*, Cambridge: Cambridge University Press.
Olsen, S.H. (1998) 'Appreciation', in M Kelly (ed.), *Encyclopaedia of Aesthetics, Oxford Art Online*, Oxford University Press, www.oxfordartonline.com/subscriber/article/opr/t234/e0027, accessed 30 March 2016.
Olson, E. (1976) *On Value Judgments in the Arts and Other Essays*, Chicago and London: University of Chicago Press.
O'Pray, M. (2003) *Avant-Garde Film: Forms, Themes and Passions*, London and New York: Wallflower.
Osborne, H. (1955) *Aesthetics and Criticism*, New York: Philosophical Library.
Paglia, C. (1998) *The Birds*, London: British Film Institute.
Pearsall, J. (ed.) (1998) *The New Oxford Dictionary of English*, Oxford: Clarendon Press.
Peckham, M. (1981) 'Three Notions about Criticism' in P. Hernadi (ed.), *What is Criticism?*, Bloomington: Indiana University Press, 38–51.
Perez, G. (1998) *The Material Ghost: Films and their Medium*, Baltimore and London: Johns Hopkins University Press.
Perkins, V.F. (1963) 'The Cinema of Nicholas Ray', *Movie*, no. 9, 4–10.

Perkins, V.F. (1969) 'Vivre sa vie' in I. Cameron (ed.), *The Films of Jean-Luc Godard*, London: Studio Vista, 32–9.

Perkins, V.F. (1972) *Film as Film*, London: Penguin. [N.B. The citations in the text refer to the 1991 imprint. To simplify, because they are numerous, they are referenced as 1972.]

Perkins, V.F. (1981) 'Moments of Choice', *The Movie*, no. 58, 1141–5. (Reprinted in A. Lloyd (ed.), *Movies of the Fifties*, London: Orbis Publishing, 1982, 209–13).

Perkins, V.F. (1982) '*Letter from an Unknown Woman*', *Movie*, no. 29/30, 61–72.

Perkins, V.F. (1990) 'Must We Say What They Mean? Film Criticism and Interpretation', *Movie*, no. 34, 1–6.

Perkins, V.F. (1994) '*In a Lonely Place*' in I. Cameron (ed.), *The Movie Book of Film Noir*, London: Studio Vista, 222–31.

Perkins, V.F. (1996) '*Johnny Guitar*' in I. Cameron and D. Pye (eds), *The Movie Book of the Western*, London: Studio Vista, 221–8.

Perkins, V.F. (2000) 'Same Tune Again!: Repetition and Framing in *Letter from an Unknown Woman*', *CineAction*, no. 52, 40–8.

Perkins, V.F. (2010) 'Ian Cameron: A Tribute', *Movie: a Journal of Film Criticism*, no. 1, 1–2 www2.warwick.ac.uk/fac/arts/film/movie/contents/ian_cameron_-_a_tribute.pdf, accessed 22 December 2016.

Piso, M. (2009; first published 1986) 'Mark's *Marnie*' in M. Deutelbaum and L. Poague (eds), *A Hitchcock Reader* (second edn), Oxford: Blackwell, 280–94.

Plantinga, C. (1993) 'Film Theory and Aesthetics: Notes on a Schism', *The Journal of Aesthetics and Art Criticism*, vol. 51, no. 3, 445–54.

Powell, D. (1950) '*Jour de Fête*', *The Sunday Times*, April 1950. www.bfi.org.uk/news-opinion/sight-sound-magazine/features/pantheon-one-s-own-25-female-film-critics-worth#powell, accessed 13 December 2016.

Pye, D. (1989) 'Bordwell and Hollywood', *Movie*, no. 33, 46–52.

Radford, C. and S. Minogue (1981) *The Nature of Criticism*, Brighton: Harvester Press.

Rawlinson, M. (2006) 'Beauty and Politics' in J. Elkins (ed.), *Art History Versus Aesthetics*, New York and Oxford: Routledge, 128–43.

Reichert, J. (1977) *Making Sense of Literature*, Chicago and London: University of Chicago Press.

Richards, I.A. (1973; first published 1929) *Practical Criticism*, London: Routledge and Kegan Paul.

Richards, I.A. (2001; first published 1924) *Principles of Literary Criticism*, London and New York: Routledge.

Ricks, C. (1996) *Essays in Appreciation*, Oxford: Clarendon Press.
Righter, W. (1963) *Logic and Criticism*, London: Routledge and Kegan Paul.
Ross, S. (2005) 'Style in Art' in J. Levinson (ed.), *The Oxford Handbook of Aesthetics*, Oxford: Oxford University Press, 228–44.
Ross, S. (2014) 'When Critics Disagree: Prospects for Realism in Aesthetics', *The Philosophical Quarterly*, vol. 64, no. 257, 590–618.
Rothman, W. (1989) *The 'I' of the Camera: Essays in Film Criticism, History, and Aesthetics*, Cambridge: Cambridge University Press.
Rushton, R. (2011) *The Reality of Film: Theories of Filmic Reality*, Manchester and New York: Manchester University Press.
Sarris, A. (1976) *The John Ford Movie Mystery*, London: Secker and Warburg (with British Film Institute).
Sarris, A. (1985; first published 1968) *The American Cinema: Directors and Directions 1929–1968*, Chicago: University of Chicago Press.
Savile, A. (1982) *The Test of Time: An Essay in Philosophical Aesthetics*, Oxford: Oxford University Press.
Schapiro, M. (1966) 'On Perfection, Coherence, and Unity of Form and Content', in S. Hook (ed.), *Art and Philosophy: A Symposium*, New York: New York University Press, 3–15.
Scruton, R. (1974) *Art and Imagination*, London: Methuen.
Scruton, R. (1999) *The Aesthetics of Music*, Oxford: Oxford University Press.
Seamon, R. (2005) 'Criticism' in B. Gaut and D.M. Lopes (eds), *The Routledge Companion to Aesthetics* (second edn), London and New York, Routledge, 401–15.
Shaviro, S. (2006; first published 1993) *The Cinematic Body*, Minneapolis and London: University of Minnesota Press.
Shelley, J. (2013) 'The Concept of the Aesthetic' in *Stanford Encyclopaedia of Philosophy*, http://plato.stanford.edu/entries/aesthetic-concept/, accessed 11 December 2015.
Shusterman, R. (1984) *The Object of Literary Criticism (Elementa 29)*, Amsterdam, K&N (Kindle edn).
Shusterman, R. (1986) 'Wittgenstein and Critical Reasoning', *Philosophy and Phenomenological Research*, vol. 47, no. 1, 91–110.
Sibley, F. (2006; first published essays 1950–93) *Approach to Aesthetics: Collected Papers on Philosophical Aesthetics*, J. Bensen, B. Redfern, and J. Roxbee Cox (eds), Oxford: Clarendon Press.
Sinnerbrink, R. (2012) '*Stimmung*: Exploring the Aesthetics of Mood', *Screen*, vol. 53, no. 2, 148–63.

Smallwood, P. (2003) *Reconstructing Criticism: Pope's Essay on Criticism and the Logic of Definition*, Lewisburg and London: Bucknell University Press and Associated University Presses.
Smith, M. (2006) 'My Dinner with Noël; or, Can We Forget the Medium?', *Film Studies*, no. 8, 140–8.
Sontag, S. (2001; first published 1961) 'Against Interpretation', *Against Interpretation*, London: Vintage Books, 3–14.
Sparshott, F.E. (1967) *The Concept of Criticism*, Oxford: Clarendon Press.
Stecker, R. (2010) *Aesthetics and the Philosophy of Art: An Introduction*, Plymouth: Rowman and Littlefield.
Steiner, G. (1995; first published 1962) 'F.R. Leavis' in D. Lodge (ed.), *20$^{th}$ Century Literary Criticism: A Reader*, London and New York: Longman, 622–35.
Storer, R. (2009) *F.R. Leavis*, London and New York: Routledge.
Thomson, D. (1967) *Movie Man*, New York: Stein and Day.
Thomson, D. (1995, revised edn; first published 1975) *A Biographical Dictionary of Cinema*, London: André Deutsch.
Toles, G. (2001) *A House Made of Light: Essays on the Art of Film*, Detroit: Wayne State University Press.
Toles, G. (2010) 'Acting Ordinary in *The Shop Around the Corner*', *Movie: a Journal of Film Criticism*, no. 1, 1–15, www2.warwick.ac.uk/fac/arts/film/movie/contents/the_shop_around_the_corner.pdf, accessed 22 November 2016.
Vendler, H. (1988) *The Music of What Happens: Poems, Poets, Critics*, Cambridge, MA: "Harvard University Press.
Walton, K.L. (2008a) '"How Marvelous!": Toward a Theory of Aesthetic Value', *Marvelous Images: On Values and the Arts*, Oxford: Oxford University Press, 3–21.
Walton, K.L. (2008b; first published 1970) 'Categories of Art', *Marvelous Images: On Values and the Arts*, Oxford: Oxford University Press, 195–219.
Watson, G. (1963) *The Literary Critics*, London: Penguin.
Wellek, R. (1981) 'Literary Criticism' in P. Hernadi (ed.), *What is Criticism?*, Bloomington: Indiana University Press, 297–321.
Wilson, G.M. (1992) *Narration in Light: Studies in Cinematic Point of View*, Baltimore and London: Johns Hopkins University Press.
Wimsatt Jr., W.K. and Beardsley, M.C. (1946) 'The Intentional Fallacy', *Sewanee Review*, vol. 54, no. 3, 468–88.
Wimsatt Jr., W.K. and M.C. Beardsley (1949) 'The Affective Fallacy', *Sewanee Review*, vol. 57, no. 1, 31–55.

Wittgenstein, L. (1989; first published 1966) *Lectures and Conversations on Aesthetics, Psychology and Religious Belief*, Oxford: Blackwell.

Wittgenstein, L. (2006; first published 1953) *Philosophical Investigations*, G.E.M. Anscombe (trans.), Oxford: Blackwell.

Wood. R. (1965) *Hitchcock's Films*, London: Zwemmer.

Wood, R. (1969) '*BANDE A PART*' in I. Cameron (ed.), *The Films of Jean-Luc Godard*, London: Studio Vista, 61–71.

Wood, R. (1989) *Hitchcock's Films Revisited*, London and Boston: Faber and Faber.

Wood, R. (1998; first published 1974) '*Written on the Wind*' in J. Hill and P.C. Gibson (eds), *The Oxford Guide to Film Studies*, Oxford: Oxford University Press, 24–6.

Wood, R. (2002) *Hitchcock's Films Revisited* (revised edn), New York and Chichester: Columbia University Press.

Wood, R. (2006) *Personal Views: Explorations in Film* (revised edn), Detroit: Wayne State University Press.

Wreen, M. (2014) 'Beardsley's Aesthetics' in Edward N. Zalta (ed.), *Stanford Encyclopaedia of Philosophy*, http://plato.stanford.edu/entries/beardsley-aesthetics/, accessed 11 December 2015.

Zangwill, N. (2001) *The Metaphysics of Beauty*, New York: Cornell University Press.

Zangwill, N. (2012) *Aesthetic Creation*, Oxford: Oxford University Press.

Zangwill, N. (2014) 'Aesthetic Judgment' in Edward N. Zalta (ed.), *Stanford Encyclopaedia of Philosophy*, http://plato.stanford.edu/entries/aesthetic-judgment/, accessed 11 December 2015.

# Filmography

*All That Heaven Allows* (Douglas Sirk, 1955)
*Ball of Fire* (Howard Hawks, 1941)
*The Best Years of Our Lives* (William Wyler, 1946)
*The Birds* (Alfred Hitchcock, 1963)
*The Bitter Tears of Petra von Kant* (Rainer Werner Fassbinder, 1972)
*Black Swan* (Darren Aronofsky, 2010)
*Blue Velvet* (David Lynch, 1986)
*Boudu Saved From Drowning* (Jean Renoir, 1932)
*Bringing Up Baby* (Howard Hawks, 1938)
*Camille* (George Cukor, 1936)
*Citizen Kane* (Orson Welles, 1941)
*Diary of a Country Priest* (Robert Bresson, 1951)
*The Diary of a Lost Girl* (G.W. Pabst, 1929)
*Doctor Zhivago* (David Lean, 1965)
*The Gold Rush* (Charles Chaplin, 1925)
*The Guns of Navarone* (J. Lee Thompson, 1961)
*The Idle Class* (Charles Chaplin, 1921)
*Imitation of Life* (Douglas Sirk, 1959)
*The Immigrant* (Charles Chaplin, 1917)
*In a Lonely Place* (Nicholas Ray, 1950)
*It's a Wonderful Life* (Frank Capra, 1946)
*Johnny Guitar* (Nicholas Ray, 1954)
*Jour de Fête* (Jacques Tati, 1949)
*The Ladies Man* (Jerry Lewis, 1961)
*Lawrence of Arabia* (David Lean, 1962)
*Letter from an Unknown Woman* (Max Ophüls, 1948)

*The Little Foxes* (William Wyler, 1941)
*The Magnificent Ambersons* (Orson Welles, 1942)
*Marnie* (Alfred Hitchcock, 1964)
*Moonrise Kingdom* (Wes Anderson, 2012)
*Mouchette* (Robert Bresson, 1967)
*My Dinner with André* (Louis Malle, 1981)
*Ordet* (Carl Theodor Dreyer, 1955)
*The Passion of Joan of Arc* (Carl Theodor Dreyer, 1928)
*The Pawnshop* (Charles Chaplin, 1916)
*The Philadelphia Story* (George Cukor, 1940)
*Playtime* (Jacques Tati, 1967)
*Psycho* (Alfred Hitchcock, 1960)
*Rebel Without a Cause* (Nicholas Ray, 1955)
*Rio Grande* (John Ford, 1950)
*River of No Return* (Otto Preminger, 1954)
*Rope* (Alfred Hitchcock, 1948)
*The Rules of the Game* (Jean Renoir, 1939)
*Ryan's Daughter* (David Lean, 1970)
*Safety Last* (Fred Newmeyer, Sam Taylor, 1923)
*Secret Sunshine* (Chang-dong Lee, 2007)
*Seven Men From Now* (Budd Boetticher, 1956)
*She Wore a Yellow Ribbon* (Jon Ford, 1949)
*The Shop Around the Corner* (Ernst Lubitsch, 1940)
*Sonatine* (Takeshi Kitano, 1993)
*Strangers on a Train* (Alfred Hitchcock, 1951)
*Trouble Every Day* (Claire Denis, 2001)
*Trouble in Paradise* (Ernst Lubitsch, 1932)
*Vertigo* (Alfred Hitchcock, 1958)
*Vivre sa vie* (Jean-Luc Godard, 1962)
*Under Satan's Sun* (Maurice Pialat, 1987)
*The Woman in the Window* (Fritz Lang, 1944)
*Written on the Wind* (Douglas Sirk, 1956)
*You Only Live Once* (Fritz Lang, 1937)
*You, the Living* (Roy Andersson, 2007)

# Index

In the index, forenames of creative personnel are given in full. The abbreviation 'n.' after a page reference indicates the number of a note on that page.

Aestheticism 20
*All That Heaven Allows* 147, 150, 152–7, 187, 220
Alvarez, A. 83
ambiguity 84, 104, 122, 168–9, 172, 180, 181, 194, 195
analysis 13, 63, 78–82
anti-aesthetic 19, 20n.4
appreciation 11, 12, 22, 30, 31, 39–41, 43, 44, 52, 54, 61–3, 68, 89
argumentation 88, 95, 107–9, 113, 191
Arnheim, R. 4, 5, 119, 120, 131–4, 136–40, 144, 160, 181, 186, 200
Austen, Jane 106
avant-garde 144

badness 164
balance 77, 104, 147, 158, 168, 187n.69, 202, 203, 208, 210
Baldick, C. 45, 84, 85, 87
Bale, Christian 122
*Ball of Fire* 48
Barr, C. 167n.49, 175–6
Barthes, R. 4n.3, 97, 110
Bateson, F.W. 85
Baumgarten, A. 17

Bazin, A. 4, 119–22, 126, 144–5, 156, 160–3, 165–6, 168, 175, 180, 200, 201, 203, 204
Beardsley, M. 4, 10, 31, 49, 50, 60, 73–5, 91, 103, 104, 200, 202
Beattie, J. 24
Beauty 17, 18, 20, 22n.8, 23, 24, 25, 26, 28, 30, 32–4, 36, 41–2, 48, 49, 54, 68, 98, 158, 188, 200, 215n.94
Beckett, Samuel 93
Bell, C. 22, 43, 44
Bell, M. 32, 47, 53n.56, 63, 77, 86, 95, 100, 105, 114
Bergala, A. 101, 125n.9, 143n.24
*Best Years of Our Lives, The* 145, 160–1, 167, 181, 182, 210n.88, 235
Beugnet, M. 64n.9, 91–3
*Birds, The* 42n.34
Bíro, Y. 206n.84
*Bitter Tears of Petra von Kant, The* 181n.66
*Black Swan* 94
*Blue Velvet* 51
Boetticher, Bud 175
Bogart, Humphrey 173

# 238  Index

Booth, W. 13, 80, 90, 93, 106, 110–11, 113, 187n.69
Bordwell, D. 46, 80, 176n.58
*Boudu Saved From Drowning* 162–7, 203n.80
Braudy, L. 4
Brecht, B. 184
Bresson, Robert 94–5
*Bringing Up Baby* 65
Britton, A. 88, 144, 193n.74
Brooks, C. 86, 88n.35
Budd, M. 30, 31, 54, 55, 107, 160
Bullough, E. 22, 23
Burke, K. 187n.69
Byrne, P. 106

Callahan, D. 48
*Camille* 65–6
canon 6, 10, 27, 63, 96
Capra, Frank 146
Cardullo, B. 160
Carroll, N. 10, 48, 61, 90–1, 93
Casey, J. 46, 68, 103, 107, 174
category 2, 6, 18n.3, 26, 52, 80, 90–5, 104, 106, 119, 134, 152n.34, 164n.46, 183n.68, 194, 199, 219
  see also classification
Cavell, S. 9, 33, 36, 40n.30, 63, 65, 68, 94, 102, 103n.53, 113–14, 121, 126, 146
Chaplin, Charles 60n.3, 93, 131, 133–5, 137–40, 163, 220
choice 6, 95, 100–2, 109, 130, 143–5, 154–6, 218
*Citizen Kane* 10, 96, 167, 181n.65, 204–6
classification 34, 54, 59, 64n.9, 85, 91n.41
  see also category
Clayton, A. 70, 78n.24, 103, 154, 155
cliché 51, 83, 86, 92, 94, 95, 99, 109, 149, 150n.30, 168, 200

Cohen, M. 4
coherence 71, 73–4, 89, 102, 137, 168, 200–1, 207, 209, 210, 214
Collings, M. 18n.2
Collinson, D. 23, 45
comparison 53, 90, 95, 99n.48, 106, 136n.18, 152n.33
complexity 30, 31, 38, 60, 74, 88, 90, 91, 104, 105, 166, 167, 180, 181, 194, 209, 210
complex word 24, 169
Connery, Sean 188, 192
convention 2, 6, 52, 54–5, 94, 99, 119, 130, 143–54, 156, 199, 218
Costello, D. 45
Costelloe, T.M. 17
criteria, evaluative 6, 33, 63, 88, 90, 92, 96, 104–7, 109, 121, 150, 180, 200, 203, 209, 210n.88, 215, 217n.97
Crowther, P. 26, 35, 38, 54
Cukor, George 1, 65

Dall, John 140
Danto, A. 97
Davies, S. 42
Davis, Bette 122, 145
Day, G. 17, 18, 24–5, 61, 68, 95, 113
Denis, Claire 92
de Oliveira, Manoel 143n.24
description 13, 50, 52, 77–82, 188
Dewey, J. 37
Dhir, M. 133, 160, 181
*Diary of a Country Priest* 94, 98
*Diary of a Lost Girl, The* 235
Diderot, D. 201
disinterest 22–3, 30, 75, 113, 219
dispositif 143
*Doctor Zhivago* 202
Donaghue, D. 23–4, 40
Doorly, P. 45, 96, 99
Dreyer, Carl 137, 181n.66

# Index

Duchamp, Marcel 19–20
duck-rabbit figure 69, 110, 132, 198
Dufrenne, M. 52
Durgnat, R. 93
Dyer, R. 42n.35
Dziemidok, B. 76

Eastwood, Clint 27
economy 84, 202–3, 215
Eisenstein, Sergei 119–20
Eldridge, R. 41
Eliot T.S. 87, 95, 169
emergence 52–4, 70, 73, 160
Empson, W. 24, 44n.39, 76, 86, 168–9
Emrich, W. 97
expectation 73, 90, 147n.29, 154–9, 194

Farber, M. 202
Fassbinder, Rainer Werner 104, 181n.66
Fogle, R.H. 108
Fonda, Henry 194
Fontaine, Joan 206
Ford, John 1, 27
formalism 7, 20, 43–4, 82
Foster, R. 219–20
*Fountain, The* 19
function 12, 42–3, 76, 128, 131, 167

Garbo, Greta 65–7, 122
Gaut, B. 120, 122, 123
generalists 104
Gibbs, J. 29, 47, 100n.49, 156, 167, 168, 175n.56, 191, 202n.78, 79
Godard, Jean-Luc 126, 210, 214–17
Goldman, A. 49, 53n.54, 74n.19
*Gold Rush, The* 133n.16, 138–9
Gombrich, E.H. 95
Granger, Farley 140, 145
Grant, J. 107, 112
Gregor, Nora 128

Gregory, André 123
*Guns of Navarone, The* 202
Guter, E. 21, 119
Guyer, P. 9, 17, 34, 38n.29, 42, 45, 49, 75

Haneke, Michael 46
Hanich, J. 80
Hawks, Howard 48, 65
Hedren, Tippi 188
Hegel, W.F. 45
Heidegger, M. 77
Hepburn, Katharine 65
Herder, J.H. 113
Herrnstein Smith, B. ii, 8, 10, 11, 13, 59, 116
Higgins, S. 132, 133n.15, 225, 227
Hitchcock, Alfred 10, 42n.35, 62, 103, 140, 145, 155, 188, 191n.71, 193n.73, 215
Horowitz, G.M. 72–3
Hough, G. 11, 44, 63
Hume, D. 4, 27, 68, 106, 107, 110

identification 101, 113, 192, 211
*Idle Class, The* 134–6
imagination 30, 34–9, 45, 55, 74n.19, 86, 94, 97, 107, 110, 112, 160
*Imitation of Life* 152n.16
immediacy 25, 28, 53, 97, 160
*Immigrant, The* 131–4, 136
*In a Lonely Place* 169, 170–4
Ingarden, R. 52n.53
interpretation 27, 35, 36n.26, 40, 61–8, 82, 83, 93, 103, 111, 112n.64, 136, 160n.41, 166n.48, 177n.60, 191, 210
invention 9, 37, 40, 64, 132–3, 137, 140, 163, 202, 220
Iseminger, G. 11, 40
Isenberg, A. 4, 48, 53, 68, 107
*It's a Wonderful Life* 146

James, Henry 24, 44, 77, 147
*Johnny Guitar* 89, 174
Johnson, Samuel 83
Jourdan, Louis 206
*Jour de Fête* 60

Kael, P. 158
Kant, I. 4, 25–6, 28–35, 38, 41–2, 45, 51, 54–5, 59
Keathley, C. 164, 165, 166n.48
Klevan, A. 1, 35n.23, 48n.45, 51n.48, 55n.58, 64n.8, 65, 68, 70, 72n.15, 78n.24, 79n.25, 95, 100, 125, 134n.17, 146n.28, 201, 206n.84
Krieger, M. 113
Kuhns, R. 70, 228
Kupperman, J.J. 110n.62

*Ladies Man, The* 93
Laetz, B. 95
Lang, Fritz 54, 194
*Lawrence of Arabia* 202
Lean, David 202
Leavis, F.R. 32, 45, 53n.56, 63, 64, 77–8, 85, 88, 95, 100–1, 102, 104–8, 110, 113, 114
*Letter from an Unknown Woman* 1, 62, 174, 206–10
Levinson, J. 26–7, 30–1, 41
Lewis, Jerry 93
Lindgren, E. 167–8
*Little Foxes, The* 145, 146, 156
Logan, W. 83
Lubitsch, Ernst 134n.17, 157
Lyas, C. 11, 110, 220
Lynch, David 46, 51

Macdonald, M. 111, 112
McDonald, R. 13, 86, 95
MacDowell, J. 147, 149, 150, 151n.32
McFee, G. 68, 97, 103

Mackail, J.W. 188
*Magnificent Ambersons, The* 96
Mann, Anthony 27
*Man with a Knife (St Bartholomew)* 98–9
*Marnie* 72n.13, 188–93, 201
Martin, A. 143, 210, 214, 215, 216
Marvell, Andrew 85n.32
Mayersberg, P. 211
medium 2, 3, 6, 20, 26, 29, 87–9, 91, 102, 105, 115, 119–26, 130, 132, 164, 173, 200, 201, 203n.81, 218
Meyer, L.B. 46, 143
Middleton Murry, J. 47, 203
Minogue, S. 107, 109n.61, 210
Mitcham, Robert 175
Mitias, M.H. 52, 53
Modleski, T. 192
Monroe, Marilyn 175, 179
*Moonrise Kingdom* 80n.27
Morgan, Frank 157–9
*Mouchette* 95
Mulhall, S. 9, 121, 146
*My Dinner with André* 123–6

Nehamas, A. 23, 35, 36, 37, 54
Norris, C. 86

objectivity 13, 32, 40, 81, 95, 107, 110–13
obtrusive 181–7, 209
Olsen, S.H. 39, 40, 61, 62
Olson, E. 43, 168, 169
Ophüls, Max 1, 62, 174, 202n.79, 209, 210
O'Pray, M. 80
*Ordet* 181n.66
Osborne, H. 61, 81, 188, 195
Ozu, Yasujiro 131n.13, 143

Pabst, Georg Wilhelm 136
Paglia, C. 42

# Index

paraphrase, heresy of 68, 87–9
particularist 104
*Passion of Joan of Arc, The* 137
pattern 6, 18n.2, 31, 41, 46, 62, 73, 75, 97, 102, 103, 110, 125, 143, 151, 169, 173, 174, 177, 181, 187–98, 199, 207, 209n.87, 210
*Pawnshop, The* 137–40
Perez, G. 209n.86, 215, 216, 217n.95
Perkins, V.F. 1, 4, 5, 29, 31n.17, 45, 88n.36, 89, 100n.49, 105, 114n.66, 121, 123, 141–2, 155, 169, 172–5, 177n.60, 199–202, 206–11, 214, 215
persuasion 9, 32, 33n.21, 36, 79, 107–9, 129, 168, 178, 191, 209, 210
*Philadelphia Story, The* 1
Pialat, Maurice 95
Piso, M. 72n.13, 188–93, 201
Plantinga, C. 3, 4
*Playtime* 181n.66
pleasure, aesthetic 2, 17, 18, 29–32, 160
Popper, K. 112
Powell, D. 60n.3
Preminger, Otto 175
prominence 6, 53, 68, 92, 166, 172–87, 192
Proust, Marcel 28
*Psycho* 103
Pye, D. 145, 191

quality, aesthetic 2, 9, 31, 48–54, 64, 69, 70, 73, 74, 76, 94, 126, 180, 209, 220

Radford, C. 107, 109n.61, 210
Rawlinson, M. 8, 28, 37, 54, 55
Ray, Nicholas 89, 169, 174, 177n.61
realisation 2n.1, 41, 77–8, 84, 104, 112, 121, 140, 174n.55, 178, 180, 192

*Rebel Without a Cause* 177n.61
Reichardt, Kelly 27
Reichert, J. 12, 80, 107
relation 6, 19n.4, 23, 24, 29–31, 36, 40, 42, 48, 51, 53–5, 72n.13, 73, 76, 78–80, 85, 86, 89, 90, 92, 93, 95, 112, 114, 121, 122, 140, 150, 154, 162n.43, 164, 174, 177n.59, 180, 187, 189, 199–218
Rembrandt 98
Renoir, Jean 126, 128–30, 162
responsiveness 11, 17, 51n.48, 76–8, 105n.56, 107, 175, 187n.69
Rettig, Tommy 175
revaluation 77, 115
rhyme 190, 195
rhythm 64, 111, 147n.29, 164, 168, 199, 206
Richards, I.A. 82, 84, 164, 168, 169
Ricks, C. 106
Righter, W. 105, 107, 109, 169
*Rio Grande* 1
*River of No Return* 175–80, 203–4, 206, 220
Rohmer, Eric. 48
*Rope* 140–3, 155
Rosenblatt, L.M. 23–4
Ross, S. 46, 107, 115
Rothko, Mark 63
Rothman, W. 126, 128–30
*Rules of the Game, The* 126–8, 146
Rushton, R. 201
Russell, Harold 160
*Ryan's Daughter* 202

*Safety Last* 91
Sarris, A. 1, 46
Savile, A. 96
Schapiro, M. 97–8, 115, 209
Scorsese, Martin 126
Scruton, R. 12, 26, 32, 33n.20, 38n.29, 52n.53, 54, 68, 78, 82, 107

Seamon, R. 63, 64
Secret Sunshine 50
self-reflexivity 126, 128n.12
Seven Men From Now 175
Shaviro, S. 64
Shawn, Wallace 123
Shelley, J. 25
Shelley, Percy Bysshe 64, 107, 110
She Wore a Yellow Ribbon 1
Shop Around the Corner, The 157–60, 181–2
Shusterman, R. 10, 62, 63, 106, 107, 112, 113
Sibley, F. 4, 8, 49–52, 69–70, 94, 104
Simon, Michel 162–3, 165
Sinnerbrink, R. 50n.48
Sirk, Douglas 147, 152n.33, 183, 184
Smallwood, P. 59n.1, 113
Smith, M. 121–2, 123n.5, 126
Sonatine 80
Sontag, S. 64
Sparshott, F.E. 9, 12, 60, 61, 82, 99n.48, 100, 108
spectatorship 3, 13, 20, 34, 38, 109
Stanwyck, Barbara 51n.48
Stecker, R. 21
Stewart, James 141n.21, 155, 157–9
Storer, R. 71, 83–4, 102
Strangers on a Train 145–6
style 5–7, 21, 29, 33, 41, 42, 44, 46–8, 59, 80n.27, 87, 88, 101, 116, 130, 143, 144, 145, 168, 188, 199, 202, 209

Tati, Jacques 60n.3, 181n.66
Thomson, D. 122, 202
Toland, Gregg 48
Toles, G. 146, 157–9, 181–3
Trouble Every Day 92–3
Trouble in Paradise 134n.17
Truffaut, François 36n.25, 202

Under Satan's Sun 95
universality 32–6, 46, 55, 104–6, 116

Vendler, H. 76
Vermeer, Johannes 28, 54
Vertigo 10, 62, 63, 70, 155, 157
Vivre sa vie 128n.12, 203n.80, 210–18, 220
von Sternberg, Joseph 46

Walton, K. 31, 39, 52–3, 94–5
Warren, R.P. 86
Watson, G. 169
Wellek, R. 59, 62, 64, 113
Welles, Orson 10, 96, 167, 201, 204
Wilde, Oscar 113
Wilder, Billy 48
Wilson, G.M. 145, 169n.53, 177n.60, 193–8, 209n.86
Wimsatt, W.K. 62, 75, 104n.55
Wittgenstein, L. 4, 32–3, 40n.30, 49n.47, 64, 69, 77, 79n.25, 105–6, 116
Wollheim, R. 103
Wood, R. 71, 88, 100n.49, 155, 183–4, 187, 191–2, 209, 216
Wreen, M. 49
Written on the Wind 51n.49, 183–7, 209
Wyler, William 144–5, 156, 162n.43, 201
Wyman, Jane 147

Yeats, W.B. 110
You, the Living 80n.27
You Only Live Once 194–8

Zangwill, N. 7, 101

EU authorised representative for GPSR:
Easy Access System Europe, Mustamäe tee 50,
10621 Tallinn, Estonia
gpsr.requests@easproject.com

www.ingramcontent.com/pod-product-compliance
Lightning Source LLC
Chambersburg PA
CBHW070326240426
**43671CB00013BA/2373**